THE
BARON
OF
ARIZONA

THE
Baron
OF

E. H. COOKRIDGE

ILLUSTRATED

The John Day Company
NEW YORK

Illustrations by courtesy of the Arizona Department of Library
and Archives and the Phoenix Public Library

Library of Congress Catalogue Card Number: 67-22931
PRINTED IN THE UNITED STATES OF AMERICA
BY AMERICAN BOOK–STRATFORD PRESS, INC.

To
"Rocky"
A. M. ROCHLEN
of Los Angeles
with gratitude and affection

Author's
Acknowledgments

It would have been impossible to assemble the story of the Baron of Arizona without the assistance of a large number of people, many of them as fascinated by the subject as the author is. I can express my thanks here to only a few by name, particularly to John L. Carpenter, of the Phoenix *Gazette,* who conducted research in Phoenix and obtained for me copies of many documents and contemporary newspaper reports; to Donald M. Powell, the chief reference librarian of the University of Arizona, for his kindly permitting me to use and quote from his excellent and well-documented study of *The Peralta Grant;* and to F. George Kay, of Wendover, England, without whose encouragement this book would never have been written.

I also wish to thank Andrew Wallace, assistant director for historical research of the Arizona Pioneers' Historical Society; Dr. Myra Ellen Jenkins, senior archivist of the State Records Center and Archives of the State of New Mexico, at Santa Fe; David O. Kelly, librarian of the University of New Mexico, Albuquerque, who kindly offered sixty-six reels of microfilms, including those containing the Muniments of the Baron of Arizona, for their guidance; and the editors of the Phoenix *Gazette, Sunset Magazine,* the Tucson *Arizona Star,* and other newspapers and journals, who gave me permission to quote from their publications, as well as the publishers of the books listed in the bibliography.

Contents

Illustrations

THE
BARON
OF
ARIZONA

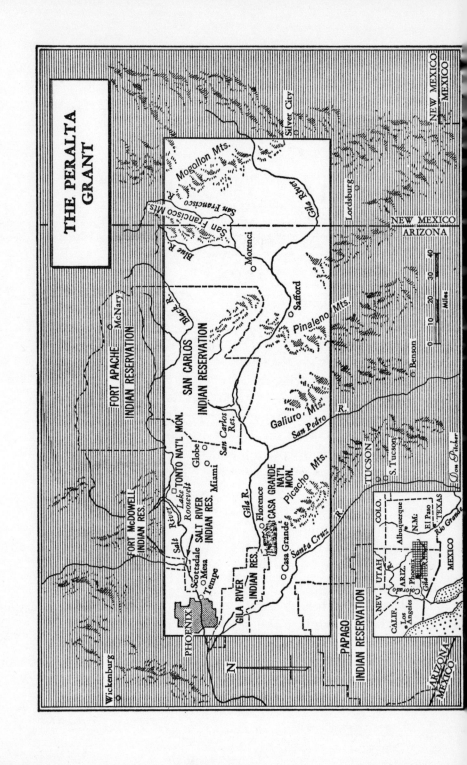

1

The Man from Frisco

Only a few passengers alighted from the stagecoach when it pulled up alongside the big rambling one-story adobe building of Hancock's store at Phoenix, Arizona. Although the distance from the railroad station at Maricopa was less than forty miles, the trip had taken more than six hours across the parched desert. It had been a long, dreary, and exhausting journey, for it was already abnormally hot on this May afternoon in 1880. For miles, all that the passengers could see to the right and left was sand and rocks of the desert, only occasionally relieved by clumps of ocotillo shrub with its long thorny stalks pointing like warning fingers toward the cloudless sky and crowned now, in the spring, with flaming-red blooms. Ahead, toward the east, the mountains rose with high craggy peaks and wooded slopes, promising shadow and rest.

"There is Phoenix. A rough place it has been, but it is growing fast into a fine township," the coachman said, pointing with his whip toward the mountains and jutting his passengers from the semilethargic state into which they had succumbed.

The entrance into Phoenix offered a pleasant surprise. The

desert had ended abruptly; the cacti and tumbleweed had given place to tall saguaro and paloverde trees throwing deep and cool shadows across the track. A carpet of tall green grass spread before the eyes of the few men in the coach, who began to observe the wide fields of corn and the growths of cotton, beans, and pumpkins.

It was not more than ten or twelve years that fruitful soil had been wrestled from the desert, and it had almost been the work of one man. In 1864 John Smith and a few hired hands had pitched their tents there, for a hay camp, when Smith had secured a forage contract for the U.S. Army outpost at Camp McDowell. Three years later a prospector named Jack Swilling came from Wickenburg. Seeing the ancient Indian canals dug from the Salt River centuries ago, rebuilt and improved by the Mormon settlers who had come and gone, and now dry and blocked up by silt, he realized the possibilities if water could be made to flow again.

Having made some money out of a gold placer, Swilling and some enterprising men staked the land north and south of the river where it was widest—between today's Tempe and Glendale—and founded the Swilling Irrigation Company. Primitive machinery, tools, and provisions had to be hauled in carts drawn by eight mules over a distance of fifty miles from Wickenburg. But within six months the first network of canals had been dug, and within a year the first crop had been gathered.

The place was called Swilling's Camp when the first settlers arrived in 1868. They included one woman, Mrs. Adeline Grey, who died in 1936. Among the canal builders was a man who had a vision and helped found—and named—a township which today is one of the twenty-five largest cities of the United States, with a population rapidly nearing the 500,000 mark. He was an Englishman, an adventurer, gambler, and drunkard, who went under the name of Darrel Duppa—his friends called him Lord Duppa—and he was reputed to be a scion of English nobility.

In his sober moments Lord Duppa was a man of culture and great charm. He was well educated—some said at Oxford University—spoke several languages, and wrote poetry. He had made his home in a ramada in New River, and it was a curious place in the flaming desert. In a way it was an English gentleman's castle, even though the roof was of willows and the walls were of ironwood, covered inside with hide. He had made himself some good furniture with quaint carvings and had built a huge Dutch oven, and not only did he have a fine collection of Mexican saddles, old guns and spurs, and Indian pottery and silverware, but he also had books, a rare commodity in those parts in the 1860's—books in English and French and Spanish, as well as in Latin.

He had come to Swilling's Camp to work on the irrigation canals, and although he was more often in a drunken stupor than sober enough to do a day's work, he was liked and, in a way, admired. Swilling, who had been a Confederate soldier and had marched in February, 1862, into Tucson with Captain Hunter's Missouri regiment, wanted to call the place Stonewall, but Lord Duppa, pointing to the ancient Indian mounds, the remnants of a forgotten Pueblo civilization, told him, "Call it Phoenix, after the mythical bird that was consumed by fire but arose resplendent from the ashes." And he made a strange prediction: "A city will arise, Phoenix-like, on this spot, great and beautiful, from these ashes of the past!" Although neither Swilling nor any of the men had ever heard of the mythical bird, they liked the sound of its name, and the place was called Phoenix. The name was made official a year later, when an election precinct was established.*

What the stagecoach passengers now saw was a pleasant town, which had rapidly developed from a rough pioneer settlement. It had four or five streets, and although most of the dwellings were still roughly built adobe houses, there were several stores, two or three hotels, a new schoolhouse, two churches, and the

*Federal Writers' Project, *Arizona* (New York, Hastings House, 1950).

first ice factory in Arizona, whose owner delivered this coveted commodity in a wheelbarrow at seven cents a pound. There was also a large assemblage of squalid shacks where there lived the Mexicans who constituted well over half of the 2,000 inhabitants.

The stage had passed Mike's Brewery and James Monihon's livery stable. After it had come to a halt the trunks were unloaded, and the passengers could, at last, stretch their legs. Most of them made for one of the many saloons along treelined Van Buren Street.

On this hot afternoon the town seemed deserted. All those who could do so were in the cool of their homes, resting until the heat eased. For a good many of the people of Phoenix, the working day began at sundown. Then the miners and prospectors from around the Vulture gold strike and the many mines to the southeast, the rangers and cattlemen from corrals that each could take 2,000 head of cattle, and the Chinese laborers digging the irrigation canals tapping the Gila River descended on the town in search of a game of faro, craps, or keno, to drink and to watch the variety shows which monotonously repeated themselves every half hour till the early hours of the morning.

One of the men who had left the stage was obviously not in search of amusement. He gave a glance at Hancock's store and then stepped out down Washington Street.

He was a tall man, still young, although his shock of auburn hair showed silver streaks above the temples. He had a serious and rather handsome face, very light blue eyes, and a darkish, carefully trimmed mustache, which did not conceal the full, expressive, and almost feminine lips. He carried himself well and strode quickly, even though his pigskin valise was packed to its limit. A silver-knobbed cane helped stamp him as a gentleman quite as much as his severe black frock coat and wide-brimmed black hat did. Despite the heat and the dust of the long journey he had just completed, he looked cool and immaculate.

He stopped in front of the Phoenix Hotel on the corner of Third Street and carefully surveyed the wood-fronted building, observing that it had a swimming pool covered with a canvas roof in the backyard. Apparently satisfied, he pushed through the doors and went to the desk. The hotel owner, Charles Salari, looked up, calculated that the visitor was a man of means, and politely asked him whether he wanted a room.

"The name is Reavis. James Addison Reavis from San Francisco," the visitor said. His voice was soft, with a trace of a Midwestern accent. "Yes, I should like to stay for a few days in this city, and I require a room."

"Well, Mr. Reavis, sir," said Salari, "you're in luck. Till Saturday we ain't overfull. I have an excellent room available right above where we are standing. Overlooking the main street. With a good and comfortable bedstead. There's a tub in an adjoining room—for your private use, of course," he added proudly. "The upper rooms ain't so good. When the prospectors and the herd hands come, they have to go, half a dozen of 'em, into one room, and they ain't got more than a bed and a washbowl—"

"Excellent," said Reavis, cutting short Salari's flow. "I shall avail myself of your hospitality. I am a representative of the San Francisco *Examiner,* and this is my first visit to this territory."

"Newspaperman, eh?" said Salari, handing over the room key. "There ain't much news for you here, not even now when we are going to be a city. Nothing, I reckon, to interest the folks on the Coast. We have two papers of our own, and I figure you want to meet Mr. McClintock, the editor of the *Herald.* A fine man and very clever. And Judge Reilly, who is a great writer for the newspapers, too."

"Yes, I shall do so," Reavis replied. "The *Examiner* is one of the great journals of the country, not barring New York. We're extending our coverage right through the Southwest, now the railroads and telegraph are opening up social intercourse and trade. My task is to arouse interest for my great newspaper among your citizens who want to be acquainted with the progress of the world at large and also to find out something more about your progress here."

Reavis turned around and climbed the stairs to his room. He rested until the evening, then washed, shaved carefully, and changed into clean linen. He appeared in the hotel lobby when darkness was falling and groups of people had begun congregating on the boardwalk, under the rows of ornamental trees which had been planted in anticipation of Phoenix's incorporation as a city. As he had surmised, his chat with the hotel owner had spread the news of who he was and of the purpose of his visit throughout the town.

In the lobby he was approached by a young man, who asked him deferentially, "Have I the honor of addressing Mr. James Addison Reavis, sir?" Being told that this was so, he explained that he was Jim Harris, reporter of the *Herald,* and that he had come to convey the compliments of the editor, James H. McClintock, who wanted a piece about Reavis' visit for the next issue of his newspaper. The editor had to attend to some business but would join them at the Maricopa saloon.

"The best in town," Harris added reassuringly.

Reavis was delighted. "Let's go have some refreshment meanwhile," he said. "I do not take spirits myself, but you must join me for a meal."

Before they had finished the meal, McClintock joined them. He was a big burly man, who had come to the territory as a prospector and in 1878 had founded the *Salt River Valley Herald.*

He stretched out his hand and said, "Welcome to Phoenix, Mr. Reavis. I am honored to meet a representative of that great paper of yours. What brings you here, sir, and how do you like our town?" Before Reavis could reply, he continued, "This is becoming a smart town. When I came here, it was not much more than a cluster of cabins. Now we are fighting to make it the capital city of the territory. When the railroad comes, as it shall soon, the Salt River Valley will be the garden of the Pacific Slope and Phoenix its most important city."

"Quite so, I am sure," said Reavis. "As you've heard, I am here on behalf of the San Francisco *Examiner*. It is indeed true that we hope to arouse interest in these important areas, of a nature which will not, of course, compete with your own publication. Important and influential people in California, such as Mr. Collis P. Huntington and Mr. Charles Crocker, are interested in this territory. I am sure you are, sir, aware of this."

He poured two generous measures of brandy into McClintock's and Harris' tumblers and, forgetting his principles for the moment, a couple of fingers into his own. Then leaning across the table and studying the editor with his steely eyes, he grew confidential.

"My mission is a matter of great delicacy and political importance. It is not confined to newspaper work. Indeed, I regard my being sent here as the benign action of the Deity," he said piously.

Glancing at young Harris and then fixing his eyes on McClintock, he continued in a low voice. "You will respect the confidence of a colleague, gentlemen. I speak openly to you because we are in the same craft. Soon enough a matter of greatest importance will become public knowledge. When there is actual news, I assure you that you will have it exclusively, even before my own journal. You will find me a useful friend, and our friendship will be mutually beneficial."

McClintock just made a grunt and with a wave of his hand encouraged Reavis to continue.

"You see before you, gentlemen, someone who has suffered

with patience the rigors of an unkindly fate, but one who has persevered. I have journeyed many thousand miles, all the way from Missouri. I have lost a dear and devoted friend, a trusted partner who died in these parts a few years ago, pursuing our quest. I have strained my own resources to the utmost; I have neglected my family—but at last I find myself at the threshold of achievement."

His voice fell almost to a whisper. "This is a rich land, a big country. There is room for everyone. The future of the United States is here. I have come here to open up this land, to stage great enterprises. I shall bring great prosperity to this territory, and I shall claim my heritage."

"I don't follow you, sir," said the mystified young reporter, but McClintock motioned him to be silent.

Reavis did not appear to be listening. He had been thinking aloud, lost in his reverie. Then he pulled himself together, and with one brief calculating appraisal of his table companions, he began talking in a firmer, more confident voice.

"I have a claim to land in this territory," he said, "to a large, a very large, stretch of land. A claim based on a Spanish land grant."

"Oh, I see," said James McClintock. "Well, there are many people who believe they have such claims. There are a lot of these floating grants, but nobody takes them very seriously."

Reavis looked up, visibly hurt. "I am aware of such claims, of course," he said indignantly. "They bear no comparison to that in my possession. My claim is based on documents which have been fully verified by no less a person than the president of Mexico and by Mr. William Gitt, the famous Spanish scholar at St. Louis. These documents emanate from the chancery of the kings of Spain."

"Well, sir, some of these grants are good and genuine, of course." Young Jim Harris intervened, feeling that his boss had been abrupt. "We have published reports of some successful claims in the *Herald*. Only a year or so ago, I remember, a Mexican peon proved his right to five hundred acres of good fruit-growing land—"

"Five hundred acres! My good friend, my claim refers to a large part of this territory and to land in New Mexico, besides that. To give you an idea how significant and serious it is, I want to tell you that I paid thirty thousand dollars for the deeds, not counting the heavy expense in pursuing my studies and searches."

"Thirty thousand dollars! Oh, my! Then surely you must have all the proper documents and get a hearing in Prescott," exclaimed Harris.

"You should find out, Mr. Reavis," McClintock said quietly, "whether the land you want to claim is not used by anyone, or reserved for the Indians, or staked out by a mining company. Such Mexican claims were investigated quite a few years back. The surveyor general, Mr. Joseph W. Robbins, rejected most of them as frauds. Folks just come here and want something for nothing. It makes bad blood with the citizens who settled here and built homesteads or worked hard on the ranches."

"I am aware of delays and difficulties," said Reavis solemnly, sensing that the editor was neither impressed nor sympathetic. "As regards the good people who settled on this land and built their homesteads, I do not intend to hurt them. The men who fought the Indians and sacrificed themselves to open up this land shall not be ignored or disturbed. And as you mentioned frauds—well, do I look like a man who would present a fraudulent claim?"

"Sure, you do not, sir," said Harris quickly, anxious to dispel any impression that McClintock intended to offend his host.

"Quite so, my friend," Reavis affirmed. "You see before you a man of mature years. I am thirty-seven years old. I have prospered in business. For close to ten years I have devoted my time and a considerable part of my fortune to the investigation of my rights. You may be sure that I would not have jeopardized my health and reputation in pursuit of a criminal conspiracy. Unfortunately, my partner in this enterprise, Dr. George M. Willing, a distinguished physician who at first acquired the deeds from a noble Spaniard, succumbed to a serious illness on his journey to these parts some six years ago. I am now off to Prescott to secure certain papers which he lodged there at the courthouse—"

"Willing?" McClintock asked suddenly. "Willing? I know that name. Was it the fellow who died in Prescott some years ago? I heard about him from Jim Monihon, who knew him. There was some rumor that Willing had been poisoned—"

"And who is this Mr. Monihon?" asked Reavis.

"Jim Monihon had lived in Prescott. He was one of the first pioneers there, back in 1867, when he first came to Arizona, soon after Governor Goodwin, and he kept a livery stable there. Now he is here in Phoenix, and I figure you should meet him. He knows about Willing's claim, and between you and me, he never thought much about it."

This was bad news, but Reavis took it composedly. "I shall be greatly obliged, Mr. McClintock, if you would be so good as to introduce me to this Mr. James Monihon," he said.

"That can be done. Come tomorrow morning to my office, and we shall pay a call on old Jim," said McClintock, rising. "And now I must be off. It's getting late. It has been interesting meeting you, Mr. Reavis."

"The pleasure is all mine," Reavis assured him.

There is a record of Reavis' meeting with James D. Monihon on that morning in May, 1880. Some years later, after Reavis had become the notorious Baron of Arizona, Monihon told all about it to Judge Sloan, later the last territorial governor, who wrote it down and recounted it in his memoirs.*

* Richard E. Sloan, *Memories of an Arizona Judge* (Stanford, Stanford University Press, 1932) .

Monihon well remembered that meeting. Reavis came to him with McClintock and asked him if they could go for a drive to the Gila and Salt River fork, where Avondale is today, and Monihon obliged. He took a liking to Reavis, "a very lively fellow, who seemed to have boundless energy and kept up an interminable flow of questions," even though he looked so serious and solemn that Monihon thought he resembled a schoolteacher or a preacher rather than a newspaperman.

They drove out of the town toward the head of the Gila River, along the cotton plantations, some five or six miles due west. There were few settlers in those days in that portion of the valley. Reavis seemed to be very pleased with the country and said, "My, this is just what I have been looking for. This is an item!"

He asked Monihon about his acquaintance with Doc Willing back in the sixties, and Monihon, who had a wry sense of humor, told him about it straight from the sleeve. Before the war the Doc had been well known in the Southwest for his traveling medicine show. Many regarded him as a charlatan even though he must have had a sound medical knowledge. Around 1860 he had gone into gold prospecting and had located a placer.

Those were the days of great finds. In 1858 Arizona had its first gold rush. Along the Gila River, some twenty miles from Yuma, gold placers were found, and by 1861 some $2,000,000 worth of gold had been taken from the region of Gila City. A year later the placers were worked out, and a flood destroyed the town. Henry Wickenburg found the Vulture Mine in 1863 and sold it for 85,000, but during the following years it yielded more than $3,000,000 worth of gold. Within less than a year more than $2,000,000 worth of gold was taken from Lynx Creek and adjacent placers in Yavapai County.

"Fellows made money quick, and some lost it even quicker when the rush was over, and with the war," said Monihon. "For a time your friend Willing must have been doing well, but when the big mining companies moved in and many prospectors had to quit from land which they had never properly staked, the placer excitement died down. Mining became big business controlled by the big fellows in the East and in California. The Doc had to wind up his Mining and Exploring Company, and when he came to Prescott in 1867, he was stonebroke."

Willing had come to Monihon's livery stable and told him he had to attend to some important business in the East, needed $250, and asked for a loan of this sum. Monihon had no intention of advancing the money but teasingly asked what security Willing could offer.

"I have purchased a Mexican land grant," he told his host. "I paid one thousand dollars for it, and it is a good claim. I have the document, and I have filed it at the Yavapai County courthouse here in Prescott. I have shown the deeds to Governor Goodwin and to Manuel Yeserea, who knows what's worth knowing about Mexican grants, and they both said the claim will stand. I want to go to St. Louis to raise capital for exploiting the land. It is a fine and big piece of land, all around Prescott and down to Florence and Pinal County. The grant was given by the Spanish kings to a Count Peralta, who was a cousin of the governor of Santa Fe."

Monihon was not impressed. There were many floating grants, and nothing good had ever come out of them, he told Willing. Nor was he impressed by Willing's offer of half a share in the claim in return for the $250 he had asked as a loan. He grew really angry when Willing developed his plan: they would fix the boundaries of the grant around Prescott, where a few ranchers had settled and gold and silver mines had sprung up, and after having had the claim established, they would sell the land back to the present owners. Thus, Willing said, no one would be really hurt, and they would make a tidy sum of money. Monihon bluntly refused to be a party to such a

scheme; he would not play a trick on his neighbors. He told
Willing that if he wanted good advice, he should quit as quickly
as he could. If the people of Prescott and Yavapai County were
to hear of the scheme, "they would probably hang you from a
convenient pine tree," he said.

Willing may have talked too much to people in the saloons
afterward, trying to raise a loan or find a partner for his scheme.
He was beaten up and told to clear out. A worse fate might have
overcome him were it not for the fact that at that time a
surveying party was in Prescott, on its way to Santa Fe. Willing
joined the government officials and traveled with them to New
Mexico. Monihon did not see him again, although he heard that
the Doc had come back several years later to Prescott, had
registered his claim, and had died soon afterward.

That was the story James D. Monihon told Reavis, advising
him to forget about the claim, which, in any case, he considered
useless. Reavis proffered his thanks for the information and
took his farewell. He did not indicate to Monihon or Mc-
Clintock what his further intentions were. He took the stagecoach to Prescott, and after twenty hours of a journey which
had to be made under military escort because the territory was
infested by hostile Apaches, he arrived at the beginning of May,
1880, in Prescott.

Prescott had come into existence largely because Fort
Whipple, established by a military column, stood nearby. The
first gold prospectors were in the Joseph R. Walker party, which
in the early 1860's had come up the Hassayampa to that area.
They were followed by Joseph Ehle and his family, who started
from New Mexico with a herd of 200, which on arrival had
been reduced to 4 cows because of constant attacks by Indians.

These settlers and gold prospectors were Confederate ad-
herents, a fact which alarmed the Government in Washington.
Moreover, news had arrived of gold strikes (Henry Wickenburg
had discovered the great Vulture Mine), and the United States

Treasury, badly depleted by the Civil War, awoke to the fact of Arizona's goldfields. President Lincoln signed the bill creating the Territory of Arizona, separating it from New Mexico.

After a three-month journey by wagon and on horseback, the first governor, John N. Goodwin, and a party of officials arrived at Fort Whipple, which was then seventeen miles north of Granite Creek. They were looking for a site for a capital because Tucson, staunchly Confederate, did not welcome the Washington-appointed officials. A few months later Fort Whipple was moved to Granite Creek, and the first legislature met there, at a small settlement named for the historian William Hickling Prescott.

The first building was a two-room log cabin, and it served as courthouse and official residence until the governor's mansion, a two-story house, and the capitol were finished. This first log cabin was later called Misery Fort, a name which it seems to have gained from the meals provided by "Virgin Mary," the first woman to arrive in Prescott, who had converted the cabin into an eating place and boardinghouse.

Prescott had a checkered history right from its beginning. It was attacked again and again by Indians, and although it grew into a township of some 1,500 persons, the site of the new capital caused dissension until in 1867 Tucson was named the territory's capital by a majority of one vote in the legislature—a victory which it held for ten years. Then Prescott declined badly, with the population falling to less than 500, mainly because of mines' failing and Apache attacks.

When in the 1870's more peaceful conditions prevailed, the little township began to pick up again. Reckless promoters in the East, as far away as Boston, Philadelphia, and New York, had been painting life in the newly discovered Southwest in very attractive colors, describing gold and silver bonanzas and luring settlers and adventurers to the new territory. In 1877, three years before Reavis' first visit, the capital had been moved back to Prescott, and it had grown to a sizable town. Around it were more than 7,000 gold mines, many small and many abandoned, although others, such as Congress and Crown King, still prospered. The mines disfigured the hills like pockmarks, but rangeland began to be cultivated. There were now many ranches and corrals; after the Civil War great herds had been driven to Arizona from Texas, and their owners had found a ready and remunerative market in the mining settlements. Cattle breeding had achieved such preponderance that beef was available for shipments to other parts of the United States, and when the railroad came, prosperity vastly increased. In the late 1870's more solid industry than prospecting had already come to Yavapai County; there were several steam sawmills, brick and lime kilns, and three breweries, and business had become so brisk that it provided livelihoods to twenty lawyers.

When James Addison Reavis arrived there in 1880, it was a pleasant and prosperous place, different from any other in Arizona, an American town which had none of the leisurely charm of the South or the Spanish influence which had softened the harshness of the lawless communities in the Southwest in the mid-nineteenth century. Prescott had been founded by a Republican administration. The majority of the town's residents had come from the East, and the officials were carpetbaggers. Southerners often found themselves ostracized, while Mexicans were reduced to menial jobs.

Prescott had a surfeit of saloons, gaming houses, and brothels, as well as a theater and several music halls. It was significant that although premises stood to supply every possible requirement in the way of pleasure and vice and the needs of clothing, food, and tools—all at exorbitant prices—there was for several years no church. It was one of the few towns where the Arizona law prohibiting women from visiting saloons and gaming places was generally ignored. Every ingenuity was used to get plenty of women into every social occasion. Tickets for the places of entertainment, dances, and concerts were the same price for a gentleman alone or accompanied; thus, a male patron could bring as many women as he wished at no extra cost.

On Granite Street stood the hotels and saloons, where dawn was regarded as closing time for the night's festivities. The notorious Whiskey Row survived as late as 1900, when Prescott's center section was swept by a fire, caused by a drunken miner's upsetting a lamp in a lodging house, and most of the saloons were burned down. Faro and craps were the most popular games in these saloons, and Reavis soon discovered that Doc Willing was well remembered there, from his previous visits with his medicine show and as an inveterate gambler.

Retracing Doc Willing's steps in Prescott six years earlier proved easier than Reavis had anticipated. In the small community the Doc's visits had been memorable events, particularly when in the saloons he had flamboyantly spun his yarn about the great land claims he had purchased from some Spanish nobleman, a claim that would make him a rich and powerful man. No one really believed these tales, but everybody liked to listen to this fluent and amusing talker.

Reavis made his rounds. He visited Moses H. Sherman, who had been the first schoolteacher in Prescott and had become superintendent of public instruction and the president of the bank, and he called on Charles W. Beach, the proprietor and editor of the *Arizona Miner*, the second oldest newspaper of the territory. At his office Beach readily provided such information as he had. He rummaged in old volumes of his paper and produced a copy of the *Miner*, dated March 20, 1874, in which "the sudden demise of the well known Doctor George M. Willing" was duly recorded. The *Miner* had reported:

We stated in yesterday's paper that Dr. Willing arrived here from the States, via New Mexico, on the previous evening. Soon after his arrival he made haste to visit us, when we learned that his object in again visiting the Territory was to secure title to some mines claimed by the Willing Mining and Exploring Company in the vicinity of Black Canon [*sic*] Creek, and a Spanish grant on the Gila river. . . .

The paper reminded its readers of Doc Willing's previous visits, since he had first come in 1864 with a prospecting party, and told how on another occasion he had been attacked by Indians, lost most of his property, and returned to Arizona in later years. "The day after he had visited editor Beach at his office," the report continued, "he was found dead at the lodging house of Mr. R. E. Elliott, lying across the bed." Beach had added a brief epitaph: "The Doctor had his faults, not the least of which was the habit of stretching the truth, but was on the whole a bold adventurer and intelligent man."

Having learned from Reavis that the dead man had been his partner in business, Beach was a little embarrassed about this epitaph, but Reavis put him at ease, saying that he was aware of the deceased's faults and talents.

Then Beach made a puzzling remark. There were some rumors in town about Doc Willing's not having died of natural causes. His demise had caused talk in Prescott because of its suddenness. True, everybody knew that the Doc had been a heavy drinker, and some believed that he had been addicted to morphine. If he had died of poison, as it had been rumored, the poison had probably been administered accidentally and by the victim himself and none else. Prescott, 5,000 feet above sea level, was no place for a man weakened by drink and morphine. Unexpected death of this kind, invariably diagnosed as apoplexy, was not uncommon in the frontier town, Beach said. It was the reason for far more sudden termination of life than the more romantic bullet.

Death which struck swiftly was always a topic for rumor, rarely a motive for legal investigation. Nevertheless, a coroner's jury was summoned and found that George M. Willing had died of natural causes. He was given a Christian burial, and nothing was said afterward.

If this disclosure worried Reavis, he gave no indication of it. He warmly thanked Beach for his kindness and inquired what had happened to Willing's possessions. He produced an authorization signed by the widow, Mary Ann Willing, and Beach directed him to Judge Henry W. Fleury who would know more of what had happened after the coroner's jury. Judge Fleury resided just across the street from Elliott's boardinghouse, where Willing had died, and Reavis went there to find out whether any of the Doc's chattels had been kept for six years since his death.

Judge Fleury was an old man; he seemed absentminded, but after some prodding he recalled the coroner's jury which had sat in his house in 1874. He carefully read Mrs. Willing's authorization, which entitled the caller to collect her deceased husband's belongings.

"Yes, there was a gunnysack somewhere," said Judge Fleury. "Mr. Elliott, the boardinghouse keeper, gave it to me, and it might still be somewhere in the attic."

He asked Reavis to come again on the following morning, and if the maid could find the sack, he was welcome to it.

The next morning, when Reavis called again, a large sack was lying on the parlor table. There was some clothing, a bag stuffed with the Doc's nerve tonic bottles and pillboxes, and a fat envelope.

Reavis could hardly control his excitement. This was the same envelope into which Willing had put his documents when they had parted in St. Louis. He opened the flap and quickly glanced at the contents. Yes, these were Willing's documents of the Peralta claim. He put the envelope into the pocket of his frock coat.

"My main business, Judge," he said solemnly, "is to secure for my friend's widow some of his personal papers. I shall not take the clothes, and I shall be obliged if you could dispose of them to a needy and deserving person." Judge Fleury asked for a receipt, which Reavis wrote out. Then he thanked the judge for his help and hurriedly returned to his hotel.

There he spread the papers on the table. He knew that the documents, of which Willing had talked so proudly, insisting that they had cost him many thousands of dollars, were vague pieces of evidence to support a claim of such great magnitude. But Reavis knew that he could improve on them.

At that moment, looking at the yellowed papers, he must have experienced his great, overwhelming vision: the possession of a realm that included a large slice of Arizona, an area that reached from the inflow of the Salt River into the Gila in the west, to Silver City in New Mexico in the east, from the peaks of the Tonto and San Francisco Mountains in the north to the Coronado in the south—12,000,000 acres of land studded with gold and silver and copper mines and with a score of townships and settlements inside its boundaries.

A realm much larger than the states of Massachusetts, Connecticut, and Rhode Island put together—the Barony of Arizona.

2

Graduate in Forgery

For the man who held between his fingers the passport to fame and fortune, there must have been as much satisfaction in the vindication of what he had felt, since his childhood, to be his rightful place in society as in the realization that the stream of money was running his way.

James Addison Reavis was born on May 10, 1843, in a settlement in Henry County, not far from Clinton, Missouri. He was the second of five children of Maria and Fenton George Reavis. His father, of Welsh stock, had emigrated from England in the early 1820's and after long wanderings had come to Missouri. In his younger days he had been a drifter, rarely keeping a job for long. All brawn and little brain, he worked as a stockman and on the riverboats working down to Memphis and New Orleans.

Fenton Reavis might never have settled down, had he not met in St. Louis a beautiful young girl and married her in 1841. Maria Dixon was half Scottish and half Spanish. She never knew her father, who, like many Scotsmen, had come to America after the Napoleonic Wars, in search of fortune in the Midwest. Her mother—of whom she always spoke as "a noble Spanish lady"—

had told her she had been an unworldly girl when she had been seduced by a rough Gaelic adventurer, who left her soon after their marriage. Her mother's family had come to St. Louis around 1768, some years after the French had ceded Louisiana to Spain.

Maria Reavis was very proud of her Spanish ancestry. From the few tales her mother had told her, she had created over the years for her children a picture of an illustrious and romantic background, a family of prestige and wealth, perhaps of nobility, which had contributed to the glory of Spain before the upstart Napoleon had come like a vandal and destroyed it. Her stories of how her mother had married beneath her to a Scottish immigrant explained her own unfortunate mistake in marrying Fenton Reavis, like her father, a ruffian from the cold north.

There was perhaps some justice in her attitude. Strikingly beautiful, with an olive complexion and jet black hair, vivacious and intelligent, she had yielded to Fenton's brief and forceful wooing, not from love but because he had been well furnished with money after six months' work on a Kansas stock farm and had promised her a life of comfort, even of luxury. But the money had gone quickly, and soon they were living in grinding squalor in the riverside slums of St. Louis, Reavis being unwilling to accept habitation among "foreigners" speaking Spanish or French just because his wife had friends and relatives among them. Thus, the marriage was not happy, and although Mrs. Reavis kept her physical beauty and proud bearing to the end of her life, her vivacity degenerated into a sour nostalgia for what might have been.

St. Louis was a roistering, prosperous town and one of the most important river ports in the New World. In less than eighty years, since a French adventurer, Pierre Laclède, had set up a fur-trading post along the west bank of the Mississippi, honoring his monarch, Louis XV, by tacking a nameboard to his shack, the town had expanded both as a trading center and as a home for thousands of Frenchmen and Spaniards.

Fenton Reavis could have found a steady job, for he could work hard if he wanted, but he was a restless man, always trying to find new opportunities and always failing because he was not clever enough to seize them. His wife, with her blend of Iberian romantic sentiments and the cautiousness and determination inherited from her Scottish father, prodded him, and he managed to save some money. One day he decided he wanted to be a farmer, and they moved to Henry County, where he bought a small derelict farmstead. By hard work he prospered for a while and later added a tannery to his property, buying and processing furs brought by trappers from Kansas. The farm was heavily mortgaged, and life was not easy for the family, to which two children were now added.

The firstborn, William, took after his father, but James, although he had red hair, which he must have inherited from his Scottish grandfather, was a "mother's boy." Maria Reavis concentrated all her affection on him. She never settled down to the hard life of a farmer's wife, and eventually she persuaded her husband to sell the property.

In 1856, with such money that was left after repaying the mortgage, they moved to St. Joseph, Missouri. By then they had five children, and Reavis senior was making one of the "completely new starts" which he regularly promised to make when things became bad and creditors were pressing.

The family had traveled by riverboat up the Missouri. It was the boom period of the steamboats on the great Western rivers. They had become floating palaces, with staterooms and first-class cabins of great luxury; with ornately furnished dining rooms, where white-gloved Negro waiters served eight-course meals; and with saloons, where gamblers played cards and roulette around the clock. The Reavises traveled as deck passengers, of course; this meant sharing sleeping accommodations on the bottom deck, beside poor immigrants and crates with tools, machinery, and household goods.

But twelve-year-old James cared little about the discomfort of their accommodations. He spent all his waking hours on the top deck and around the glittering staterooms, admiring the well-dressed gentlemen and elegant ladies. Some of the wealthy passengers noticed the handsome and well-spoken boy, chatted with him, and gave him cookies and sweetmeats, and for a few days James lived like Little Lord Fauntleroy, petted by the fine ladies and laughing and playing with boys in velvet suits and silk bow ties.

It was his first encounter with wealth and luxury, and it must have made a deep and lasting impression on the boy, even though he already knew from books something about the life of great and mighty people.

His mother had channeled all her frustrated hopes into her children, particularly into her favorite son, James. Mother and son lived in a dreamworld. The child was told that poverty was wicked, a state suffered by the weak and not an infliction by an unkindly fate. Bestowing on James a possessive, protective love, she spoiled the child and set him against his father, the man who had failed her in her hopes and dreams of a life of wealth and dignity.

It was typical of the woman's monomania about her noble Spanish ancestry that she turned to books. Whenever she had a little money to spare, she would buy tattered copies of Spanish romances and novels recounting the exploits of Spanish conquistadors in America. Bizarre and often farfetched, the stories had a basis of truth in that the authors had used historical reports and memoirs of Spanish monks and royal officials for their highly romanticized tales. She read them to James and explained to him passages in English when he could not grasp the flowery Spanish.

James devoured these picaresque tales, and he loved to listen to the stories which trappers, who brought the furs to his father, told of fights with Indians and of the thrilling adventures of the first American pioneers in the Far West. Although he had little formal schooling, James Reavis acquired a great facility with words and a distinct gift for expressing himself on paper in a fluent, if flowery, manner. Perhaps it was not only his mother's influence but also an inherent gift of the gab, which came down to him from the Welsh ancestors on his father's side. It certainly stood him in good stead in later years, when he became a persuasive talker and a journalist of undisputed talent.

Some ten years earlier St. Joseph had become one of the main gateways to the fabulous West, after James W. Marshall had found the first few ounces of virgin gold on Sutter's farm, forty miles from Sacramento, and the California gold rush had begun. The great stampede to the new Eldorado went by four main routes from the East. One was the sea route all the way down the coast of South America, around Cape Horn, and up to San Francisco, lasting many weeks and wrought with the risk of yellow fever and tropical disease; however uncomfortable in often unseaworthy boats, only the wealthier gold seekers could afford this route. The thousands and then the tens of thousands who made the journey overland, starting by mail coach or wagon train and often continuing on horseback and by mule, could choose three main routes. First, there was the famous Platte River Trail, from Omaha and Salt Lake City along the Humboldt to Sacramento. Those coming from New England converged on St. Louis and St. Joseph to take the Southern Trail to Santa Fe, the old fur-trading route, and hence the Spanish Trail to San Bernardino. Finally, after Congress had appropriated $300,000 for a road from El Paso, Texas, to Fort Yuma, California and Arizona were opened to emigrants from the Southern states.

When the Reavis family came to St. Joseph, the California gold rush had been over for some years, but emigrants were still coming in droves. When the gold rush started in 1848, California had a population of some 20,000, not counting the Indians; by 1854 more than 200,000 had reached the "Golden State," and the Missouri traders and promoters had grown rich during those years when a seemingly interminable flow of humanity passed their towns. In 1855 James watched the wagon trains assemble every day on the outskirts of St. Joseph—many scores of families, lone prospectors, young married couples, itinerant merchants, adventurers, all starting a new life, all full of hopes and great expectations, unperturbed that the journey, which might take months, made the destination seem as remote as the moon.

They were being lured to the West by extravagant promises and descriptions of unscrupulous agents, who grew fat on the gullible migrants. An idea of the methods of persuasion used by those mid-nineteenth-century land agents can be got from a statement made by a politico–*cum*-promoter, John S. Watt, who for a short while in 1860 held the exalted position of a delegate to Congress from New Mexico. Extolling the riches which awaited the pioneers in Arizona, he wrote:

> An Italian sunset never threw its gentle rays over more lovely valleys or heaven kissed hills; valleys harmonious with the music of a thousand sparkling rills; mountains shining with untold millions of mineral wealth, wooing the hand of capital and labor to possess and use it. The virgin rays of the morning sun first kiss the brow of Arizona's lofty mountains, and the parting beams of the setting sun linger fondly around their sublime summits, unwilling to leave to darkness and night such beauty and such grandeur. If there be a single thought which lights up the ofttimes gloomy pathway of the faithful legislator, it is the sweet reflection that he has been instrumental in protecting the rights of feeble people. . . .

"Instrumental" Mr. Watt may have been, if not in protecting, then surely in luring many thousands of feeble people into the professed paradise, which was in reality to a large extent parched desert before the pioneers, in hard toil and at the price of many lives, turned it into habitable areas.

By the late 1850's the eastern parts of the United States were crisscrossed by a fairly extensive system of railroads. But they stopped at the Mississippi. The westernmost point was St. Joseph, the terminus of the Hannibal and St. Joseph Railroad. Beyond the banks of the Missouri and Mississippi were the Great Plains, where, in the opinion of businessmen and railroad builders of the East, only trappers and hunters and savage Indians dwelled.

It was not until September 16, 1858, that the first Overland Mail service started, from Missouri to California, by Fort Smith in Arkansas, then in a wide sweep to the south through Indian territory to Texas and through New Mexico to Yuma and San Francisco. John Butterfield, who inaugurated this first transcontinental link, had engaged on a gigantic enterprise: a route of more than 2,700 miles, with 139 stage stations along it and with hundreds of horses and mules, drivers, stationmasters, and armed guards to accompany the coaches. The first journey was completed in twenty-five days, the coach arriving on October 10 and encountering no trouble from Indians.

That young Reavis was at Tipton, Missouri, on that great occasion is unlikely, but he must have been at St. Joseph in April, 1860, when the first Pony Express left the town for Sacramento. Many years later he mentioned in one of his letters to Collis P. Huntington, the great California railroad builder, that he and his mother had been among the vast crowd who had bidden the first rider Godspeed on his lonely trip. He also mentioned that for six months not once did he miss the start of a Pony Express on its weekly service, and only rarely did he fail to be present when the incoming rider trotted in, exhausted, after maintaining the average of 8 miles per hour on his day-and-night ride over 2,000 miles, but still ready to enjoy free drinks in the saloons, recounting stories of deserts and mountains, Indian ambushes, and encounters with outlaws.

It seems that at that time James Reavis either had a job at St. Joseph or came to town on some commissions for his father, who had moved to Montevallo, Missouri, where he had opened a dry-goods store.

By the time James was seventeen, Missouri was in an upheaval. Under the Compromise of 1820 Missouri had been admitted to the Union as a slave state, but slavery had been prohibited in the Louisiana Territory north of Arkansas, a prohibition that remained merely on paper. Since 1850 St. Louis, that great jumping point to the West, had steadily sunk into a state of political turmoil over the slavery question. The majority of the inhabitants of Missouri, including Reavis' parents, regarded themselves as Southerners and supported slave labor, to which the South owed its cotton prosperity.

With the outbreak of the Civil War, Missouri became a bewildering area; its authorities were at first loyal to the Union. Yet when in 1860 the six Southern states followed South Carolina in proclaiming secession, Missouri, though it did not pass any ordinances of secession, sent representatives to the Confederate Congress. Soon it found itself a battleground, invaded by both sides, and the people in many districts lived under military occupation, hardly knowing whether the troops in temporary possession of their town or county should be regarded as friends or enemies. Reavis' parents lost their modest property when the store in Montevallo was burned down in a skirmish between Union and Confederate troops.

Inevitably, feeling ran high, and under the impetus of national and state patriotism youngsters heeded the call to arms. James had the chance of joining either the Unionists or the forces of the secession, for both of which recruiting officers were busy in Springfield and St. Louis. In the latter city, on the Mississippi, stood the great United States Arsenal, packed with

60,000 firearms and large supplies of ordnance. The secessionists in the southwestern part of the state formed companies of minutemen, and when Union General Nathaniel Lyon marched with 6,000 men against Springfield, he was met by 20,000 Confederates at Wilson's Creek and killed with many of his officers. It was during that ill-fated Unionist sally into southwestern Missouri that Fenton Reavis' store was destroyed.

James' mother had no doubts about which side she should support. It was heroic resistance by the forces of the glorious past against the assault of the *Yanqui* invaders. She told her son that this was his chance to emulate the descendants of conquistadors who under the pennants of Castile had waged war against the English looters and buccaneers. Soon after the Battle of Wilson's Creek, James Reavis joined the Confederate Army.

He enlisted in Hunter's regiment of the Eighth Division of the Missouri State Guard. But after the first great clash between the Unionists and Confederates, the battle moved to the east, into Kentucky and Tennessee, and he was not the first man in uniform to discover that war is boredom and that the chances of attaining glory are few and far between. Member of a force, callow and untrained, which suffered bewildering changes of command and embarked on activities which faded into nothing, Reavis was soon disillusioned as only a dreamer who has never faced reality could be.

After a few months he left his regiment but, still in search of adventure, joined Captain Lowe's company at Springfield. It seems that he resented discipline, and when the company was sent into action along the Mississippi, his enthusiasm for military service rapidly faded. It was when he was serving with Captain Lowe at Springfield that he first discovered the talent which was to become his lifetime preoccupation—the ability to imitate other people's handwriting with a perfection that amounted to genius.

He had felt homesick from the very first day of his service; a "mother's boy," he hankered after his home, where every one of his whims had been indulged. The officers of Hunter's regiment did not grant furloughs easily, and this, it seems, was the reason why he left for Captain Lowe's unit, where discipline may have been less rigid. It was the custom for a military pass to be written in full by the officer—not merely to be signed. A pass could require all persons to provide food, shelter, and transport for the bearer and could mention, if the mission was not secret, the itinerary of the soldier. Thus, Reavis had a document of several lines to forge, as well as his lieutenant's signature.

Purloining an appropriate sheet of paper from his officer's tent, he squatted on his straw bed one night and by the light of an oil lamp forged his first pass. His penmanship had always been commended by his schoolteachers, and he found it easy to complete this little forgery. The next morning he showed the pass to his sergeant and the camp guard, and it was accepted as genuine without question.

He went home, told his mother of his heroic, though fictional, adventures, explained that jealousy of his youth had hitherto prevented his promotion, but told her he had been promised an officer's commission in due course. When he had to return to camp, his self-assurance waned as soon as he approached the tented lines, and soon he was writing himself another furlough pass. If some of his comrades envied him for getting leaves so often, his absences were not particularly noticed by his officers. He practiced his art of forgery with great success, and he became so cocksure that he was unable to keep the secret to himself. He told his fellow soldiers how he got himself the furloughs and demonstrated the ease with which he could imitate signatures. He did not need much prodding when some of the fellows offered him a few silver dollars for his help, and he turned his talent into a remunerative business. Over and over he produced passes and excuses for fatigue, not only for himself but also for trustworthy buddies.

When some sergeant or officer at last became suspicious, Reavis absented himself. By now he had acquired a taste for military service, which appeared to be pleasant if one knew how to turn it into a discreet source of financial reward and to intersperse it with periods of comfortable rest. He had been using his penmanship for forging orders for requisition of provisions, mules, blankets, and other articles, which he sold at bargain prices as soon as he had procured them from traders and farmers. For a youth of eighteen or nineteen, James Reavis showed an astounding acumen for smart and risky deals and the ability to persuade people either by smooth talk or intimidation.

Having deserted Captain Lowe's company, Reavis enlisted once again, with Colonel Thomas Catron's artillery regiment, but his officers saw little of him because after a few months he obtained leave to be married.* Even during his short service he had been absent several times, forging orders for requisitions and selling the supplies thus obtained during furloughs, which he procured for himself by more forged passes. Eventually he decided to try his luck with the Union forces. The fortunes of war had turned against the Confederates, who had fallen back to the Memphis–Chattanooga line and had lost Vicksburg, giving the Unionists command of the entire Mississippi area and cutting off Texas, Arkansas, and Louisiana from the Confederacy.

Whatever Reavis' loyalty to the South and his dreams of glory may have been, he realized that victory was now on the side of the enemy, and he quickly joined the winning side. Of the many gaps in the life and career of James Addison Reavis, none is more mysterious than the year 1865. Shortly before the end of the Civil War he enlisted in a U.S. Army regiment, but his ill practices, which he was able to perpetrate unpunished for so long in the Confederate forces, were soon discovered, and Reavis disappeared.

* Which he was not.

He went to Brazil. It was a very long and expensive journey, considering the disrupted means of transportation in those chaotic times immediately after the end of the Civil War. But he must have had good reasons to remove himself to a distant country and thus to escape the jurisdiction of the United States authorities. He probably had a tidy sum of money, acquired by his shady deals during his Army service, but nothing is known about where he stayed in Brazil and what he did there. At his trial, thirty years later, he maintained an obstinate silence about any period in his life when setbacks or poverty spoiled the image of success which he was so anxious to preserve even if an explanation might have aided his defense.

At the end of 1866 he suddenly reappeared in St. Louis, the city he knew well from the days of his childhood. He was now twenty-three years old, toughened by his military campaigning, over six feet tall, with a shock of red hair and a broken nose. His mother was dead by then. She did not return to the story which was pieced together years later, when the nemesis of the law finally caught up with James Reavis and his whole life was investigated. He was not anxious to meet his father, who had in any event gone off in search of work in areas less affected by the war than Missouri, but he made contact with his brother William, who had some lowly, menial job in the city. During the following two or three years James drifted from one job to another; this perhaps was not entirely his fault.

Economic recovery after the Civil War was fitful and impaired by the prolonged conflict over the Reconstruction Acts and by the Fourteenth Amendment, which provided that the war debts of the Confederate government should never be paid and former masters never be compensated for their slaves. There was general uncertainty in the business community, and widespread corruption in the administration did not help matters. However, within two or three years St. Louis, perhaps more than any of the other cities in the Midwest and South, experienced a boom, largely caused by increasing westward migration. Within two decades the population of St. Louis had jumped from 8,000 to almost 250,000, and by the early 1870's, it had become the sixth largest city of the United States and one of its most important trade centers.

When Reavis arrived in St. Louis, trade was still in bad straits, and he was unable to find a job that suited his ambitions. Remembering his mother's words, he would not soil his hands with menial work or toil on the river as his father had done. It took him awhile to land on his feet. At one time during his Army service he had been employed as a wagon driver and muleteer. On this experience, glowingly recorded in a testimonial bearing the signature of Captain Lowe—which Reavis wrote for himself—he got a job driving horse streetcars on the Olive Street line; later he became a conductor and worked in a ship chandler's shop and as a clerk in a clothing store. These were not jobs he would have taken from choice, and so he drifted from one to another, until he was hired by a wholesale saddle and leather manufacturer as a traveling salesman. This was much more to his liking, and he made good money, traveling for his boss all over Missouri and Illinois.

About 1869 James Reavis had saved enough money to launch out on his own. During his travels through the Midwest he had seen how the real estate business was developing by leaps and bounds, and he decided to set himself up as an estate agent. He opened a small office on Olive Street, one of St. Louis' main thoroughfares. His agreeable manners, fluent sales talk, and obvious shrewdness soon attracted some good clients. Within months he had firmly established his business and made enough money to invest a small capital in several building plots.

During his stay at Montevallo some years earlier, when his father ran the store there, he had met a neighbor's daughter, Ada Pope—a pretty, if simple, girl—and had come to an understanding with her. He was now thinking of marriage, but he

decided to wait until his business would allow him to provide
for a family. Ada came to St. Louis, where she stayed with an
aunt. The two young people were now going out together and
became officially betrothed.

Reavis was handling land claims for some of his clients. On
one occasion a man who had sufficient faith in the future to buy
a stretch of land some thirty miles from St. Louis came to him
for advice. The hitch was that the titles to the land were not
clear, and some people were questioning his rights to it. Reavis
went out to search among the papers and documents which the
family originally owning the property had accumulated over
two generations. The documents were probably insufficient to
provide evidence for the registry, but the inevitable result of
Reavis' search was that he returned triumphant, producing
documents from the late eighteenth century which had eluded
previous searches. On yellowing ragged paper, grimy with the
dust of years and with ink faded to an almost indecipherable
sepia in places where the light had reached it, the newly
discovered document was accepted by both sides as genuine.
The deal was satisfactorily completed, and Reavis' grateful
client presented him with a generous bonus. This was probably
Reavis' first excursion into big-time forgery, and it may be
assumed that encouraged by this success, he embarked on many
others.

He may by then have discovered that his penmanship and
imagination, coupled with his lately won experience in real
estate conveyances and land claims, could be put to excellent
use. It was, therefore, with keenest interest that he listened to a
story which a visitor spun out on an autumn day in 1871 at the
little office in Olive Street.

The stranger was a man in his early forties, balding, of
medium height, and of a tense and lively disposition. He
introduced himself as Dr. George Maurice Willing, Jr., and

mentioned that he had come upon a recommendation of Colonel Byser, a St. Louis property owner for whom Reavis was acting.

"I am told that you are well versed in land claims, Mr. Reavis," the visitor said. "Indeed, Colonel Byser assured me that there is no better man in this city who can bring anything out of a property deal."

"Well, sir, I pride myself to understand my business," Reavis replied with a smile. "And I shall be honored to be of such assistance as I can possibly render."

The story Dr. Willing told Reavis was one the young estate agent had heard a few times before—a story of a Spanish land grant, purchased from some poverty-stricken Mexican beside an evening campfire in the desert of the faraway Arizona Territory. Doc Willing was no mean talker, and Reavis, who usually monopolized a conversation, had difficulty in stopping his flow and intercepting a few relevant questions.

What Willing told him—and as later events proved, it was a tale whose gist was embellished with greatly imagined embroidery—was that some seven years earlier, one day in October, 1864, he had met an elderly Mexican at Joe Kayer's saloon on a mining location some thirty miles southeast of Prescott, where men from the Copper Mountains congregated. The Mexican told him that his family owned the rights to a large estate in Yavapai County.

"I have considerable mining interests in that part of Arizona, have founded the Willing Mining and Exploring Company, and I was the owner of a considerable fortune," Willing said. "Prescott was then the capital of the territory, before some ill-advised legislators had it moved three years later to Tucson, and I have been elected as territorial delegate to Congress. Naturally, I was interested in the Mexican's claim, as it might have interfered with my own substantial interests in the area around Prescott. The fellow told me that his elderly father had the relevant documents. We rode to a camp near the ranch of Hank Cordes on the Agua Fria River.

"There I met the old man, who must have seen better days. His name was Miguel Peralta. He showed me his documents, and although my knowledge of Spanish is slight, I realized even after only a superficial examination—and I am sure you will agree with my judgment when you yourself scrutinize them— that this claim was well founded."

Willing took out a large envelope from his frock coat pocket and spread a few battered and brittle papers on Reavis' counter. The estate agent viewed them with growing interest.

"As you can see, they concern an old Spanish land grant given to the Peralta family in the eighteenth century, a grant which is valid under the Treaty of Guadalupe Hidalgo and must be honored by the United States Government. I decided there and then to purchase the claim, and after some hard bargaining with that shrewd old Mexican, I paid twenty thousand dollars for it."

"That was a great deal of money, sir," Reavis remarked.

"It was perhaps; but as I mentioned, I had very substantial means at that time, and I decided it was a fair price to pay for land exceeding two thousand square miles."

Seeing that Reavis was not convinced that someone would pay such a large amount over a campfire for a rather vague claim, he added, "Well, I did not pay in cash. I gave that fellow Peralta two bags of gold dust, some nuggets, six mules, saddles, tools, and prospecting equipment. It came, in my estimation, to at least twenty thousand dollars if you realize that prices of tools and equipment were extremely high in those days and those parts."

"And you have a document in your possession that can be proved to confirm the quitclaim or transfer of the land grant to yourself?" Reavis asked with professional solemnity.

"By heck, sir, I have and I haven't," was Willing's reply.

"You see, the deal was made at the camp, in a wild country. In those days the Black Canyon was a dangerous place. There were many holdups, and Apaches were roaming all over the place, being kept in some order only by the Army cavalry at Fort Whipple. However, we did sign a document, and here it is."

He pointed to a greasy, crumpled piece of brownish paper. "Well, I know it does not look like a proper deed, and that's the trouble of it. I had to find some paper in the camp, a stout piece of paper, and that was all I did find, a piece of wrapping. So I wrote it all down, and as there was no opportunity to have it signed and sealed by a notary or judge, I had it witnessed by two men. I asked that old Mexican to come with me to Prescott and have the document drawn up properly, but the fellow refused. He was determined to move on to some other mining location, now that I gave him the mules and the equipment. However, I did go to Prescott myself with the document and showed it to several respected men there, to Judge Fleury and to James Monihon, who kept the livery stable, and they all agreed that the claim was a good one."

"So you did register the claim at Prescott then?" Reavis inquired.

"Well, not at that time. They did not understand it, and they told me I should have to go to Santa Fe, where the Land Registry for the Territory of Arizona was. The territory had only been quite recently detached from New Mexico, and everything concerning government business was in a turmoil. Sometime later I had a bad turn in my fortune. I lost a very considerable part of my capital, and there was also some domestic trouble of a delicate character—"

"Oh, I fully understand, sir," Reavis assured him, sensing that his visitor felt embarrassed to continue. "I had my ups and downs in my life."

"Yes, who hadn't? You see, I had a disagreement with my good wife. We—or rather she—lived then at Sacramento in California. I had to travel a great lot, on business, and my good Mary Ann was unhappy about it. To cut a long story short, I was away from our home for some years, and I could not address my mind to the pursuit of the claim which I had acquired. Now I have consulted several important people in this city, and they suggested, as did Colonel Byser, that I should entrust the matter into your good hands, my dear Mr. Reavis."

Reavis must have realized that Doc Willing's story had only a remote resemblance to the events that had really happened between the purchase of the documents in 1864 and his arrival in St. Louis in 1871. Subsequently he discovered many other details, which Willing had wisely omitted to mention, things which were not favorable to the pursuit of the claim. When he suggested that Willing leave the documents with him so that he could more carefully examine them, mentioning that he had good knowledge of Spanish, the Doc told him that he would rather take them with him. He promised to return the following day with "a famous Spanish scholar," who would assist them in the examination. Reavis probably thought he would never see Willing again and may have cursed himself for having been uncooperative; his interest in the Spanish grant had been kindled.

But the next day Willing reappeared, and with him came a small elderly man with a shifty look and oily manners. Reavis knew of him and had wanted to meet him for some time. He was William Gitt, known in St. Louis as the "Spanish Land Grant Gitt" of doubtful repute. The three men were from then on closeted together for several hours each week, Gitt explaining and translating the documents and advising on the legal complexities.

It has never been established what the value, if any, was of the documents which Willing had brought along. There is no doubt that Willing had some documents referring to a Spanish land grant, but Reavis subsequently manufactured such a vast number of forged documents, maintaining even in his "Confessions," published after his trial, that some of them were not faked but were original papers brought by Willing and old Gitt, that it is impossible to say whether any of the deeds he registered in 1883 originated from Willing.

During the months following Willing's first visit, Reavis was preoccupied with other business, and although he met the Doc regularly, he did not pursue the matter with great energy.

One reason for this hesitation may have been that he had learned some details of Willing's past which did not encourage him to go into partnership with the volatile former physician.

Doc Willing looked older than his forty-two years. It was part of his stock-in-trade to do so. A carefully trimmed goatee, flecked with silver, gave him a dignified air, not spoiled by the merriment of his piercing dark eyes. He came from a respectable family of Philadelphia. His English ancestors had belonged to the upper middle class; some had been landed gentry in Lancashire, the English northern county famed not only for the manufacture of cotton textiles, but also for its shrewd businessmen and for the best comedians ever to grace the music hall stage.

He had a good education, qualified as a physician, and married a beautiful girl, Mary Ann, the daughter of a well-to-do merchant. His father, George M. Willing, Sr., was a prosperous businessman. But the young medico was temperamentally unsuited for a dignified, though modestly rewarded, profession. He enjoyed good living, and even more, he enjoyed feminine companionship. He soon gained a dubious reputation as a doctor who indulged in undue familiarities with any attractive female patient and as a man given to gambling and drink. Very early in his career he got into trouble, having discovered that the practice of a discreet abortionist was more rewarding than that of a general practitioner. There were some untoward mishaps which brought him to the attention of the authorities and his medical colleagues, and he was compelled to quit his hometown hurriedly.

Like so many social misfits of his generation, Dr. Willing saw the Far West of the 1850's, as remote from the Eastern seaboard as Africa in time and social attitudes, as both a refuge and a goal. He owned up to his father, who gave him a sum of money in an effort to save the family honor, and young George boarded a ship at Baltimore for the long trip around the Horn to California. Mary Ann, who loved him dearly in spite of his failings, went with him, and for a time they settled down in Sacramento, where he established a medical practice. It would have prospered, had he not been bitten by the bug of prospecting. One day, without good-byes, he left his home and office and went to the mining fields, changing his comfortable life for that of a rough prospector. Like tens of thousands, he found only disillusionment, but he was not a man to give in and return like a prodigal son.

He discovered that traveling as a medical charlatan through the new settlements and mining locations which were springing up, like mushrooms after a torrent, all through the Southwest was a more rewarding occupation than chasing the evasive fortune from gold or silver strikes. He set up a traveling medicine show, combining charlatanism and some useful medical work.

In a small wagon, sometimes alone, sometimes with one or two hired assistants, he journeyed thousands of miles across California, Arizona, and New Mexico, even as far north as Utah and as far east as the Rio Grande and Santa Fe, selling "nerve tonics," aphrodisiacs, abortifacients, hair restorers, and little phials and boxes with pills and powders for every ill and ache that might afflict man and woman.

His "Mesmeric Balsam" and his "Strengthening Remedy" became as popular with the tough prospectors and cowhands as his "secret tonics," which he claimed to have concocted from ancient Navajo and Hopi Indian recipes, did with superstitious Mexicans and mestizos.

Northeastern Arizona had been his favorite marketplace, even though it was still a wild area in the late 1860's. Although Prescott had lost its status as the territory's capital in 1867, it remained an important center of the mining industry, which greatly expanded with the introduction of machinery. There were more than 7,000 gold mines in the vicinity, ever since the gold rush in 1858, when rich placers were found near the Colorado River and at Gila City. Money was aplenty, and Doc Willing could always reckon on collecting a few hundred dollars on each of his visits to the area.

With his phials and capsules he distributed a printed leaflet with "an honest and unconditional warranty," stating that he was prepared "to forfeit $500 here and now if my Mesmeric Balsam does not cure any of the Seminal Weakness and Private Disease and clear up any trouble and unpleasant discharges, and clear up all that within one month."

It seems that the lotions and ointments did help; otherwise Willing would have risked a very rough welcome when he returned to the same locality. Perhaps the pleasant manner in which the medicines were to be taken increased his popularity: "Mixed with water or coffee, but preferably with whisky."

But it must also be recorded that Dr. Willing on many occasions did useful work in bonesetting, in bullet extractions, and even sometimes in midwifery, and he was as ready to work as a veterinary surgeon on a burro, a horse, or a cow as on a human being. He was greatly liked by a vast number of people who possibly saw him only once a year on his ceaseless travels.

Not least of his popularity was among the Indians whom he befriended. To the peaceful Papagos he was a welcome friend, but he could also safely traverse the Apache territory, when the tribes were on the warpath and Victorio and Geronimo had vowed to avenge their great chief, Mangas Coloradas, who had been killed by the soldiers of Colonel J. R. West's California Volunteers when he had come to their camp near Fort McLean to offer peace.

Willing could cross unmolested even Cochise's territory, where the Apaches almost ceaselessly attacked settlements and (according to a report in the Prescott *Arizona Miner*) had committed many atrocities between 1864 and 1869, killing 301 pioneers, wounding 53, and carrying several white women and children into captivity.

As already mentioned, Willing had embarked on various prospecting schemes, but by 1867 he must have gone broke, being compelled to ask James Monihon at Prescott for such a paltry loan as $250 and offering him his alleged Spanish land grant as security or in partnership.

What Willing had been doing afterward and where he had been before he appeared in 1871 in St. Louis, Reavis never discovered. Willing had little money then, asked Reavis for small loans, and pressed him to pursue the Peralta claim.

Although Reavis treated the Doc with caution, he struck up a friendship with William Gitt, the crooked lawyer, and had various business dealings with him. He bought several Spanish claims from him, and he must have used his penmanship and improved on these dubious documents which Gitt brought him, because some of the smaller claims were accepted by the land commissioners. Reavis made good money out of these deals.

He was now quite prosperous. He had embarked on profitable real estate speculations in Missouri, owning more than 1,000 feet of frontage of property in St. Louis, near the Old Catholic Cathedral, in Florissant Street, and in the new quarters around Forest Park, and he had also purchased land in Illinois and sold it for farmsteads with a good profit.

Willing had brought his wife to St. Louis, and Reavis, missing his mother's care, became a frequent visitor to their home. Mary Ann was a long-suffering, neglected wife; her husband was a heavy drinker, he was taking drugs, and he often had violent tantrums. Little wonder that she found solace in talking to the polite young estate agent for whom she felt motherly affection. There is no suggestion that any but purely platonic relations existed between them. Mrs. Willing cooked meals for Reavis, mended his linen, darned his socks, and grew to like and trust him.

From time to time Willing disappeared for spells of varying duration, returning sometimes with money, on other occasions in rags. He continued to press Reavis to pursue the Peralta Grant, and by the end of 1873, Reavis had made up his mind.

The financial crash in 1873 had brought about a disastrous slump in trade and real estate values. There were runs on the banks, and deprived of credit, speculators were selling property while buyers were difficult to find. Reavis lost most of the money he had invested. In the general panic he had sold out too early; values recovered when the worst calamity was over.

There may have been other reasons why Reavis decided to close his estate agency and depart with Willing for the Southwest in search of the Peralta fortune. During the crash he had apparently involved himself in some fraudulent deals. He had always sailed near the wind, and when some of his clients or opponents enlisted the help of the authorities, he must have realized that it was time to leave St. Louis and chance his luck elsewhere.

Willing had mentioned, in a casual way, that there was a small matter to be settled concerning mines located on the Peralta Grant land. He had assigned mining rights to Florin Massol, a merchant in Sacramento, in return for a small loan he had badly needed during one of his visits to California some years before. He suggested that Reavis go to Sacramento and negotiate with Massol, while he would proceed directly to Arizona and file the documents with the authorities in Prescott. Willing chose the overland route, by Topeka and Albuquerque, and set off from St. Louis in January, 1874, taking all the documents with him. Reavis was to follow by the sea route via Panama to San Francisco.

For some reason he postponed his departure for more than six months. He may have been pressed by the Pope family to keep his promise and lead his fiancée, Ada, to the altar before his departure, or he may have still had to wind up some business. The marriage took place on May 5, 1874. The couple had a short honeymoon, which was the last time Ada Reavis saw her husband for several years. Three weeks after the wedding James Reavis embarked at New Orleans on the 1,400-mile sea voyage to Colón in Panama, and after crossing the isthmus, he sailed to San Francisco.

Six years were to elapse before he reached Arizona.

3

At the Golden Gate

When James Addison Reavis arrived in San Francisco, the city was recovering from the financial crisis that had hit the nation a year before. Based on paper money, American economy had experienced since the close of the Civil War a succession of booms and depressions. The "Great Reconstruction," overexpansion in business and trade, currency inflation, and reckless speculation had brought about a sad decline in business practices throughout the United States.

In the struggle for the control of the railroads, constructed in the East at an amazing pace, Cornelius Vanderbilt had pitted his millions against Jay Gould, Daniel Drew, and Jim Fisk. The corruption in President Grant's administration led to the great Crédit Mobilier scandal. This French banking syndicate had financed the Union Pacific Railroad. Men such as the United States Vice-President Schuyler Colfax, Secretary of the Treasury W. A. Richardson, and many members of Congress had been accused of bribery, some escaping impeachment only by resignation. President Grant's secretary, O. E. Babcock, was implicated in the Whiskey Ring. Senators, judges, and entire state legislatures were bought by business promoters just as Western cattlemen bought steers.

In 1873 the failure of Jay Cooke and Company, the great Wall Street brokerage house which had financed the Northern Pacific syndicate, had led to a run on the banks. Many became insolvent, and hundreds of industrial and commercial enterprises, deprived of credit, were driven into bankruptcy. Much of the American business expansion had been financed from abroad; a financial panic in Vienna spread to other European money market and stock exchanges and resulted in the withdrawal of foreign capital from the United States. Widespread unemployment—more than 2,000,000 jobless in the Eastern states—led to labor riots.

Yet all this was happening in the face of technological progress that within a few years had reached undreamed-of peaks, with new railroads opening up vast areas of great mineral wealth and farming opportunities. The first transatlantic cable had been laid, linking America with Europe by a tick of the Morse telegraph; Bell had devised his first workable telephone; Edison, at the age of twenty-two, had invented the stock ticker, sold his rights for $40,000, and founded his "invention factory" at Menlo Park, New Jersey, where he was working on the first electric bulb; and Charles Brush had built a dynamo engine which was to revolutionize not only lighting but also industry.

The use of the sewing machine, invented by the American Elias Howe, spread throughout the world; Sholes and Remington had produced the first typewriter; in Philadelphia Bullock had invented the web printing press, soon followed by Campbell's and Tucker's rotary press. The Westinghouse air brake made high speed of railroad trains safe; Pullman introduced the first dining and sleeping cars on the rapidly expanding American railroad system.

Iron was being converted into steel in scores of big new steelworks by the new Kelly and Bessemer processes, opening a new era in machine industry. Oil wells in Pennsylvania marked the beginning of commercial exploitation of petroleum; the invention of concrete and the adoption of the English portland cement resulted in a fantastic building boom.

The depression of 1873 had affected California to a lesser degree than it had the industrialized and densely populated East, with its great influx of immigrants. Until the advent of the Pacific railroads, California had, in many ways, remained isolated from the rest of the United States and had developed its own way of life, still fashioned in the ranch country after leisurely Spanish tradition. The discovery of silver and gold in the new territories in the West and the Southwest, the great bonanzas in Nevada and Colorado, had thrown up men in San Francisco who vaunted their careers from poverty to fabulous riches, men as greedy for the next million as they had been for their first silver dollar, whose business interest and political influence reached far beyond the boundaries of California. Boom or depression, the Golden Gate city was full of people determined to make their fortune.

It is one of the many puzzles in the life of James Reavis that when he landed in San Francisco in 1874, he stayed for only a short time in the city which offered rich opportunities to a man endowed with brains and initiative. After his long sea voyage he had arrived in poor health. He may have contracted malaria, although there is no record of any serious illness in his later life.

Bad news awaited him at the shipping agent's office where he had asked Willing to direct his communications. There was only one letter from the Doc, announcing his safe arrival at Prescott, but this missive had been dated several months back. Another, a brief official communication, was from the sheriff of Yavapai County, informing him that Dr. George M. Willing had suddenly died at Prescott on March 29. The only address found among Willing's papers was that of the shipping agent in

San Francisco, and the notification of the sad event was sent there to await Reavis' call.

He had arrived in San Francisco equipped with some good introductions. In St. Louis he had known James O. Broadhead, a lawyer of nationwide repute, who became a Congressman from Missouri and was later president of the American Bar Association and the U.S. minister to Switzerland. Broadhead had conducted for Reavis a few of his more respectable legal deals, and he had given him letters of introduction to important people in San Francisco and Sacramento. Reavis also had such letters from William Gitt, the "Spanish Land Grant Gitt," who at one time had lived in California and Mexico and knew certain people there who might have been useful to Reavis, although they may have been on a different level from those to whom Broadhead had written his introductions.

During his short stay in San Francisco, Reavis did not avail himself of any such connections as he might have formed on the strength of these letters. The news of Willing's death was, of course, shattering. Without Willing and without the Peralta documents, Reavis could hardly hope to make progress in Arizona. His funds were low, and he decided to go to the country to recover from his sickness. He stayed for more than two years in the south. For a time he worked for an estate agent in Tulare County, taught school at Downey, and took intermittent jobs, until he returned to San Francisco.

There was a striking contrast between the south and north of the state. San Francisco, Sacramento, and Stockton were cities with vigorous communities, a thriving business life, and a surfeit of promoters, financiers, and speculators. Many of them had made their fortunes during the great gold and silver rushes twenty years earlier.

The south was still Mexican frontier land, thinly populated with vast ranchos, small cattle market towns, and a constant flow of huge cattle herds—a romantic feature of Southern California and a vitally important one to its economy. A drive of several thousand head of cattle across a distance of 500 miles, from the ranchos to the northern market towns, was a familiar sight, as were the *vaqueros,* cowboys, and drovers.

Reavis soon learned that a cattle buyer or drover was a man who commanded great respect. The drover came from the upper country, often carrying many thousands of dollars' worth of gold in his gunnysack to call on the rancher, who, living like a feudal master is a sumptuous *casa* surrounded by a host of servants and attendants, extended lavish hospitality to the visitor. In the cattle towns, hotels and saloons vied for the drovers' patronage, and professional cardsharpers, rogues of all kinds, and highwaymen addressed their particular attention to them. Deals between seller and buyer, often amounting to a small fortune, were clinched by a handshake, and although the rancher knew that a steer sold by him for $20 would probably bring the drover six or seven times that amount in a northern market, there was no bad feeling about it on his part.

Most of the rancheros were rich men and, at least for a generation or two, had lived "like princes in the keeping of their houses and bountiful in all manners of things." Their *casas* were hung with precious tapestries and furnished with fine furniture and precious ornaments. They and their ladies dressed with exquisite, if flamboyant, elegance, and it was not unusual for a ranchero to pay $2,000 or $3,000 for a costume, embroidered with gold and silver, with silver-trimmed saddles and spurs made of solid gold, not to mention the jewelry which went with the dress.

Like most Californians, the ranch owners and drovers were inveterate gamblers. When drought ravaged the country and vast herds perished, many of them found themselves impoverished and even penniless because they had never had the prudence to salt away at least some of their profits. But they rarely changed their habits, and living beyond one's means was an accepted way of life.

What must have aroused Reavis' particular interest were the stories of the Spanish and Mexican land grants in California. After the war with Mexico the Treaty of Guadalupe Hidalgo had provided that the United States was "to recognize all legitimate titles to every description of property, personal and real, existing in the ceded territories." Ever since, there had been an endless flow of claims and litigations. In a single year 800 claims, involving some 20,000,000 acres, were heard by the Private Land Claims Commission, and more than 500 were approved.

Reavis discovered that in many cases, even if a claim appeared frivolous or outright fraudulent, the land commissioners and courts solemnly examined it if the claimant was willing to advance generous fees for such an examination, which involved the search and translation of old Spanish documents. He also discovered that a large proportion of such fees went into the pockets of judges and officials and that bribery was accepted as a matter-of-fact premise for getting a claim settled. Men such as William M. Lent, one of California's greatest promoters, who had grabbed vast stretches of the Barbary Coast, and George Hearst—the father of William Randolph Hearst—who had made a huge fortune during the gold rush and later in the Nevada and South Dakota silver bonanzas, boasted that they acquired an old Spanish grant of 48,000 acres in San Luis Obispo County for 60 cents an acre, knowing how to deal with corrupt officials.*

Many landowners and users were ready to settle out of court with the claimants, rather than to risk prolonged litigations and to employ unscrupulous lawyers who sometimes played into the hands of their adversaries. Reavis must have felt that the dubious practices adopted by at least some of the land commissioners might not greatly differ in the Territory of Arizona. This

* John Bruce, *Gaudy Century* (New York, Random House, 1948).

augured well for such hopes as he still nursed for the Peralta Grant.

When Reavis returned to San Francisco, the city was in the throes of frenzied financial speculation, so reckless and extravagant as never before in its fantastic history since the days of the gold rush. Bayard Taylor, writing of Eldorado a quarter of a century earlier, said:

> Of all marvelous phases of the present, San Francisco will most tax the belief of the future; its parallel was never known, and shall never be beheld again. Like the magic seed of an Indian juggler, which grew, blossomed, and bore fruit before the eyes of the spectators, San Francisco seemed to have accomplished in a day the growth of half a century.

These words could well be applied to the scene which unrolled before the eyes of James Reavis. He remembered the stories told about the California gold rush when he was a boy in Missouri. Then the miserable little village of Yerba Buena—the spearmint village—had a population of 800, housed in a cluster of rough adobe shacks and log cabins. Two years later it had become San Francisco, crowded with 30,000—and soon 50,000—persons—a rough polyglot city hurriedly erected of wood and canvas, whose notoriety for crime, murder, and robbery spread over the world.

Now, in the mid-seventies, it was a beautiful place, sprawling from the hills to the marvelous sweep of the bay and the Pacific, with great thoroughfares; ornate buildings; the sumptuous mansions of the rich on Nob Hill (called Snob Hill) ; the nine-story Palace Hotel; the California Theatre, which William Ralston, one of many millionaires, had given to the city.

Although San Francisco now claimed to be "the best-governed city in the United States," after years of lawlessness, murders, the Vigilantes, and public hangings, it was still a wicked place in the eyes of New England Puritans. Moral values were topsy-turvy. A populace of two dozen nationalities, from Spaniards, Mexicans, French, Irish, Germans, Hawaiians, and Chinese to a contingent of former members of an Australian penal colony, reveled in merrymaking, never missing a festivity, whether gaudy Irish frolics on St. Patrick's Day, high jinks of the miners who came to town for a special beano, a Mexican fiesta, a French *quatorze juillet,* or a Chinese New Year. Carnival seemed to last all the year round, with hard work in between, not the other way around, and the innumerable saloons, music halls, and variety shows were never short of customers.

Prostitution was considered a civic necessity, and the many bordellos were as lavishly furnished and ornamented as the elegant French restaurants and the theaters where the high and mighty found their amusement. The "gilded madams"—among them were some of San Francisco's great beauties—were regarded with indulgence, indeed with undisguised admiration by the menfolk; leading citizens tipped their hats to them in the streets, when they went by in all their silken finery. If a ditty proclaimed that:

> The miners came in forty-nine,
> The whores in fifty-one;
> And when they got together
> They produced the city's son.*

there was much truth in it. Many a distinguished "Frisco" family had sprung from such a copulation, and many a son from a respected home had led a courtesan to the altar and made her a lady.

If San Francisco was a sinful city, it was also a place of refinement and sophistication. The hardworking, hard-playing tycoons had wives who cultivated literary salons and patronized

*Herbert Asbury, *The Barbary Coast* (New York, Knopf, 1933), p. 31.

artists, painters, writers, and musicians who had come from the East, attracted by the glitter and the money the city offered. The conversation in these salons centered on the paintings of Millais and Rossetti, Verdi's new operas, and Oscar Wilde's plays. Edwin Booth scored triumphs as Hamlet at the Bush Street Theatre; Adelaide Neilson appeared as Juliet; famous English actors and Italian singers, visiting New York and Boston, were lured by lavish money offers to cross the continent and perform in San Francisco. The city's 200 "upper families" were bent on adding culture to graft and extravagance.

Although the depressions of 1873 and 1875 had caused temporary unemployment, the rapid spread of industry and the building boom created ever new opportunities. Simple handicrafts had developed into great manufacturing enterprises of machinery, shipbuilding, milling, brewing, wood, furniture, and papermaking. Wool production had risen to 30,000,000 pounds; the San Joaquin Valley had become a fabulous domain of cattle breeding controlled by two men, Henry Miller and Charles Lux, whose empires reached into Oregon in the north and into Mexico in the south.

San Francisco financiers controlled the Nevada silver mines; the Comstock Lode and Washoe Valley provided fantastic bonanzas. Enormous fortunes were made. Real estate was snapped up and rose in value by leaps and bounds. Immense sums were invested in town lots and buildings, which mushroomed everywhere. Lots in the city, bought a few years before for a few hundred dollars, brought $30,000 and more for their owners. Loans were advanced against flimsy or without any securities; property was mortgaged at its full value, lenders being convinced that the value would continue to rise.

This seemingly all-embracing, yet, in fact, extremely frailly based prosperity had brought about a bedlam of speculation. People from every walk of life—banker and barkeeper, doctor, stevedore, schoolteacher, barber, storekeeper, miner, laborer, housewife, prostitute, Chinaman—were seized by this virulent fever. Everybody was playing the stock exchange, encouraged by a dozen newssheets published or backed by dubious financiers, promoters, or outright crooks. They spread a thousand rumors, tips, and every sort of tittle-tattle about the floating of new stock issues, discoveries of new bonanzas, industrial schemes, and property deals. Talk in the saloons centered on nothing but on how to make easy money.

A handful of tycoons, all of whom had started from humble beginnings, were in control of finance, business, and railroad construction—men such as Collis P. Huntington, head of the Central Pacific and Southern Pacific railroad syndicate; George Hearst, who made his fortune in the Nevada silver mines; William C. Ralston, the president of the Bank of California. If Huntington regarded himself the uncrowned ruler of California, Ralston could have laid claim to this position not only because of his wealth, but also because he was the most spectacular and trusted figure in California's public life.

In contrast with the morose and secluded Huntington, Ralston led an exuberant life, taking a prominent part in civic affairs and giving generously to public welfare. He had created a vast business empire, not only in California, but also in Nevada, New Mexico, and Texas. He was the head of the Washoe silver mining syndicate, had promoted the San Joaquin Valley irrigation scheme, had built the dry docks at Hunter's Point, controlled a string of woolen mills, sugar refineries, and machine, hardware, and furniture factories. He had financed the building of the Grand Hotel and the Palace Hotel in San Francisco, in those days the two most luxurious caravanserais in the United States, and he had given the city the California Theatre. He was one of the first men to envisage the possibilities of petroleum mining when oil was found on a tract of land in Santa Barbara County. For a while petroleum became the object of a speculation fever, which soon died down because, apart from oil lamps, nobody wanted petroleum, and financiers could not see how to make profitable use of it. The advent of the combustion engine and the automobile was still a quarter of a century away.

Ralston had made his fortune from the Comstock Lode silver mines. But there were other syndicates exploiting the great Nevada silver bonanza—one headed by Adolph Sutro, another by James Fair and John W. Mackay. In 1873 the Fair syndicate tapped one of the richest veins, which in the course of time yielded more than a billion dollars' worth of silver. Mackay later became one of the backers of the Peralta Grant and paid Reavis a monthly retainer. Speculation in mining stock reached colossal proportions in San Francisco. Four hundred million dollars were poured into mining development to the detriment of California's great agricultural resources, which were starved for capital.

Crooks took advantage of the public's readiness to invest money in any, however dubious, mining scheme. Two slippery promoters announced the discovery of great diamond deposits in a remote spot of the Rocky Mountains in Colorado. They salted the "mine" with low-grade rough diamonds, which they had bought cheaply in London, and produced certificates from bribed "experts."

The Colorado Diamond Company floated its stock, and it was snapped up by eager and gullible investors, mostly small people, who sank their savings into the crooked enterprise. Ralston was taken in by the con men, and when Clarence King, a Government geologist, exposed the fraud, panic broke out; on August 25, 1875, this led to a run on the supposedly impregnable Bank of California. The crash came like a thunderbolt from a blue sky. The collapse of the Bank of California led to a disaster that struck not only the "Golden State" but also business throughout the United States. Nearly all San Francisco banks suspended operations; several other banks collapsed in Los Angeles and even in New Orleans, Boston, Philadelphia, and New York. William C. Ralston committed suicide, adding to the panic that swept the West and caused many bankruptcies in cities hundreds of miles distant.

Yet such was the resilience of American enterprise that in spite of the dried-up credit, business recovered within an astoundingly short period. One reason for this was the great boom in railroad construction.

What James Reavis had witnessed in St. Louis a few years before now seemed chicken feed compared with the events in San Francisco. One might have expected that he would have tried his luck once again in the real estate business or in land speculation, of which he had shrewd knowledge. But he must have hankered for a long time after the dreams of his youth—to become a journalist and writer. There was also a more mundane reason for his decision to seek a job with a newspaper. What he had seen of the gullibility of San Francisco folk during the turmoil of wild speculation encouraged him to resume his efforts for the Peralta claim, after the setback caused by Willing's untimely death. He realized that as a newspaperman, he could gain useful contacts and possibly backers for a scheme which now began to ripen in his mind.

Newspapers abounded in San Francisco. There were the *Chronicle*, the *Call*, the *Bulletin*, and the *Examiner*. Even those which were controlled by native tycoons and politicians maintained up to a degree the honorable tradition of press freedom which James King, the first editor of the *Bulletin*, had established. Fighting corruption, he was killed by a bullet from James S. Cassey's revolver, whose corrupt political practices he had exposed.

The newspapers were as vigorous and noisy and gay as their readers; there was nothing about them of the sepulchral solemnity of their New England contemporaries. Only the people of

San Francisco could support journals which treated the earthy politics and social life of California with outspoken sarcasm and humorous zest. Likewise, only in San Francisco could the Democratic machine be run by a blind saloonkeeper, Chris Buckley, who judged people by the firmness of their handshakes and made and unmade Senators, governors, and state legislators.

And only San Francisco could for many years sustain and admire a lovable lunatic who believed he was the emperor of America, styled himself Norton the First, strutted through the streets in a resplendent uniform, with plumed hat and saber, levied his imperial taxes in the saloons, presided over the festivities of the populace, and was invited as a court jester to the mansions of the rich and mighty, until he was buried with regal pomp in 1880, having always provided good copy for the newspapers.

Reavis presented himself to every one of the editors in turn. But although he was a suave and quick-witted talker, he failed to get a job as a reporter. There were many skilled and even brilliant journalists in San Francisco, and none of the editors was prepared to hire a man without any experience in news-paper work. However, the editor of the *Examiner* suggested he see the manager, who was looking for an advertising and sub-scription canvasser. Reavis took the job, which brought him at least onto the fringe of the newspaper world.

At that time the San Francisco *Examiner* was a moribund paper, the only one in the city which was losing circulation. It had got into bad straits during the depression, having backed the wrong horse and attacked Collis P. Huntington and the Southern Pacific syndicate. Huntington had done his best to undermine the paper's existence by withdrawing advertising contracts and inducing his business associates to do likewise. Jay Gould, involved in a struggle with the Southern Pacific, had provided money for the paper, reasoning that it might be useful to have a stake in California politics, but he was growing tired of paying its losses.

Reavis went immediately to work. He decided to concentrate on obtaining advertising contracts from big business concerns, rather than on peddling at the doors of tradesmen and store-keepers. After scanning for a few days the volumes of the *Examiner*, he asked the manager why he did not carry announcements of the Southern Pacific, which appeared in all the other newspapers in the city. He was told that the paper had brought on itself Huntington's wrath. Reavis suggested that he go see Huntington, but the manager laughed it off.

"You'll never even get near that big fellow," the manager said. "It is easier to get an interview with the President of the United States at the White House than with Collis P. of the Southern."

This was a challenge which Reavis decided was worth taking on. He had heard of Huntington, and he knew that this choleric, unyielding great boss, who firmly believed that God had selected him to be the dominant figure of the West, had erected a wall of exclusiveness around himself that few uninvited people ever succeeded in piercing. Reavis did exactly that. He saw Huntington, and when he left the office in the great building of the Southern Pacific on the corner of Fourth and Townsend Streets (people used to say that the real seat of power and government in California was there, not at the capitol in Sacramento), he had a contract in his pocket.

The *Examiner*'s manager could hardly believe his eyes when Reavis brought it to him. It was a contract for regular insertions of all announcements and timetables of the Central and Southern Pacific Railroad, for two years and worth several thousand dollars. Overnight Reavis became a person of consequence at the *Examiner*, then located in a small dilapidated house in Sacramento Street. There were no conditions attached to the generous advertising order. Huntington—so Reavis reported—

had told him he did not mind if the *Examiner* continued to attack him.

How did Reavis secure this contract? It was some years before it transpired how he succeeded in ingratiating himself into the charmed circle of the Southern Pacific bosses, whose ruthless policies and fabulous wealth were bywords throughout the United States. To comprehend how an adventurer such as Reavis could strike a bargain with these men who subsequently backed his fraudulent career, we must briefly consider the era of the great railroad and financial syndicates which dominated the West.

Collis Porter Huntington was born in 1821 in a village in Connecticut, where his father was a small farmer. As a schoolboy, he bought and sold trinkets and watches from schoolfellows. In his teens he was buying pawn tickets in New York and selling the articles he redeemed at a few cents' profit. In 1848, with $1,200, he had gone West, when the West was still really wild, and after some years of commercial enterprise, which he was later unwilling to discuss, he emerged as one of the richest men in California. With a partner, Mark Hopkins, he ran large hardware stores, which supplied miners and prospectors during the gold rush.

In 1861 he became interested in railroads. At that time Asa Whitney, the great pioneer of railroad development in the West, was agitating in California for a railroad across the Rocky Mountains, to link the West and the East, an idea generally regarded as crazy. But another railroad prophet, Theodore Judah, found a long and easy ascent of the Sierra Nevada, by the way of Dutch Flat. He persuaded the California legislature to pass a law authorizing a survey and paying $35,000 for the exploration.

Seven men formed a syndicate: Collis P. Huntington, Theodore Judah, Mark Hopkins, Leland Stanford, L. A. Booth,

Charles Marsh, and James Bailey. Five surveys were made, and eventually a company, called Central Pacific Company of California, was floated, with a nominal capital of $8,000,000, for the construction of a railroad from Sacramento to the eastern boundaries of the state.

Huntington and his partners were at first after Government subsidies and the prospects of lucrative freight and passenger service with the Washoe silver mines; it is doubtful that they really envisaged a transcontinental rail link. Almost immediately a wrangle ensued with the Government in Washington, because at the same time the Union Pacific Railroad Company, formed in New York and financed by the French Crédit Mobilier, had started a similar scheme from East to West. The French bankers had bought scores of Washington politicians and could dictate to Congress.

The Pacific Railroad Bill had stipulated that the Union Pacific should connect to the Central Pacific, after the latter had crossed the Sierra Nevada. But the bosses of neither the Union nor the Central had any intention of agreeing to this compromise, and the rivalry between them resulted in the epic and famous construction race. The reason for it was simple. The Federal Government had granted large subsidies, consisting of 12,800 acres of public land per each mile of track and credits of $16,000 for every mile of railroad across the plains and up to $48,000 per mile in the mountains.

Building westward from Omaha, the Union Pacific expected to reach the California boundary before the Central Pacific crossed the Sierra Nevada, but Huntington and his partners were quicker.

Charles Crocker, whom Huntington had put in charge of the construction work, had sent agents across the Pacific to recruit Chinese coolies. Within a few months many shiploads of Chinese workers arrived in California, and soon some 9,000 of them were toiling from dawn to dusk, hewing, blasting, digging, and driving their way through the mountains. There were no bulldozers, steam shovels, or steam drills to ease the work. Huntington's motto was "Quick and cheap!" The Central Pacific Railroad was built by hand. Many of the Chinese workers perished in the snow and ice of the Sierra Nevada and in the parched deserts the railroad crossed.

As construction progressed, it became evident that the tracks of the competing lines would meet in eastern Nevada or possibly in Utah. In addition to the control of future traffic, each of the railroad companies stood to gain more than $3,000,000 in Government credits and 1,280,000 acres of public land for every 100 miles of track laid down at the expense of its rival.

The labor force employed by the Union Pacific consisted of former soldiers and immigrants, most of them newly arrived Irishmen. They were called Terriers, because they dug the way terriers do for a bone. By 1869 the two railroads were running parallel, the Central Pacific building on higher ground than the Union Pacific, but the two tracks were separated by only 100 feet. Pitched battles took place between the two rival labor forces. Some of the Irish and former soldiers cut the Chinese down by gunfire; the Chinese retaliated by rolling huge boulders down onto the Union Pacific track, destroying work completed at a hard toll.

Eventually, by forceful intervention by the Government in Washington, a compromise was reached between the rival railroad syndicates. The Central Pacific and the Union Pacific established a junction at Promontory, Utah. The event was celebrated by a ceremony of nineteenth-century pomposity and strangely out of place in the wild desolate heart of the Great Basin. To the accompaniment of top hats, frock coats, long speeches, and numerous toasts, a golden spike was driven into the track to unite the rails of the two roads, and a dramatic telegram was sent to President Grant: "The last rail is laid, the last spike is driven, the Pacific Railroad is finished."

America had a railroad from coast to coast. Financiers had gained millions of public money, but the full impact of the rivalry was still some years away, when by cutthroat competition the standard fare from the Midwest to the Coast dropped from $100 to a nominal $1 on the Santa Fe Railroad for a trip from Missouri to Los Angeles. The Southern Pacific, too, was prepared to carry passengers at a loss, in the hope that they would settle in the areas served by the railroad. Pioneers literally stepped off the train at fuel stops and started farming within walking distance. Touts employed by the company and con men swarmed around the trains at every whistle-stop and pointed to stunted trees growing in the desert, festooned with fruit—fruit which had been hung there in the morning.

If pitched battles had been fought between the workers of the railroad companies for the possession of every pass and every road across the mountains, they were nothing compared to the battles fought out in the lobbies, bars, and smoke rooms of the Capitol in Washington and the capitols of the state legislatures. By every means, fair and foul, by blandishment, promise of office, bribery, and blackmail, the rival syndicates asserted their domination.

The completion of the Central Pacific was only one, if a major, step in the great scheme of the "Big Four." Huntington was determined to gain the coveted prize—to open up Arizona and New Mexico. New rich gold and silver strikes were reported from these territories; news reached San Francisco of great copper deposits at Santa Rita and of the untapped mineral wealth of the Ortiz Mountains. The Big Four now began to push the railroad from San Francisco and Los Angeles to Yuma, to extend the track across Arizona and New Mexico toward El Paso in Texas and on to New Orleans.

In this bold undertaking Huntington and his partners encountered a rival as powerful and ruthless as they themselves: Jay Gould, the New York tycoon, who had financed the construction of the Texas Pacific. He had already sunk capital into the Atchison, Topeka and Santa Fe Railroad, which had fought its way across Kansas and Colorado. The Missouri, Kansas and Texas Railroad had started at about the same time. Between these and several other companies there was bitter rivalry to reach the Indian Territory, which was to become the state of Oklahoma.

The financial crashes in the mid-seventies had caused setbacks to many of these plans, and it was not until the spring of 1877 that the Southern Pacific arrived at the west bank of the Colorado, but the Federal Government, under Jay Gould's sway, refused to allow an extension of the track into Arizona. It was not until 1879 that the Southern Pacific at long last entered the territory; its trains reached Adonde. On March 31, 1879, the first train steamed into the hurriedly erected little stop at Gila Bend, and on April 28, it arrived at Maricopa, still thirty miles away from Phoenix.

Of the seven men who had started the Central Pacific, only three had remained partners: Huntington, Hopkins, and Stanford. The man who had initiated it all, Theodore Judah, had fallen out with the financiers and, on a journey to New York in an endeavor to obtain financial backing and regain control of the company, died of yellow fever when he was crossing the Isthmus of Panama. The other three were either eased out by Huntington or backed out when they lost the courage to invest still more capital during the race against the Union Pacific.

However, Huntington had been joined by another man— Charles Crocker, who was later to play a decisive role in financing James Reavis' claim to the Barony of Arizona. From then on the Big Four became the great tycoons of the West, controlling not only the Central and Southern Pacific but also nineteen other railroad companies, harbors, shipyards, and scores of industrial enterprises in California and the Southwest.

While Huntington was the dominant member of the syndicate and the master lobbyist with the Federal Government, Charles Crocker looked after the actual business management. Hopkins controlled the organization and legal matters, and Stanford—now a Senator—concerned himself with the finance and state politics in California. Thanks to this teamwork and immunity to ethical precepts, the Big Four created for themselves a dictatorial position in the business and political life of the West.

In addition to the railroad construction companies, they had formed the famous Contract and Finance Company, which embarked on financial and exploitative enterprises concerning land, mines, real estate, and industry. Assets of this company were transferred to the Big Four individually, and they made huge personal profits out of Government subsidies and land grants meant for building railroads. Minority stockholders were kept in complete ignorance about what was going on. The amount of profit and details of financial operations were a closely guarded secret. When questions became too awkward and newspapers exposed the bribery of members of Congress, vital documents relating to dubious transactions were destroyed and official enquiries evaded.

When James Reavis came to Huntington on behalf of a second-rate newspaper canvassing for a paltry advertising order, he arrived with the right sort of proposition in the right place at the right moment.

"I know your interest in Arizona," he told Huntington. "My work for the *Examiner* is only incidental. I am in the possession of documents which will make me the owner of vast estates in Arizona and the western parts of New Mexico, of land that will be fought over by the railroad companies."

He explained briefly, precisely, and almost convincingly the possibilities which the Peralta Grant offered.

It may be that Huntington did not believe a single word of it.

He was not a man to be taken in by a penniless adventurer. But he recognized in Reavis a man he could use. If Reavis went with his "irrefutable evidence" of his land claim to the rival company, Jay Gould would mobilize a small regiment of lawyers and venal officials. He would use the Peralta claim as yet another obstacle to throw across the way the Southern Pacific was to take.

Huntington realized that Reavis, even if he were probably only a small-time crook, could become dangerous if he were to join the rival camp. The Big Four boss did not want more trouble in Arizona than could be avoided. It was better to render Reavis harmless. The more land through which the Southern Pacific was to run that was in their hands or in the hands of men who were in their pockets, the better, Huntington decided.

He gave him the advertising order for the *Examiner* as a first gesture of his favor. He was careful not to get personally involved with Reavis and told Charles Crocker to "keep an eye on that fellow." Then, in the summer of 1878, when the rivalry between the Big Four and Jay Gould became particularly acute, James Reavis was summoned to Huntington's magnificent mansion on Nob Hill. It was an invitation that ranked almost with one to the Pope's private audience at the Vatican in Rome.

In the presence of Charles Crocker, Reavis told Huntington such details about the Peralta Grant as he could muster, carefully omitting to mention the late Dr. Willing's part. He explained that he would have to conduct careful and costly research in Arizona and Mexico before he could register the claim.

He did not talk only about the Peralta Grant. He developed before the two tycoons a bold plan for the irrigation of large areas of the Arizona desert and painted a word picture of thousands of square miles of rich farmland and pastures for cattle. He had briefed himself on the possibilities which the opening up of Arizona would offer. He surprised his listeners by his knowledge of Joseph Glidden's invention of the barbed wire, only recently patented in Chicago, and told them that the fencing up of pastures would revolutionize the range country, make stock farming vastly more profitable than ranging, and speed up the settlement of the great Western plains. He spoke of the control of innumerable gold, silver, copper, zinc, and ore deposits which had hardly been tapped.

Huntington and Crocker must have recognized that however vague the evidence of the Peralta Grant might be, James Reavis was a man of unusual intelligence and drive and the sort of man who would make most people believe in his claim. Even so-called experts of the Government would probably accept it, at least to the extent of assessing it worthy of examination. Reavis talked of Gila Bend, Maricopa, Phoenix, Casa Grande, Florence, and Prescott as if these places already belonged to him.

Seeing Huntington and Crocker grow increasingly interested, Reavis became bold:

"I would deny Gould's Texas Pacific the right of way over the land of the Grant, and at the same time recognize the right of the Southern Pacific and grant you the right of way through my property," he said, "providing you would make a contract with me to the amount of fifty thousand dollars."*

But Huntington was not prepared to rush matters. He was careful not to become too closely involved with Reavis, at least not yet. He promised he would provide finance, but the claim would have to be properly registered. What Reavis did not know at that time was that Huntington was secretly conducting negotiations with Gould through middlemen and that he hoped to arrive at a compromise with his rival.

The interview proved somewhat disappointing, but Reavis

* See "Account of Incidents Connected with the Peralta Grant," letter from J. A. Reavis to James O. Broadhead in 1894 (original in the Missouri Historical Society collection of the Broadhead Papers). The contract was eventually signed on September 17, 1881.

continued to meet Charles Crocker and told him that in order to pursue his claim, he needed publicity. Some he could obtain through the San Francisco *Examiner,* but he suggested that Crocker finance a journal which he wanted to start. Probably without Huntington's knowledge, Crocker gave Reavis $2,000, and Reavis began to publish the *Weekly Advertiser* at Sacramento, the state capital.

Reavis fully proved his flair for journalism. The *Advertiser* was a lively well-edited newspaper. It survived for eighteen months, against the competition of old-established papers and in spite of difficulties in obtaining advertising.

Then, in 1879, Reavis received another summons to the palatial office at the corner of Fourth and Townsend Streets. Crocker told him that the Southern Pacific was now ready to assist him to go to Arizona and set the ball rolling.

It was Reavis' idea that he enter Arizona in the role of a newspaperman. He closed down the Sacramento *Weekly Advertiser,* equipped himself with credentials from the San Francisco *Examiner,* and set off in May, 1880, for Phoenix.

He had concealed from Huntington and Crocker that he still had to recover Willing's documents and that if he did recover them, they were the property of Mary Ann, Willing's widow. Undoubtedly he had already decided to use his penmanship in the production of such additional documents as he would need to prove the claim.

At long last the curtain was going up on the tragicomedy of the Peralta Grant, a drama that was to be enacted by a splendid performer and to keep his audience spellbound for almost fifteen years.

4

The Peralta Grant

After his visits to Phoenix and Prescott in the summer of 1880, James Reavis returned to San Francisco. He had in his possession the documents he had found in Willing's gunnysack at Judge Fleury's house in Prescott and a notebook in which he had recorded everything he had heard from James Monihon and the people in Arizona with whom he had discussed Willing's claim.

He had also kept the notes made during the talks with Willing and William Gitt, six years earlier in St. Louis. Willing had supplied a mass of information about his travels in the Southwest and had rattled off the names of places in Arizona and New Mexico where the Peralta family was supposed to have lived and of people supposed to have known the Miguel Peralta from whom he had bought the claim. But when Reavis had plied him with questions of a more exact nature, Willing would confirm only a few details and contradicted still others.

William Gitt, the crooked lawyer, had produced a few Spanish documents which at that time appeared to have some relevance to the Peralta Grant but now only added to the confusion. Thumbing through Willing's documents, Reavis realized they provided not even a remote basis for filing a claim that would be worthy of official scrutiny.

There was the scrap of the old wrapping paper on which Willing and the old Mexican had signed the agreement providing for the transfer of the claim to the Doc, bearing two hardly decipherable signatures of the witnesses, two hoboes Willing had accosted in the Black Canyon camp. The agreement was dated October 20, 1864, but Reavis found out during his visit to Arizona that Willling could not have met that legendary Miguel Peralta before 1867—if he ever met him at all. There was no mention in the agreement of the amount Willing had paid for the claim, and Reavis had never believed that he had given $20,000 worth of gold and equipment for that scrap of paper and a few dubious documents.

Willing had told him that Peralta had gone to Wickenburg to start prospecting as soon as he received the payment. Inquiries Reavis had made in Arizona confirmed that a Mexican family named Peralta had lived near Wickenburg in the late 1860's but had long since gone away, probably to Mexico.

The other documents which Willing had received from Peralta contained only vague references to the grant, which seemed to be just one of those floating Spanish grants held by many Mexican families, peddled all over the West, and usually sold for a few dollars. If Reavis had qualms about further pursuing the matter, he must have weighed them against Huntington's and Crocker's promise to finance the claim. He had already involved himself too deeply and had spent too much time and money to abandon his plans. Above all other considerations, the prospect of mulcting the bosses of the Southern Pacific was sufficient inducement to smother any doubts he may have had.

He realized, however, that he would have to start afresh and produce a set of documents which would stand up to examina-

tion. He was determined to produce them by forgery; the basis
he needed for the start was in the Willing documents. He went
to work with his usual zest.

First of all, he had to settle some of the "small matters"
Willing had told him about, such as the assignment of the
mining rights within the supposed Peralta estate, which Willing
had made over to the Sacramento merchant Florin Massol.
Then he had to come to an arrangement with Mary Ann
Willing and have the claim transferred to his own name.

He went to Sacramento and persuaded Florin Massol to
relinquish the rights in return for a promise to repay Willing's
old debt of $3,000 plus interest—if he got the claim accepted by
the United States authorities. It was an empty promise, but
Massol agreed.

Many years earlier the Massol family had befriended Mary
Ann Willing when the Doc had been in practice in Sacramento
and after he had left her, going off with his traveling medicine
show. Mrs. Massol persuaded her husband to sign away the
rights to Reavis, believing that Mary Ann would benefit.

For several months thereafter, Reavis traveled widely. In St.
Louis, Gitt had mentioned that some important papers relating
to the Peraltas were in the records of the Mission of San Xavier
del Bac near Tucson. He had also advised Reavis to go to
Mexico and Guadalajara to ascertain the existence of cedulas,
or Spanish royal decrees, relating to the Peralta family. There
was, of course, not a shred of evidence that the Miguel Peralta
of Wickenburg was related to the great Spanish family and to
Don Pedro de Peralta who in 1609 was governor of New Mexico, founded Santa Fe, contributed a great deal to the colonization of the Spanish colonies in North America, and, having displeased the Holy Inquisition, fell from royal favor and in 1710
was jailed at the Perea monastery at Bernalillo.

But Reavis reveled in stories of Spanish conquistadors which
conjured before his eyes the exciting tales he had read with his

mother. He decided to cross the continent and go to Philadelphia and Washington because the ancient records of the San Xavier Mission had been sent by Bishop John B. Salpointe of Tucson for exhibition at the great Centennial Fair at Philadelphia.

The inspection of these records proved entirely fruitless, but during his journey Reavis visited Mary Ann Willing, who had gone to live in Kentucky. She welcomed her old friend with open arms and had little hesitation in putting her signature under a deed which in return for the promise of a payment of $30,000—if the claim was accepted—assigned all her rights in the Peralta Grant to James Addison Reavis.

He also made a stop in St. Louis, where he saw his wife, Ada, for the first time after more than six years. They had little to say to each other. Two years later Ada Reavis brought a suit against her husband on the ground of desertion, and the divorce was made absolute in 1883.

After his return from the East to California, Reavis traveled to Mexico. He arrived in September, 1880, and stayed through the winter months in Guadalajara and Mexico City. He made friends with Don Manuel Cordero and Don Justino Rubio, the archivists at the state archives in the respective cities.

It may be imagined how diligent his search had to be. With infinite patience and caution, Reavis selected the rooms, the shelves, and the moldering ledgers which were to have his attention. He perused the documents in the appropriate places with such assiduity that soon he could memorize the style of language, even the idiosyncrasies of the scribes who had at the relevant time recorded the facts. He examined the texture of the paper, the penmanship, the hues of the faded inks.

Weeks of courteous contact with the archivists and their assistants built up a trust in his honesty. It was natural that they should be only too ready to help this quiet, studious, and charming American, so proud of his Spanish blood, in his efforts to aid Mexican settlers in the territories which the republic of Mexico had lost to the land-grabbing *Yanquis*.

Reavis examined and studied hundreds, perhaps thousands, of cedulas, royal edicts, deeds, mission reports, and maps concerning ancient land grants. In his mind emerged the background of a great family of Spanish grandees in every detail, so that it is understandable that it became real to him. Just as in his childhood he had believed the vague and nostalgic tales his mother had told him of the aristocratic Iberian blood in her veins, so now he began to accept that what he was devising in his imagination was truth.

He repaid the courtesy of the Mexican archivists by filching as many documents which would serve his purpose as he could without fear of discovery. He had made transcripts of many others or had them copied and photographed with the archivists' permission. With a trunk stuffed with these copies and a bundle of the stolen originals, he made for San Francisco.

During the following months he lived the life of a medieval monk engaged in producing an illuminated manuscript or incunabula.

James Reavis was much more than a crooked forger. The history of New Spain, unfolded by the material in the archives, fascinated him. He had been painfully reading and translating the stilted and outmoded language of the past, noting the changes of style and wording which had occurred. He assimilated the finer points of Spanish title and rank in army, church, and colonial government. He was able to read the quaintly ornate calligraphy of the scribes of past centuries with as much ease as the printed characters of the final edicts for Don Juan Bautista de Anza, the governor of New Mexico.

He studied the ancient maps drawn by Marcos de Niza, who in 1539 led the first Spanish expedition into the region which was now Arizona, in search of the legendary Seven Cities of Cibola of the Zuñi Indians. He examined reports which Father

Francisco Kino had written for the viceroy after his exploration of the San Pedro and Gila Rivers and Valleys and his visit to Casa Grande in 1694.

He noted the outmoded terms for money, lineal measures, and geographical locations and compared the paper and inks of documents issued in Madrid and Seville with those produced by the Jesuits in New Spain. While he crammed his brilliant but perverted mind with this mass of historical data, he also launched into practical experiments. Inks had to be mixed to produce many different shades; chemical methods of fading the inks and yellowing the paper had to be devised. Acids which would erase writing on genuine documents or turn a piece of parchment blank were needed. Pens had to be fashioned out of quills, and brushes for decorative initials and titles handmade because no suitable artist's materials were obtainable. Wax for seals needed to be compounded in the right crimson of the Inquisition authorities and the right blue for the royal cipher. Molds had to be cut, sometimes in wood and more often in lead.

Slowly but surely, with all the genius of his penmanship and intelligent application, after he had searched and procured the appropriate kind of parchment and old paper and had processed the paper and ink, emerged a set of documents that created a great and glorious family—a family that existed only in his imagination.

The first thing was to create the founder of the line. Obviously the family name had to be Peralta, to forge a link with the only tenuous, genuine morsel of fact in his possession, the Willing deed. The splendid personage Reavis saw in his mind and now proceeded to turn into a historical figure was Don Miguel Nemecio Silva de Peralta y de la Córdoba. He was the son of Don José Gaston Silva Carillo de Peralta y de las Falces de Mendoza, his grandmother being a scion of the great De las Falces family, related to Philip IV, father-in-law of Louis XIV of France, the *Roi Soleil*. His mother was of no less ancient ancestry Doña Francisca María de García de la Córdoba y Muniz de Pérez.

Don Miguel was born in 1708, and in 1727, during the war against France and England, he entered the service of his king, Philip V as a lieutenant in the royal dragoon guards. In 1742, at the age of thirty-four, Don Miguel was appointed *visitador del rey*, a sort of royal inspector, of the city of Guadalajara in New Spain and sailed to the New World.

In the mid-eighteenth century the viceroyalty of New Spain was a well-ordered colonial kingdom. Its capital, Mexico City, was the metropolis of European life and culture in all North America; its trade and the richness of its gold and silver mines were the envy of every nation. Its northern borders extended from the Presidio of Los Adaes in Louisiana to a chain of Jesuit missions in Lower California. One of the chief figures of the bold expansion to the north was Father Francisco Kino, a courageous Jesuit explorer who became a mission builder, ranchman, cattle king, and great prospector on the frontiers of Sonora, Arizona, and California. By 1750 the Spanish frontier had pushed across Sonora and Arizona as far as the Gila and Colorado Rivers.

James Reavis provided a pseudohistorical but extremely plausible tale of Don Miguel's service in New Spain by producing many documents. One, bearing the signature of King Philip V, ordered his subjects in New Spain "to obey and respect Don Miguel de Peralta y de la Córdoba, who represents me, and to favor and support this Royal Inspector as one who represents my person, and do whatever may be necessary to do in order to execute that which I have directed in my previous secret instructions." The king charged his good and loyal vassals "to do that which you ought, and which it is your obligation to do and I will consider myself well served; but if on the contrary you should do otherwise, it will be much to my Royal displeasure."*

Equipped with such splendid credentials, Don Miguel rendered good service to his king and, as Reavis explained in another document, was charged with the examination of the accounts of the viceroy's treasury, controlled by the Jesuits. For a long time the king had been displeased with the falling receipts in precious ore and taxes from the colonies. Indeed, none other than Don Miguel de Peralta had discovered the reasons for this deficit and was instrumental in provoking the royal decree which in 1767 expelled the Jesuit fathers from all the Spanish dominions, including New Spain.

By a royal cedula in November, 1744, King Philip V had already signified his intention of bestowing on Don Miguel a grant of large estates in the Colorados. Unfortunately, the king died two years later, in the midst of the War of the Austrian Succession, but his son, Ferdinand VI, confirmed the grant and also promoting Don Miguel to the dignity of a captain general. In 1748 the new king signed a document, which Reavis produced in all its splendor:

> The King, Viceroy, Governor and Captain-General of the Provinces of New Spain and President of My Royal *Audiencias.*
> Whereas in view of the merits and services, therefore I order the Commander-in-Chief, on behalf of Don Miguel de Peralta y de la Córdoba, Captain of Dragoons, agreeably to the petition of the Royal Inquisition in New Spain, and the recommendation of the Council of Commerce and the Judges of Appeals . . . and in consideration of and by way of recompense for great and valuable services, also for his manner of bringing to a speedy and successful termination important battles in the service of the King:
> I, the King of Spain, by this mandate and public decree, in accordance with the customs of the Crown, do recommend to his Excellency the Viceroy of New Spain to grant and concede to Don Miguel de Peralta y de la Córdoba, according to common measure-

---

* Rufus C. Hopkins, *Muniments of Title of the Barony of Arizona* and *Translation into English* (San Francisco, Bancroft, 1893) .

ments . . . three hundred square leagues, or nineteen thousand two hundred million square varas of land which shall be situated in the northern portion of the Viceroyalty of New Spain; and shall be in such shape as not to interfere with grants previously made; they shall however include all lands, waters and streams, all minerals and all other belongings.

And I declare the honorable title of Don Miguel de Peralta y de la Córdoba to be Baron of the Colorados, declaring him at the same time to be a Grandee of Spain.

Thus be provided, ordered and signed. Done at Madrid on the twentieth day of December One thousand seven hundred and forty eight.*

This, then, was the Peralta claim. It was the pivot on which the great land claim depended. But Reavis knew, of course, that many more documents would have to be produced, showing the progress in delineating the estates which the viceroy of New Spain and the Inquisition authorities in Mexico were supposed to have selected and bestowed on Don Miguel de Peralta, obeying the king's command.

Reavis produced a lengthy report of the Inquisitors, dated October 10, 1757, confirming that the grant should include the Gila River area around the Mission of San Xavier del Bac and measure "eighty thousand varas from North to South and two hundred and forty varas from East to West." Another document under the squiggly signature of the Marqués Agustín de Ahumada de las Amarillas, viceroy of Mexico, dated January 3, 1758, finally outlined the boundaries of the Peralta Grant.

Reavis knew that the process establishing Peralta's title would have taken many years. The mills of Spanish colonial administration ground slowly in those days, and he allowed fourteen years to elapse between the first royal edict and the final settlement of the grant.

He sent Don Miguel de Peralta on a long and dangerous

* Royal patent submitted in the Petition of Claimants and Exhibit AAA at the trial of James Reavis. (Copies in the University of Arizona Library and the library of the Arizona Pioneers' Historical Society, Tucson.)

journey through the promised estates, from Guadalajara, to the foothills of the Sierra Madre and across Sonora, passing today's Nogales, and along the Santa Cruz River to the San Xavier del Bac Mission. It was one of the twenty-four Jesuit missions which Father Kino had established in 1700, and it was the most noted because its founder spent there many years of his service in Arizona, preaching to the Pima, Papago, Maricopa, and Yuma Indians.

Fact and fiction were cleverly intertwined in the story of the first Baron of Arizona, Reavis having used genuine records of the Jesuit and Franciscan missions in the Pimería Alta, mentioning that Father Kino was the first white man who had ever visited Casa Grande on the Gila River. That Reavis amassed all the skill and knowledge he needed for his conspiracy is testimony both to his intelligence and to his unremitting application.

At San Xavier, Don Miguel de Peralta and his retinue were welcomed by Father Francisco Pauer, the head of the mission, and by two officers of the viceregal garrison only recently established at Tubac in the Santa Cruz Valley.

The viceroy had appointed Father Pauer to adjudicate the final demarcation lines of the Peralta Grant. The priest must have been a perfect host; not only did he provide comfortable accommodations, but he also accompanied Don Miguel and a posse of royal dragoons for several days and many miles on an inspection of the estates through the San Pedro Valley to the Gila.

A lengthy copy of Father Pauer's report was attached to the documents. It described in detail the ceremony by which Don Miguel de Peralta formally took possession of his royal grant:

> Proceeding to the base of the Maricopa Mountain, which is the eastern extremity of the Sierras Estrellas on the River Gila in Pimería Alta, on the thirteenth day of May, A.D. 1758, at six o'clock in the morning, the day being splendid, all the parties in

interest cited, and being present for the measurements of the land of the Barony of Arizonac, titles of Grace of the Most Excellent Señor Don Miguel de Peralta y de la Córdoba, Baron de Arizonac, Caballero of the Chamber of His Majesty, Grandee of Spain, etc., etc., holding his titles in his hand, said:

Having reduced the measurements of this Barony of Arizonac . . . to varas of the common Mexican measure, the result being 53,333,333,333 and one third common Mexican varas, and for the south boundary which is the same as of the north, of thirty ancient leagues, or two hundred-forty thousand ancient varas, the result is four-hundred thousand common Mexican varas.

No person having presented himself to object, the measurement is proceeded with. Don Cristóbal Vega and Don Andrés Gálvez are appointed measurers, and they are of the highest intelligence. Having presented themselves before the adjudicator and accepted the charge, they proceeded to execute their commission and have found a great and high rock at the foot of the Sierras Estrellas, mentioned above, which is at their extreme point; and we who have seen this singular rock, truly admire the marvel which the Supreme Creator placed in this delightful valley. As there is neither mount nor hill towards the north, east or south which obstructs the view from this magnificent rock of which we speak, we ascended to the summit of this rock and looking round from the height of seven or eight or more varas, there is an unobstructed view towards the north, east and south, and we saw at a great distance the valleys of the Gila and the Salado and the Santa Cruz, all grouped in this charming place; and we believe that there is nothing in the world so singular; we descended from the rock, and ordered to be designed on this said rock the diseño* of the said Barony of Arizonac, and it was so designed; and with ceremonies appropriate for the purpose of consecrating it to its destiny; wherefore, it is named the Initial Monument (*Monumento Inicial*) for the center of the west boundary.†

The adjudicator duly issued a certificate, dated May 13, 1758, confirming that the land of the grant had been properly surveyed and measured and that a marking stone engraved with

---

* The Spanish word diseño (verb, disenar), meaning design or draft, in this case means the outline.

† Muniments of the Barony of Arizona, pp. 108–110. (two reels of microfilms in the Zimmerman Library of the University of New Mexico, Albuquerque.)

the outline and the Peralta arms had been set up and a map of the estate inscribed.

Don Miguel then left for Mexico, and the documents issued by the adjudicator, Father Pauer, were registered at the *residencia* of Guadalajara a year later.

Don Miguel de Peralta had thus taken formal possession of his grant, but he still needed a royal endorsement. For ten years he did nothing about it. The reason for this—according to various letters Reavis produced—was that in 1751 the Apaches came from the north, invaded the missions, were joined in an uprising by the usually peaceful Papago and Pima tribes, and committed murder, arson, and robbery, forcing the priests to flee. Those Jesuit fathers who did not manage to escape to southern Sonora were killed. The silver mines were overrun, and all the mining equipment was destroyed. It was not for four or five years that the missionaries returned to Pimería Alta, and by then Don Miguel was involved in a bitter quarrel with the Jesuits.

When the Jesuits were expelled and all mission property in New Spain was transferred to royal *comisarios,* Don Miguel felt that he would require a confirmation of his grant. He submitted a petition to King Charles III, who had followed his brother Ferdinand VI, and the grant was duly confirmed by a royal cedula dated December 2, 1772. But Don Miguel had to wait another three years until he received the approval of the High Court, in a document dated January 22, 1776.

The first baron never really enjoyed his estates in faraway Arizona. It appeared that he visited them only once, in 1778, although he maintained a garrison there and erected several buildings near the ruins of Casa Grande, which he named La Hacienda de Peralta. Almost constant attacks by the Apaches must have made life on the Gila unpleasant, although Father Francisco Tomás Garcés, of the Franciscan order, who had come to Pimería Alta in 1770, headed a flourishing mission at San

Xavier del Bac, and traveled widely in the area. In 1774 Father
Garcés and Father Juan Díaz accompanied an expedition led by
Governor Juan Bautista de Anza to lay out the first route
between the Franciscan missions in Arizona and those of Cali-
fornia. Two years later Garcés entered the present region of
Prescott, where his reception by the Yavapai tribes was friendly.

Don Miguel had been preoccupied by other business in
Mexico. As a soldier and an administrator, he had served five
Spanish kings, from the Seven Years' War to the Napoleonic
Wars, had seen Charles III raise Spain to the highest position of
power and influence she had enjoyed since the sixteenth cen-
tury, and had helped Viceroy Gálvez expand the colonial em-
pire far to the north. He lived to see the foundings of San
Francisco, Los Angeles, and San Diego, the emergence of the
United States from colonial rule, and the slow decline of Span-
ish power in America. He had amassed a large fortune, owned
estates in Jalisco and Sonora, with rich ranchos at Ahualulco,
Guda, and Etzatlán.

In 1770, at the age of sixty-two, still a bachelor, he led a
young noblewoman to the altar at the Church of Etzatlán. She
was Sofía Ave María Sanchez Bonilla de Amaya y García de
Orosco, the daughter of the governor of Nayarit. For eleven
years the couple remained childless; but their prayers were
heard, and in 1781, when Don Miguel was seventy-three years
old, Doña Sofía gave birth to a boy. He was born at Cumpas on
Yaqui River, on one of the baron's estates, not far from the
present-day border of Arizona. He was baptized Miguel Silva
Jesús.

There must have been some malicious gossip about the legitimacy of the child whose mother was almost forty years younger
than his father, because Don Miguel de Peralta took pains to
establish it beyond any doubt. When the boy was seven and a
pupil at the Franciscan College of Querétaro, the baron ordered
the public notary, Don Juan Ballesteros, to draw up a last will

and testament and also a certificate establishing the legitimacy
and nobility of his son and heir.

Three witnesses, all noble officials of the court of Viceroy
Gálvez, testified that the baron and his wife were true Chris-
tians, of pure Spanish blood, free from any mixture with Moors,
Jews, or Indians, which could not have been otherwise as Don
Miguel de Peralta was not only a grandee of Spain but also a
knight of the Order of the Golden Fleece and of the Order of
Montesa, a gentleman of the King's Bed Chamber, a member of
the Royal Collegium, and a Knight of the Order of Our Lady of
Guadalupe.

The testament contained a special clause referring to the
estates in the Barony of Arizonac and los Colorados:

> I constitute and appoint as my sole and universal heirs, my wife
> Doña Sofía Ave María Sánchez and my son Miguel Silva Jesús de
> Peralta y de Amaya impartially to the end they may take and
> enjoy and inherit in full property and dominion . . . the Barony
> of Arizonac, known as the Hacienda de Peralta . . . under the
> obligation to respect the franchises and privileges, which in the
> name of the King of Spain were granted to the Pima Indians,
> who have several rancherias within the limits of the said Barony.

Don Miguel had thus shown a touching, if most unlikely,
concern for the Indians. The reason Reavis included this clause
in the testament was that he must have envisaged difficulties
with the United States Government concerning the Indian
reservations which had been established on the land he was to
claim under the Peralta Grant. By including this reference, he
obviously intended to placate the officials who were to examine
the claim.

The baron had safeguarded the inheritance of his family,
although there was no need for him to hurry. He lived for many
more years and died in 1824, still a sprightly gentleman in full
possession of his faculties, at the amazing age of one hundred

and sixteen. Indeed, Reavis might have extended his long span of life even further were it not for the need to introduce the second baron into the complex web of the Peralta history.

The patriarch died suddenly on a journey from his estates in the province of Hermosillo to Guadalajara. On February 2 the obsequies took place at the Cathedral of Santiago, at a Guadalajara, with all the pomp due his rank, and he was buried at the Belen cemetery, on the banks of the Río Grande de Santiago.

A document including a long inventory of the baron's possessions showed that Doña Sofía and her son, Don Miguel Silva Jesús de Peralta, had come into a great inheritance. In addition to the Barony of Arizona, they were left estates in Sonora and a ranch at Ahualulco in Jalisco, with several thousand head of cattle, 200 goats, several hundred sheep, pigs, oxen, and mules, a stud with broodmares, and riding horses. There were several fine houses in the towns of Etzatlán and Guda and a *palacio* at Guadalajara.

The second baron, a handsome officer in the royal cavalry, could confidently look to a comfortable and illustrious future. However, when continuing the history of the Peralta family, James Reavis stopped short of providing more documentary evidence about the life and career of the second baron.

All that was learned of him from the documents was that he had married, in 1822, at the age of forty-one. His bride was Doña Juana Laura Ibarra; she came from a very respected and noble family of Guadalajara, whose ancestry went back to Don Francisco de Ibarra, governor in 1565. Like his father, the second baron remained childless for many years. His marriage was, however, blessed with a daughter in 1832. The girl was baptized Sofía Laura Micaela.

The second baron apparently never made an effort to visit his estates in Arizona, but this was not particularly astonishing, considering that Mexico was rent by civil wars and eventually involved in a conflict with the United States which ended in

1848 with the peace Treaty of Guadalupe Hidalgo, in which the republic of Mexico was compelled to cede many of its northern provinces to the victorious enemy. The new frontier now ran along the Rio Grande; California and New Mexico had become part of the United States, and this included the Territory of Arizona and all the estates of the Peralta Grant.

Wars and revolutions, civil strife, and economic upheavals must have ruined the second baron. In the early 1860's, an impoverished old man, he found himself somewhere in Arizona, in a last desperate quest for his long-forgotten estates. At the Black Canyon he met Dr. Willing and across a campfire sold him his inheritance.

Thus ended the chain of events which started in 1748, with James Addison Reavis as the final link in the story of the rise and decline of the Peralta family. Out of nothing Reavis had created this noble family and had endowed its members with great achievements and ill luck, transferring the figments of his imagination onto plausible historical documents. He did not yet know that this was but the first installment of a thrilling story and that he was to be compelled to produce yet another, a romantic story that would have done credit to an Alexandre Dumas or a Charles Dickens.

He was confident that he now held irrefutable evidence of the existence of the Barons of Arizona and of the rightfulness of his claim to the Peralta Grant.

5

The Baron Takes Possession

When James Reavis alighted on Sunday, September 3, 1882, from the train at Tucson, he had every reason to look confidently to the future. He jauntily walked through the sun-baked Congress Street—which the Mexicans, who provided three-quarters of the city's population, still called Calle de Alegría, or the street of pleasure—toward the Mesila Hotel, Tucson's best.

He had settled his business with Charles Crocker to his full satisfaction. He had been paid $5,000 on signing the agreement in 1881 and had received several payments on account of the sum of $50,000. Crocker had provided him with a first-class counselor, Harvey S. Brown, the company lawyer of the Southern Pacific.

Reavis' arrival in Tucson was not unexpected, although nobody there was looking forward to it. During 1882, several months before James Reavis descended upon Arizona, strange stories began to circulate in the territory, and local newspapers reprinted interviews he had given to San Francisco reporters. He had shown them documents, so impressive that they prompted the journalists to describe them as "conclusive proof of Mr. Reavis's rightful claim to a vast stretch of land in Arizona and to mining rights in some of the richest silver and copper districts."

The people who remembered Reavis' previous visit and his inquiries about Willing and the Peralta Grant were not unduly worried, even though the newspaper stories had caused consternation among the settlers and the townfolk of Phoenix.

However, hardly anybody in a responsible position believed that such an absurd claim, which, if validated, would dislodge and ruin thousands of landholders, could be taken seriously. At first the Arizona papers treated it all as a huge joke. The *Arizona Gazette* gave Reavis a cutting welcome:

> His Royal Nibbs, J. A. Reavis, who lays claim to nine-tenths of Arizona, arrived in Tucson on Sunday morning. On Monday, as early as business hours would warrant, he was placed under arrest for having, while on route to this city, attempted to occupy the sleeping berth of a domestic in the family of a prominent citizen of this city, who was returning by the same train. He avoided incarceration by paying a fine and apologizing to the young lady, and it is truly hoped that he is as penitent as his apology would indicate him to be.
>
> On the trip down, Mr. Reavis took occasion to pour into the ears of the passengers who prefer to kill time listening to him rather than viewing the dreary desert landscape, the story of his acquisition of the Spanish grant and his future course when it is fully confirmed by Congress. Mr. Reavis is in no hurry to effect a settlement with those who occupy his broad acres.*

It was true that Reavis had had an embarrassing experience on his train journey from San Francisco, having taken a berth reserved for a woman passenger. But this was obviously a

* Phoenix *Arizona Gazette,* September 7, 1882.

genuine mistake. His connection with the Southern Pacific was such that he surely did not need to use a mean ruse in order to obtain a ticket or a sleeping berth. Careful not to make enemies in Tucson, he immediately proffered his apologies and paid a five-dollar fine.

Reavis visited the office of the surveyor general, Joseph W. Robbins, told him that he intended to file a claim, but added that he would first go to Safford to make inquiries about the late Dr. George Willing's estate in Arizona, having acquired rights to the probate from the wife of the deceased.

A few days later the Tucson *Citizen* and the *Star* published brief notices, saying that "Mr. J. A. Reavis of San Francisco, who claims to possess rights to floating Spanish grants in the Yavapai and Graham counties, supposedly given to a Spanish nobleman named Miguel Peralta by the King of Spain, is making an effort to clarify the legal position."

At Safford, the little town settled by Mormon farmers, Reavis deposited at the courthouse of Graham County copies of deeds showing that Willing's rights had been assigned to him.

After his return to Tucson, he invited newspapermen to his hotel and showed them some of his documents. The stories published after this interview renewed uneasiness in Arizona. Although the *Star*, in a laudable effort to calm the worried citizens, declared on October 21, 1882: "From the appearance of this case there is little danger . . . and it is likely that continuance will be had . . . or the petition will be refused at once" the editor added a warning: "Reavis is determined to fight every inch of ground to obtain the land and doubtless has some powerful backing behind him. . . . He is systematically working to obtain proper and lawful title to his old Spanish Grant."

He certainly did just that, even though at first he seemed not in a hurry. He paid another visit to the surveyor general, asked many questions, but told him that he would not, at present, register his claim. Then he left Arizona and did not return until March, 1883.

Everything had started peacefully and without much public attention. The citizens of Tucson were much more concerned with the grave news which had reached them from the Indian reservations. A medicine man had stirred up the war spirit in the San Carlos Reservation northeast of Tucson, and when a unit of the Sixth Cavalry rode into the White Mountains to arrest him, Chief Geronimo, who had caused untold trouble for twenty years, had led his men to open mutiny. Several soldiers, including Captain Hentig, were killed, and the Apaches swarmed out from the reservation, attacking, burning, and plundering ranches and killing several settlers. A month after the outbreak Geronimo's men attacked the Indian agency at Camp Goodwin, killed the police chief and wounded the sub-agent, and then cut out for Mexico. Troubles with the Indians continued for a long time and occupied the settlers' minds much more than Reavis' land claim.

To his satisfaction, Reavis had discovered in Tucson that the story was largely one of what had not been done. Nearly eighteen years had passed since the first attempts at sorting out the land claims emanating from the Treaty of Guadalupe Hidalgo and the Gadsden Purchase. The first Americans who came to the Peralta barony in 1846 were members of the Mormon battalion which fought as part of the Army of the West against Mexico. In June, 1850, John R. Bartlett was appointed the United States commissioner for delineation of the new boundaries with Mexico, and from then on the work of delineation and the exploration of the newly acquired territories made some progress, although it was extremely slow and muddled.

The Government in Washington seemed to have cared little what was happening in the Southwest. The experts who had been sent to the Far West knew about the main trails and all about California. But they had no conception whatever about Arizona and the adjoining areas of New Mexico. Their natural reaction was that the United States had obtained a rather poor bargain from Mexico, having paid $15,000,000, whatever benefits there might have been strategically. The territory appeared to be a largely worthless waterless waste of parched desert and inaccessible mountains infested by hostile Indians, cutthroats, and renegades from a dozen races and twice as many Mexican half-breeds. It was true that considerable wealth was being mined in some districts, but for every genuine gold or silver placer there were ten fabled veins which did not exist.

The men who were assigned to assist Commissioner Bartlett, particularly Colonel J. D. Graham, Major W. H. Emory, and Lieutenant A. W. Whipple, each commanding small U.S. Army units, were left to their own devices. It required many weeks, often months, to get word to Washington and back. The officers and their men, left without instructions and, what was even worse, often without pay and funds to carry out their work, had an unenviable task. All the time they had to cope with sustained attacks by the Apaches.

It was not until 1854 that some order was brought into the work of the commissioners. The southern area of the territory was wild and unsettled, apart from wagon trains crossing it from the East toward California, used by pioneers and hopeful prospectors attracted by the gold rushes there and by trappers and fur hunters. During the height of the gold rushes immense flocks of sheep and herds of cattle from New Mexico and Texas were driven through southern Arizona destined for the California markets, but no raising of livestock was attempted on any large scale until 1858, when William Oury brought four bulls and a number of heifers from Kentucky. Oury started his ranch a few miles from Tucson, and his Kentucky cattle were the first blooded stock brought to Arizona. Another pioneer was Peter Kitchen, who came in 1854. By the early 1860's he had taken a thousand acres of rich bottomland around Nogales and raised large crops of grain, potatoes, and greenstuff and an abundance of fruit and melons, as well as large herds of cattle and several hundred fine hogs. He became a wealthy man by selling his produce to the citizens of Tucson. But for many years the area around Tucson, "the desert oasis town," remained wild and lawless.

The surveyor general for Arizona, who had been appointed in 1863, made a report on the natural resources but failed to provide a usable survey. Arizona was thereupon attached, for surveying purposes, to the New Mexico Land Registry at Santa Fe, and another effort was made to survey it and to disentangle the many land claims which were being filed at Santa Fe. About all that resulted was that an expedition fixed a base line and then went home. Five years later a halfhearted attempt was begun to work out who owned what. By the time James Reavis appeared on the scene, fewer than 8,000,000 acres had been surveyed, and ownership had been confirmed for a mere 250,-000 acres.

In another attempt to disentangle the mess, Washington next sent an expert to Mexico in 1874 to try to find the original documents relating to Spanish and Mexican grants of land. In Mexico City he was told that not many records were retained there because the area of the Pimería Alta had belonged, under the Spanish rule, to the Provincias Internas, and had been governed from Guadalajara. There the Mexican officials regretted that the majority of documents had been destroyed in a fire some years before. All these difficulties and the absence of original documents confirming land grants in Arizona (and in California and New Mexico) were duly reported to Congress in Washington, and little happened afterward.

Reavis knew all the relevant details of this report, number three of the Second Session of the Forty-third Congress. He had obtained transcripts of it during his visit in Washington in 1880.

Under an act of Congress the owner of a land grant (dating back to Spanish and Mexican rule), or his descendants, or persons to whom the grant had been assigned—as it was by Peralta to Willing and by Mrs. Willing to Reavis—had to file a claim with the United States surveyor general in the state or territory in question. The surveyor general had to examine the supporting documents, make all necessary investigations, and submit the claim with a report containing his findings to the Secretary of the Interior. This member of the Government had, in turn, to examine the claim and report and, if he found the claim valid, to lay it before Congress. In each case a special bill had to be passed, either finally validating or invalidating the claim.

Reavis had studied this complex and cumbersome procedure. He had read what Carl Schurz, Secretary of the Interior from 1877 to 1881, had said in a report to Congress:

> After thirty years more than a thousand claims have been filed with the Surveyors General, of which less than 150 have been reported to Congress, and of the number reported Congress had acted upon only 71. The operation of the law was a failure, amounting to a denial of justice, both to the claimants and the Administration of the United States.

The fact that so few claims had been dealt with did not worry Reavis at all. That the legal process was so extremely slow did, in fact, suit his purpose. The uncertainty in which settlers and landholders would have to live for years was a weapon which he was determined to use to his advantage.

When he again arrived in Tucson in March, 1883, he came with a devilishly clever plan for a cold war to be conducted by means of a propaganda which was very much ahead of his times. Before leaving San Francisco, he had already started a long-distance bombardment. In a series of articles, dealing with the development of Arizona, which he wrote for the San Francisco

Examiner but left unsigned, he extolled the prospects of the Peralta Grant, describing the "irrefutable evidence" in favor of this claim.

The *Examiner* was taken over by George Hearst, who had made his millions from the Comstock Lode silver mines and who, by 1880, had set his heart on becoming a Senator. Hearst had advanced loans to the *Examiner* and, when the managers had been unable to repay them, assumed control of the paper in October, 1880. He hired Emanuel Katz from the San Francisco *Chronicle* as general manager, provided new finance for hiring skilled journalists and improving the printing plant, and moved the offices from the dingy shop in Sacramento Street to new large premises in Market Street. The paper gained circulation, not the least because Hearst ordered the editor to attack the Big Four, whose business methods were causing much resentment.

Although James Reavis continued his secret connections with Huntington and Crocker, he also succeeded in ingratiating himself with George Hearst. The new proprietor of the *Examiner* had been buying up land and mining claims in California and Nevada and became interested in Reavis' scheme in Arizona, although Reavis did not disclose its extent to him. Reavis managed to use the newspaper for his purpose, either with or without George Hearst's approval.

This time Reavis came to Arizona with two men, who for a long time were to remain his faithful shadows. One of them, who was constantly conferring with Reavis, signed the hotel register as Cyril Barratt, attorney, of Los Angeles. He was in his mid-forties, balding, and fat. Despite an attempt to appear dignified and comfortably off, his badly cut suit was old and greasy. He was a confirmed drinker, and Reavis occasionally ordered him out of a saloon when he found him boasting of his lucrative law practice "back in civilization." In fact, Barratt was a disbarred attorney, wanted for malpractice and graft in California. Reavis had found him in a gutter in San Francisco, beaten up and bruised by some crooks with whom he had fallen out.

The other of Reavis' companions was a thickset swarthy man, who called himself Pedro Cuervo. He was only a little over five feet tall, but he was a strong fellow, who exuded evil from every inch of his stature. Mexican or mestizo, he had a habit of suddenly laughing uproariously, exposing a mouth full of decayed teeth, but his dark little eyes remained absolutely mirthless. There was talk among the saloon girls of Tucson that he was a nasty customer, demanding sadistic practices of a kind which even these hardened and resigned providers deemed dangerous. The grapevine spread the warning that his advances should be repulsed. The three had arrived with several trunks, most of them containing documents, copies, and transcripts; one ancient Spanish cedula was supposed to be a roll forty feet long.

On March 27, 1883, Reavis, accompanied by his "attorney" and his bodyguard, who carried two trunks, appeared at the office of the surveyor general. The documents, which included the original cedula bestowing the grant, the deeds made out by Father Pauer at San Xavier del Bac delineating the boundaries of the Peralta estates, and many supporting documents, were duly submitted, and James Addison Reavis formally registered his claim against the Government of the United States.

The surveyor general and his clerks sat with Reavis deep into the nights, examining the documents. They must have been staggered. On the face of it, Reavis had a very good case. His claim included land on which nine cities and townships were located—Phoenix, Tempe, Mesa, Casa Grande, Florence, Globe, Safford, Clifton, and Morenci—several hundred mines, including the fabulous Silver King Mine; and the copper deposits of Globe, San Carlos, Miami, Ray, Morenci, all in Arizona; and the Mogollon Mountains across the border in New Mexico.

Mr. Robbins told him that he would register the claim, as it was his duty, but that only the Government in Washington and finally Congress could decide its validity. He, the surveyor general, would have to make a careful examination, not only of the documents submitted, but also at the archives in Mexico, before sending his report to Washington. This might take a very long time, maybe years. In the meantime Reavis was not entitled to disturb the people who settled on the claimed land.

"I am fully cognizant of the legal position, Mr. Surveyor General." Reavis replied. "I do not propose to disturb anyone, although I shall, of course, take measures to safeguard my rights and make sure that the value of my land is in no way debased."

At first Reavis established his headquarters in Phoenix, where he hired several rooms at Salari's hotel. With Barratt he was busily preparing lists of landholders and mineowners, mixing rarely with the townfolk, whose resentment he sensed. Shortly after his arrival his brother William joined the party, along with two or three clerks whom Reavis had recruited. Reavis called on M. H. Sherman, the superintendent of public instruction, who had been entrusted by the Arizona legislature—usually called "the thieving thirteen"—to select a location for the future University of Arizona. In addition to looking after education, Sherman was the president of the Bank of Phoenix, and he was impressed with the amount of cash Reavis deposited in the account he opened.

When Sherman asked Reavis whether he intended to buy land, his new client replied with a smile that he did not need to do this as the land was already his by right. He even offered to select some suitable lots and donate them for the site of the proposed university. Reavis had undergone a marked change. Suave and polite as ever, he now began to display ostentation where before he had been diffident and modest. He complained about the poor comfort at the hotel, and one day the Reavis party left Phoenix, having loaded a large number of trunks and boxes onto two wagons.

A little later the citizens of Phoenix learned that the Baron of Arizona had gone to the area where, according to his claim, had stood La Hacienda de Peralta, south of Casa Grande.

If genius is the ability to take infinite pains, then Reavis was a genius. He had created the Peralta family; now he decided to create their ancestral home, which the first baron was supposed to have owned in his halcyon days. In his forged documents Reavis had told how Don Miguel de Peralta had built the hacienda in 1778, on his only visit to his Arizona estates. So Reavis now decided to conjure up the ruins of this imaginary place. There were some ancient ruins on the austere, though beautiful, small plateau, 1,500 feet high, about 1 or 2 miles from the ruins of the Casa Grande. Here, Reavis decreed, had stood La Hacienda de Peralta.

This was Papago country. The Papagos were the most friendly and civilized Indians of Arizona, who had themselves suffered from attacks by savage Apaches for generations. Reavis recruited a number of them and began to build his new home, living in the meantime in a rough log cabin. Pedro Cuervo trained and harshly bossed a few Papagos and Mexicans into a small private army, which now guarded the area.

The spot was called Arizola, and it proved a good choice for Reavis' headquarters. To the south were the banks of the Santa Cruz River, which provided the water direly needed in this arid desert country. A few miles to the north was the Gila River, which could be used as a waterway right up to Phoenix, some thirty-five miles away. Although isolated, Arizola was thus not cut off from the two most important towns in southern Arizona: Tucson was sixty-five miles to the south, and the Gila River provided communication to Yuma and California to the west.

It was beautiful and romantic country, too. Though in the midst of the Papago desert, it did not lack forbidding and grandiose scenery. To the north was the chain of the Table Top Mountains and the graceful outline of the 5,800-feet Antelope

Peak. The whole area was steeped in history and Indian legend and superstition. The Papagos called it the land of the tarantula because it teemed with the dreaded poisonous trap-door spider—although its poison never killed a man. The soil was honey-combed with the spiders' burrows, each a small round box comfortably lined with the silky web and provided with a veritable trapdoor, made of earth and silk, which could be opened and closed at the will of its owner.

It is little wonder that later in his career the baron was often referred to as the Tarantula of Arizona, a human spider that went out hunting for prey and retired to his fortress behind the trapdoor whenever he sensed danger.

The ancient city of Casa Grande was built at the dawn of history, but even its newest buildings were at least 800 years old. The Casa Grande tower has been called the first skyscraper of America; it still stood 4 stories high, 40 feet wide, and 60 feet long; its adobe walls were 4 feet thick. To provide the floor poles, the Indians must have brought the ironwood and juniper from some 50 miles away, probably floating the timber on the Gila River, as there were never trees in the surrounding desert. Near the great tower stood twelve or more houses, covering 2 acres of land, surrounded by thick mud and stone walls, each building with several rooms. A second compound consisted of buildings stretching over 900 square yards of more primitive architecture and believed by archaeologists to have been built more than 1,000 years ago by the Aztec Hohokam Indians.

It may well be that Reavis intended to set up his residence in this ancient desert city, which must have been at one time the capital of an Aztec kingdom. Perhaps he saw himself as a modern emperor, a successor to the rulers who reigned here at the time when the Christian Era was beginning in Europe.

For one reason or another Reavis decided, however, to build his home a mile or so away from Casa Grande. At first it was only a sturdy loghouse providing modest comfort. Then Reavis brought craftsmen from Phoenix and Tulsa, and they built him a mansion designed by a San Francisco architect.

It became the fanciest house in the Territory of Arizona, erected of red bricks specially made at the Phoenix kiln works, redwood, and other imported materials. The windows were tall and arched, framed in granite and carved stone, in a sort of Gothic style, with shutters and grilles in wrought iron. The doors were paneled and richly finished with wrought hardware and had thresholds of cast brass. Roofs, made of rounded baked clay tiles in several variegated colors, sloped to a fine portico and several covered patios, supported by slender balusters and pillars. There were ten rooms, some very spacious, with floors either of ornamental Mexican stone tiles or polished parquetry. Flush lavatories and a bath with walls of Dutch tiles had tap water.

When, in 1885, a Japanese engineer installed the first electric plant in Phoenix, operated by a steam engine burning cordwood, Reavis seriously contemplated introducing electric lighting at his Arizola palace; but the Phoenix powerhouse—which had the distinction of being the first electric plant in the West— was soon abandoned because the process of producing electricity proved far too expensive and complicated. But in every respect, Reavis' baronial hall was a magnificent building, which could easily vie with the governor's residence. In the course of time Reavis lavishly furnished his residence and added several outbuildings, servant quarters, stables, and store sheds, fortifying the place, for good reason, with tall stone walls.

Seventy years later, when the Barony of Arizona had become a nightmarish memory, the palace of Arizola was rediscovered by the U.S. National Park Service. By then it had been used for many years as a barn and stables by a farmer, Fred E. Gack, whose family had bought the place from Reavis' creditors after his trial and conviction.

In 1953 Farmer Gack told a newspaper reporter: "We used to

live in the baron's palace for almost forty years, and a fine place it was. But the family grew up and moved away, and the house was too big for me and my wife and children. I had a smaller, snug stone house built nearby and used the big place for storage and for stabling animals."* Now, at the time this book is being published, the palace is in a rundown condition, the floors have sagged, the wood trim is rotting away, and the bricks and tiles are scattered. But without Gack's maintenance the house would have fallen to rubble long ago. He also saved the baron's palace from destruction by bulldozer. Some years ago a new highway was planned to run through a corner of the estate, but at Fred Gack's request, the highway was routed around the house. Motorists now pass the old tumbledown ruin, probably without a glance at it and ignorant that it had once been the fortress of the bad baron, from which he ruled his realm. In April, 1965, an expert was sent to Arizola by the National Park Service to find out whether the place could be restored and preserved as a public amenity and a historical monument; he reported that it would require considerable expense and that it was not worth it.

Reavis did not wait until his palace was completed. It was from the original glorified log cabin at Arizola that the great conspiracy was put into motion.

His next move struck Phoenix in the early summer of 1883, a few weeks after he had formally registered his claim. It was the announcement that his San Francisco attorney, Harvey S. Brown, had concluded negotiations with Colonel James M. Barney, president of the Silver King Mining Company. Barney had recognized Reavis' claim to the properties of the company and agreed to pay him $25,000 in royalties.

It was the custom of the leading citizens of Phoenix to dine at one of the hotels every Friday evening and discuss the town's affairs. The news that the Silver King Mining Company, with lawyers on its payroll who could achieve legal triumph out of a

---

* Phoenix *Arizona Republic*, September 29, 1953.

misplaced comma, had capitulated to Reavis without a fight staggered these men.

The Silver King had begun working only ten years earlier, but it was already Arizona's richest silver mine, yielding more bullion for the small amount of work needed than any other silver vein in the Southwest. It was discovered in 1871 by soldiers who, trying to knock off a piece of rock which would not break, saw silver. They told four ranchmen—Long, Mason, Reagan, and Copeland—who lived near Florence on the Gila about it. These men started prospecting in 1875 and immediately struck the bonanza. A year later Long and Copeland sold out to their two other partners for $130,000, and six months later Mason and Reagan sold a half interest to Colonel Barney, for $300,000 in gold coin. A few years later the mine produced at least $6,000,000 worth of silver a year, and the value of the property was estimated to be $50,000,000.

The payment Colonel Barney made to Reavis was nothing compared to the vast fortune the mineowner had amassed. But to the farmers and property owners the apparent admission by the mightiest and richest mining company in Arizona that Reavis' claim was true, with all its terrifying implications for their future welfare and security, was a body blow.

At their new residence near the Casa Grande, Reavis and Barratt began to recruit and brief their agents and rent collectors. The news of these promising jobs had spread among just the sort of men Reavis considered most suitable for his purpose. The Southwest was still a happy hunting ground of crooks, malcontents, renegades, and diehard adventurers who regretted the decline of a man's right to do as he pleased, always provided that he could be certain of outshooting the fellow likely to thwart him. Con men from California, Texans who had deemed it wise to get out of their own country, swarthy Mexicans escaping a bloody feud, former prospectors who had spent their younger days vainly seeking for the fabled ore—the usual regiment of parasites who battened on the decent citizenry—all avidly listened to Reavis' and Barratt's instruction and liked what they heard. Reavis, a dedicated admirer of authentic-looking documents, saw to it that his emissaries were equipped with all necessary and impressive papers.

At first these agents swarmed into the towns, carrying newly printed posters, pinning and pasting them at every vantage point. One went on a sheriff's notice board, while the official dazedly looked on; others were pasted on doors of churches, at the courthouse, at railroad stops, and at livery stables or displayed in the saloons. Barratt visited editors and demanded that the text of the poster be inserted into the next issue of their newspapers as an advertisement for payment in cash.

The poster announced that all persons occupying land under any and every title or by duration of tenure were "to communicate immediately with Mr. Cyril Barratt, attorney-at-law and agent general, representing Mr. James Addison Reavis, for registering tenancy and signing agreements, or regard themselves liable to litigation for trespassing and expulsion when the Peralta Grant is, as it must be, validated by the U.S. Government."

Reavis had chosen his words carefully. No statement appeared in regard to confirmation of the claim, because no such approval had been given by the surveyor general. But to simple people, the mere threat of possible litigation and the fact that not only the Southern Pacific but also the Silver King Mining Company had already entered into agreements were proof enough of the validity of the Peralta Grant.

The reaction to these announcements was to bring normal activity in many of the affected townships almost to a standstill. Crowds gathered in front of the posters, reading and rereading the brief notice and anxiously discussing the threat. In the saloons, people talked about sending a deputation to Reavis;

still more wanted to take justice into their own hands and run him and his henchmen out of the territory.

But no one actually did anything. After a few days the excitement subsided. There was a portentous lull, until Barratt and a few of the agents, with copies of the documents, began to call on farmsteaders, property owners, and storekeepers.

They cunningly made their first demands modest. They shuffled through a pile of documents and said that Mr. Reavis' aim was to develop his estates but that he had no desire to drive his tenants away. They told stories of settlers in New Mexico and California who had slaved for five or ten years and were suddenly told to get out when similar claims were validated with the full authority of the Government in Washington and the courts of law. This, they said, Mr. Reavis did not want to happen in Arizona. He was prepared to sign quitclaims and to issue deeds of perpetual tenure to the present owner, in return for modest payments of rent.

The agents seemed extremely accommodating. There was nothing more natural than to sign a simple document which they presented and make a small payment on account, with the assurance that this would guarantee security of tenure. Many people, frightened by the rumors—semiliterate small farmers and tradesmen worried about losing a thriving store or workshop—signed and paid up, easily intimidated by all the legal verbiage. Their reward was an imposing-looking deed and receipt, bearing Reavis' signature and embossed seal.

It was unfortunate that there seemed, at times, to be confusion about what these receipts were really for. One agent would pocket the money, hand over the deed, and assure the client that he would not be troubled again. Then another agent would turn up a week or two later and demand another payment, presenting a different deed. In vain the indignant tenant would thrust forward the receipt as proof. This, the second collector would explain, was merely a receipt for a part payment, not for the completion of the deed safeguarding tenure.

When a recalcitrant farmer or trader proved uncooperative, Barratt would call on him, accompanied by Pedro Cuervo or another tough-looking and armed Mexican. If such an intimidating visit still bore no result or when the obstinacy of the "tenant" was really marked, two or three horsemen would descend on the building, kicking servants about, taking away a horse, a pig, or a sack of grain, and, in a few instances, even setting fire to a barn. It was a crude form of the modern protection racket—and it worked. When people complained to the sheriff, Reavis indignantly denied any connection with the toughs and declared that he did not employ outlaws.

More important landowners and townspeople were visited by Reavis, who conducted the negotiations with utmost politeness. He always left before a document was signed or cash handed over, leaving the completion of the business to Barratt. He succeeded in shrouding all his activities in mystery. He rarely entered a town, visiting mainly farmers of substance and mining enterprises. He evaded newspaper reporters and refused admission to those who came to his palace.

In the saloons, at the stagecoach and railroad stops, in the cattle markets, in the churchyards on Sundays, wherever men gathered, the grumbling and cursing grew as one settler recounted his troubles with the baron's agents to another. Even those who had staunchly refused to pay and had been left alone were worried what the future might hold for them. It was widely noted that there seemed little rhyme or reason in the amounts of rents and quitclaim payments Reavis demanded. An elderly poverty-stricken farmer would be asked to pay more than his vigorous and obstinate neighbor with twice as much land. Sometimes Barratt, an agent, or even Reavis himself would sign a quitclaim in return for hospitality, a meal or a few drinks; on other occasions threatening demands for as much as $1,000 would be made.

In July the editor of the Phoenix *Gazette,* Homer McNeil, fired a broadside against the "baron." Under a black streamer headline WHAT ARE YOU GOING TO DO ABOUT IT? he asked his readers:

> Are you going to sleep on your rights and allow this scheme to be consummated without as much as a protest? Your course must be peace or war! What shall it be? It is for those interested to decide. The *Gazette* cannot fight this battle for you, much as it wishes it could. Its mission is ended when it warns you of the danger that menaces you. It now tells you that this danger is imminent, and that prompt action is demanded.*

The *Herald* followed suit, warning that Reavis' emissaries suggested to the newcomer or timid settler that payments under a deed of quitclaim provided security, whereas in fact the deeds sold by Reavis could not give any legal warranty or assurance of title should the Peralta Grant be ever validated by Congress.

A few respected citizens of Phoenix called on Colonel Barney and the managers of the Silver King Mining Company, asking them to lend their company's wealth and power for a battle against Reavis. But this suggestion was shrugged off, and the deputation was told that the company's accountants and lawyers had advised making the best arrangement with Reavis because one day his claim might well succeed.

For months Phoenix and the other towns seethed in a mixture of fear and anger, clinging to the hope of some last-minute news that the whole thing was a hoax. But those who wanted to resist were bitterly disappointed.

In October the surveyor general, Joseph Robbins, had ordered one of his senior clerks, Rufus C. Hopkins, an expert on Spanish land grants, to travel to Mexico and examine the Peralta documents at Guadalajara. Reavis, who had become friendly with Hopkins, offered to accompany him and introduce

* Phoenix *Gazette,* July 2, 1883.

him to the Mexican officials whom he had met during his research work at the archives. Robbins, suffering from tuberculosis, was desperately ill, and Hopkins agreed without consulting him. Reavis took with him Andrew Squires, an attorney from Cleveland, and they traveled by the Santa Fe Railroad to Deming in New Mexico and thence to Chihuahua, where they took the stage to Durango and finally reached the old Mexican capital.

At the Guadalajara archives Reavis took charge of everything. He introduced Hopkins to his old friends Don Manuel Cordero and Don Sebastián Baltrand, adroitly selecting documents he wanted Hopkins to see, and he took care of the elderly official's welfare and comfort. Hopkins was a tired man of over seventy, glad to have all this assistance. They stayed in Mexico for several weeks, and when they returned after New Year, 1884, to Phoenix, they learned that the surveyor general, Joseph Robbins, had died and had been succeeded by his chief clerk, Royal A. Johnson.

To him Hopkins made his report, stating that he had seen the royal cedulas pertaining to the Peralta Grant, and although he mentioned that there was some doubt about the king's signature and that in some of the documents the name of Peralta was not mentioned, he concluded that, in his opinion, Reavis' claim was well founded.

The new surveyor general was not impressed by Hopkins' report, but he could do little for the moment. Reavis pestered him to send a report to Washington supporting the claim and to do this without delay "in the interest of the people of Arizona and in order to end their uncertainty and insecurity." Johnson refused, but Reavis now announced that "following Mr. Hopkins's favorable report," it was only a matter of time until the Secretary of the Interior and Congress would confirm his claim. This resulted in many people's volunteering to make payments for quitclaims before it would be too late.

Reavis was now talking of being prepared to renounce the claim for a payment of $300,000,000 by the United States Government. He spread rumors that the Government was indeed prepared to offer him $100,000,000 and make the Peralta estates into public lands which would be leased to the present owners. The Phoenix *Herald* expressed the fears of the citizens:

> Mr. Reavis is a bright, farseeing man. He foresaw that by doing what he has done the title of the lands throughout the whole county concerned would be clouded and that the prosperity of the country would cease and transactions in real estate would be throttled. Such has been the case so far as influences could work in so short a time. We learn that within the past few days one or two pending transactions in real estate have been declared off on account of the Reavis claim.*

In fact, there were many more cancellations of property deals. The rumors that the claim would be soon validated had a disastrous effect on business. No one dared to buy and sell land or to build on land which could be taken away.

While the *Herald* and the Florence *Enterprise* had begun a concerted attack on Reavis, appealing to the citizens to form committees, to petition Congress, and to collect funds with which to employ lawyers, one of the leading Phoenix newspapers, hitherto hostile to Reavis, remained strangely docile or silent. This paper was the Phoenix *Gazette,* published by Homer McNeil.

McNeil had come to terms with Reavis. The editor was a wealthy man, but most of his wealth was invested in property in the city. He became seriously worried that one day all this would belong to Reavis, who could not be expected to show mercy. McNeil decided that prudence was the better part of valor. He arranged a secret meeting with Reavis, paid him a

* Phoenix *Herald,* August 9, 1883.

sum of money—the exact amount was never disclosed—and promised to cease attacking him in his newspapers, all this in return for a deed transferring to him in all perpetuity the land in his possession claimed by Reavis.

In order to make this deal legal, it was necessary to register it with the Land Record Office. McNeil may have hoped that a kindly disposed clerk would file the deed quietly and that publicity could be avoided.

He was mistaken. Three days later the Phoenix *Herald*, the fiercest of the *Gazette's* competitors, broke the sensational news in big black type that the city's leading publisher had succumbed to Reavis:

> Saturday last a deed was filed in the Recorder's office by which J. Addison Reavis for the alleged consideration of $60 transfers to Homer M. McNeil, the publisher of the *Gazette*, all rights and titles claimed by the former to certain property held by McNeil in this city.
>
> There is a clause in this deed which reveals the true inwardness of Reavis's endeavor to get individuals to acknowledge his claim so far as to purchase from him what he does not, and never will own.
>
> The document is a regular Bargain and Sale deed by which the grantor (J. A. Reavis) makes certain reservations and among them is the clause referred to which reads thus: "Grantor reserves to himself and his heirs the right to sue for and obtain legal recognition by the United States Government of his title to aforesaid premises."
>
> A purchase from Reavis under such a deed is nothing more or less than entering into a contract with him to become interested with him in securing his title. This is the game that Reavis is trying to play, and this is the game in which the *Gazette* publisher has been induced to take a hand against the people of the valley.
>
> Great indignation is developing at the sell-out business and there is a movement afoot among business men to withdraw from that paper.*

* Phoenix *Herald*, November 15, 1883.

Under the prevailing atmosphere in Phoenix this was a fatal blow against the *Gazette*. The *Herald* called the deal a treachery against the people of Phoenix and the territory, accused McNeil of having gone over to the enemy, of having been bought by Reavis, and called the *Gazette* "the Reavis organ." The outcome was that McNeil hardly dared show himself in public. Several hundred readers canceled their subscriptions on the same day the *Herald* disclosure was published; many traders and storeowners relinquished their advertising orders. It seemed that the *Gazette* was ruined.

Nothing was left to McNeil but to repent with utmost humility. He begged two members of the legislature, Judge A. D. Lemon, and two or three other distinguished citizens to act as his witnesses at the cancellation of his deal with Reavis. He withdrew the document from the Land Record Office, canceled it by drawing lines in red ink across the pages, and then returned it to Reavis. On the following day McNeil published in the *Gazette* a lengthy explanation, hoping to placate his readers and advertisers:

> Everyone is apt, in some period of life, to commit an error and in this instance, we will not deny that such has been our fate. The object of the proprietor of this paper in securing from Reavis a title was to place himself in a position, where, should the latter be successful in the confirmation of his grant, the paper and our property would be entirely removed beyond the reach of his wrath, and being placed in such a position of independence, we could fearlessly espouse the cause of the people and oppose the purpose of the land grabber.
>
> Last summer, when we began the agitation . . . prominent business men and influential citizens asked this paper to desist in its course, fearing temporary depreciation in the real estate market. We complied. In this second instance our object was misrepresented and snap judgment was being taken as to the honesty of our purpose.

This morning a movement was set on foot to boycott the *Gazette,* and that, too, without a hearing.*

Few people believed in this explanation which smelled strongly of hypocrisy, and the *Herald* was quick off the mark to reply:

It is an ingenious but weak defense the *Gazette* of yesterday evening makes. No one thinks for a moment that Mr. McNeil was so foolish as to pay Reavis $60 in coin for his deed, yet the former has placed in the hands of an adventurer a powerful weapon towards influencing the action of the Surveyor General. . . . This community is not as blind as a bat nor as dumb as an ox, that it can neither see nor hear, and it is no wonder that so much indignation is now entertained at the conduct of the land grabber's organ, the *Gazette.*†

All this happened when Reavis was away with Hopkins in Mexico. The newspaper polemic which followed McNeil's inglorious capitulation to the baron had caused more confusion among the citizens and added to their fears. Barratt and his agents were busily mulcting the baron's "tenants" and extorted more money than ever before. When Reavis returned to Arizona with yet more evidence in support of his claim, and after Hopkins had made his report, which confirmed the existence of documentary proof at the Guadalajara archives, he was determined to silence his journalistic opponents.

* Phoenix *Arizona Gazette,* November 15, 1883.
† Phoenix *Herald,* November 16, 1883.

6

The Gun and the Pen

Close to the southern boundary of the realm the baron had successfully claimed for himself was a small settlement named Florence.

It was a small oasis of green grass and shady trees in the wide brown desert dotted by cacti of a thousand different species. To the northwest Poston's Butte raised its conical mass into the sky, its sides pockmarked with silver mine shafts. To the north and east the serrated peaks and points of the range dominated by the Superstition Mountains, inhabited by the *espantos* and *ánimas*— the souls of murdered men who return to torment their killers— made a lacy pattern against the sky, the innumerable colors of their rocks contrasting vividly with the blue of the firmament above and the monotonous hues of the desert below.

It was understandable that a squad of Italian-born troops, serving in the United States cavalry on the Indian scouting patrol, should have looked around them, as they squatted by the campfires, and remembered the brown hills of Tuscany in high summer. They dubbed the encampment after the queenly city of their native country.

Levi Ruggles, a Yankee, and his family, who came by wagon train in 1866, were the first white settlers; the town developed so quickly that within four years it had a population of 600. Soon it became a trading center for the prospectors and miners and an important stage stop, rousing hopes of a brilliant future for "fair Florence wreathed in Gila green, a city yet to be, I ween. . . ."

For the embattled outpost that stood firm against the attacks by nomadic Apache Indians had one great advantage: it had been erected on the banks of the Gila River, "the flowing water that is salt," which before the Gadsden Purchase had been the boundary between Arizona and Mexico. And thirty miles north of Forence was the Lost Dutchman Mine, around which were woven many stories of fabulous gold strikes. A young Mexican lover, fleeing the wrath of his sweetheart's father and finding refuge in the north, was supposed to have made the find. Soon a prospectors' camp sprang up, and they mined as much gold as they could carry. But the Apaches came and massacred them all, 400 men, women, and children—with one exception, an old Dutchman who had hidden himself under a bush.

This Dutchman with a flowing white beard, who was named Jacob Wolz, staked his claim, and from 1870 to 1884, when he died at Phoenix, the mine was his. As stories of the Dutchman's gold spread around Florence, many prospectors tried to trail him into the mountains, but he outwitted them or killed them. Wolz is said to have boasted of having killed eighteen men, including his nephew. When he died, with a shoebox full of the coveted ore under his bed, he gave with his last breath his secret to a friendly neighbor. He told him that the entrance to the mine was concealed under ironwood logs covered with rock. And he mentioned a landmark, a paloverde tree with a peculiar pointing branch. Thousands of prospectors have searched ever since for the Lost Dutchman Mine, but it has never been found; many people of Florence said that Wolz "never had nothin' up there nohow." Although the gold mine was never located, silver was struck, and Florence's prosperity flourished for a time.

Except for the fact that it had become a trading center for the silver mines and that it could claim to be older than most of the settlements in the Gila River Valley, by the time it had become one of the vassal towns of the Baron of Arizona, Florence was little different from half a dozen other struggling shabby one-street towns in the Arizona desert county.

There was the main street, fringed with large one-story buildings with adobe walls and high peaked roofs of timber—Levi Ruggles' house; the Mason Apartments, which housed the first store and the post office; the house of Major Pauline Cushman, who had been a Union spy during the Civil War, had been sentenced to death by the Confederates, but had been saved and commended by President Lincoln as "the bravest of women"; the stage office of Wells Fargo; and a long string of saloons.

In the few side streets were the ugly but comfortable residential houses and stables of the traders and silver brokers, and on the corner of Eighth Street was the wooden building of the first Roman Catholic church in central Arizona. In these side streets lived the law-abiding citizens, for the chief thoroughfare was a raw and boisterous place.

When the miners came into town after a good week's work, or when some prospector determined to set the desert alight in celebrations of what he believed to be a lucky strike, the center of the town became a scene of drunken fighting and escapade.

"You sure can't be too careful about stray bullets in this town" was the inevitable, if kindly, warning the stranger received when he checked in at a lodging house or chatted over a drink in the big saloon next to the Wells Fargo office, which was on the corner of the rutted track proudly called Fifth Street.

It was good advice. Wild shooting just for the hell of it was a nightly occurrence, and major gun battles were not infrequent.

And there was still danger from marauding Apaches: until 1886 their famous chief Geronimo terrorized southern Arizona, and it was not until the end of the century that the Apaches were contained.

The citizens of Florence were proud to point out to a stranger their sheriff, Pete Gabriel. Pete, they explained, was full of lead. Bullets had entered his body, including one just below the heart, when a gunman, named Joe Phy, emptied his pistol into the lawman one night in a saloon. Despite the fact that the shots sent Gabriel to the floor, he was able to draw his gun and kill his adversary before he collapsed from loss of blood.

There was another man in Florence of whom the citizens spoke with pride.

Beyond the Wells Fargo office stood a long squat building in gray adobe. A sign above the door announced that these were the premises of Tom Weedin, printer and publisher. A smaller tablet proclaimed that it was also the editorial office of the Florence *Enterprise*.

Tom Weedin's horizon as a publicist did not extend far beyond the narrow borders of his township. His editorial enterprise did not envisage much more exciting news than lists of births, marriages, and deaths, the notices of auctions and church socials, and a certain amount of enthusiastic, if long-winded, publicity for the ever-burgeoning economy of the young territory, of which Florence was a microcosm.

As a matter of business routine, he at first regularly published the long and expensive announcements of the leasehold and royalty dues which the baron's agents brought to his office. He was paid for the advertisements, and he published them as editorial matter, as was the custom. In Tom Weedin's newspaper, as in most American journals of his times, it was always difficult to know which literary effusion was paid-for publicity and which a product of the editorial pen. No one considered this sort of journalism unethical, still less that it was bribery.

With a circulation of a few hundred copies and only a single sheet to be filled once weekly, Weedin was editor, chief reporter, advertising canvasser, and head printer. He made his livelihood not from his paper but as a jobbing printer for the trading community. The sheer mechanics of his work left little time for the finer ideals of trenchant and forthright journalism. Weedin was not, in fact, a champion of the oppressed. He considered his newspaper a source of modest income, not a public service.

Yet he became a fearless fighter for justice and freedom. His readers made him that. Men came to his office and cursed the baron as they told Weedin of the money the agents had extorted from them. One or two elderly couples who were scratching an acre or two of soil to feed themselves and to produce some potatoes and meager poultry to sell to the townfolk came to him to beg for advice on what they should do to keep away their tormentors. In Florence there was the suicide of a spinster, who had kept a small haberdashery store, after one of Reavis' agents had visited her and demanded payment under the threat of eviction. As in other parts of Reavis' realm, real estate deals had come to almost a standstill in Pinal County. Some of the smaller mining companies, frightened by the claim, had laid off men or had cut the wages of those retained.

The sheer injustice of the evidence collected moved Weedin to act. He began to print brief factual stories of a few score words. They brought in a steady stream of visitors and letters from farther and farther afield, with more revelations of the ruthless methods Reavis was employing. Weedin knew nothing of the finer points of law, and at first he did not even question Reavis' rights. He confined his editorials to attacks on the knavish methods, pointing out that the Peralta claim had not been approved and might never be confirmed. He did not mince his words. Libel in those days was not something that bothered a journalist. If an important man in public life was libeled in a newspaper, he had the choice of two methods in dealing with lies and innuendo: either he bribed the editor, or he arranged that his printing press was smashed and the insolent writer was run out of town.

In the late autumn of 1883, at the height of the polemic between the *Herald* and the *Gazette* in Phoenix, Reavis arrived in Florence with a party of San Francisco businessmen, trying to sell them rights in a newly discovered mineral deposit in Deer Creek in Pinal County. The land belonged to two or three families who had been settled there for a generation. Although nothing came of this deal, Reavis' implied claim to this land brought the anger of the local population to flashpoint.

Weedin now kindled the flame of resistance that was to spread across Arizona and finally devour the bad baron. When he began to attack him in the slender columns of the Florence *Enterprise,* Reavis adopted the first of the traditional methods of silencing a mischievous journalist: he tried to bribe him.

One morning, looking dignified as always, in a frock coat and black top hat, Reavis knocked on the door of Weedin's tiny office. He was charming and polite. He explained that he had come to talk things over.

"I have been greatly perturbed that your highly reputable journal should adopt this unkind attitude to my fully documented claim to the Peralta Grant," he told the editor. "I have been an editor myself, publishing a fine newspaper in the capital of California, and I treasure the principle of press freedom in our great democracy. But your attacks seriously impair my plans, supported by leading companies and distinguished businessmen men and financiers, to open up this wonderful country of Arizona to civilization and prosperity. Your antipathy to these plans does no service to your community."

Weedin scowled but listened silently.

"However that may be," Reavis continued, opening his leather bag, which he clutched in his lap, "I feel that this might be due to the fact that your own progress has somehow been frustrated. I desire to say that I recognize the need in an orderly community of a well-established and responsible organ of public opinion. And your excellent newspaper is such an organ—"

Weedin, guessing what was to come, began growling his protest.

Reavis waved his hand. "Allow me one moment, Mr. Weedin, sir," he said with a cold smile. "Let me first indicate the practical proposition I wish to make as a token of my esteem for you."

He withdrew two canvas bags from his portmanteau and placed them on Weedin's desk. They clinked dully.

"Gold," he said. "Gold, assayed and worth one thousand dollars, sir."

Without waiting for a reply, he added hastily, "A first installment. I did not wish to travel with more wealth from Phoenix. But there would be further donations for the development of your excellent journal."

Weedin looked at Reavis for a long silent moment. Then he slowly stretched his arms and pushed the two bags to the edge of his desk. They fell into his visitor's lap.

"Vamoose," he said. "Quickly. If you don't clear out this very moment, I shall throw you out on your damn neck."

Reavis changed color. He rose, put the bags into his portmanteau, and crossed to the window.

"You will regret this cavalier treatment," he said. He glanced down at the yard. Two children were playing there beside a woman sitting on a chair, knitting in the shade of a saguaro tree. "Your family?" he asked and, without waiting for a reply, made for the door. He paused as he opened it and turned around.

"A pity if any harm came to them," he murmured. "A great pity. They are cute kids."

The door closed silently. Tom Weedin sat at his desk, thinking. Then he banged the desk with his fist and reached for a sheet of paper and his pen.

The editorial in that week's issue of the Florence *Enterprise* was the most forthright the paper had ever printed. Weedin appealed to the people of Florence to form a committee, to collect contributions toward a fighting fund, so that "the brazen fraud of James Addison Reavis should be fought tooth and nail." He suggested that an honest attorney be hired and sent to Washington, if need be, to plead with the Government and repulse such evidence as Reavis had produced, "evidence which is fraudulent and must never be accepted by the Land Office and Congress."

On the face of it, Weedin's call to arms was a futile attempt against the phalanx Reavis had erected and manned by clever lawyers, such as Harvey S. Brown in San Francisco and Senator Roscoe Conkling in New York. But Tom Weedin was made of the hard stuff that was characteristic of Arizona editors. The newspapers of the territory had always been particularly vigorous. In the early days the portable printing presses and a few forms of type had often preceded the picks and shovels of the pioneers.

The fact that only a couple of hundred people had just settled to found a community did not deter these journalistic pioneers from bringing out newssheets. The *Weekly Arizonian* appeared in Tubac in 1859 when the town was just a hutment camp with only a handful of white settlers, many of them illiterate cutthroats from Sonora and outcasts from the East. Most of these early-day editors could shoot and write with equal facility.

The news they published was brief and to the point: "Charlie Genung is in town from Peoples Valley to buy some bacon. The weather is cold in his locality and there is little news. Yavapai Indians annoyed neighbors last week and ran off a couple of mules. Several rangers pursued and killed several of the redskins. George Brown got a bad arrow wound in his shoulder."*

Complaints of libel were invariable registered at gunpoint or, if the infuriated reader was a "gentleman," with a challenge to a more formal pistol duel. That a newspaper editor was rather like a clergyman or a physician was admitted, and in a duel the gunshots were made to miss the target; the purpose was to restore honor by the gun, not to kill the offender. Equally the newspapermen preferred a policy of coexistence and fired skyward as a gesture of honorable defense or, for reasons of discretion, just ducked behind the comforting cast iron of the printing press when a plaintiff burst into the office.

The editors had good reasons for disliking gunsmoke, and most editorials in these local newspapers demanded a cessation of celebratory "shooting up the town" by cowboys after a rodeo or by miners on a hilarious visit. But as a rule the editors did not discourage the use of the gun if the target was redskins. Their wrath was invariably directed against the so-called weak-kneed handling of the Indian problem by the federal authorities. Ten years earlier, killings by Indians in Arizona were counted in the hundreds; attacks on isolated farms and murders by marauding Apaches still took place. Arizona's editors, to a man, felt contempt for the Yankee policy of Washington of providing large Indian reservations and pampering the redskins, at least within the territory. The correct locale for a removal of the "savages" was advocated as a graveyard: "a remote island in the Pacific or, if Washington preferred it, right among the tender-hearted Easterners in Boston."

By 1884 things had become more civilized. But the spirit prevailed. Week after week the *Enterprise* came out with a different story about the baron's tyrannical oppression. A sense

* From an actual news column of the Prescott *Arizona Miner.*

of justice, as well as a nose for a good story, prompted Tom Weedin to continue his fight with all the vigor which was typical of Arizona's newspaper tradition. Weedin knew that he was only a small-town David assailing a Goliath who had all the strong armor supplied by the tycoons and politicians in San Francisco, New York, and Washington. But he did not cringe when his adversary resorted to strong-arm methods.

One day the Florence *Enterprise* appeared with a headline in the largest black type its editor was able to find in his font case. It briefly, but pointedly, proclaimed OUTRAGE, and under it Weedin reported how his workrooms had been broken into one night, the type scattered into the road outside, some furniture smashed, and a printing press overturned. Only his speedy arrival from his home a block away had prevented a fire, started in the paper store, from burning down the shop. Weedin had seen two figures galloping away into the darkness, and he did not hesitate to name them as the baron's henchmen.

It was never established whether Reavis had sent these men to make his threat true, but if he had, hoping that strong-arm measures would achieve the desired result, he was mistaken. Tom Weedin was now more determined than ever to go all out in his fight.

Several new champions arose to ally themselves with the Florence editor in an attempt to run Reavis out of the territory. The most important and most effective of them was Clark Churchill, the attorney general of Arizona. He owned property in Phoenix, and although Reavis had not dared to try extortion on him, his land was as badly threatened by the baron's claim as that of those who had been under pressure.

In his private capacity, Churchill filed a court suit demanding that Reavis should show cause of his claim, and failing this, the court should "quit" title to land holding within the area claimed under the alleged Peralta Grant." It was a clever move to force Reavis to appear in court and be examined in public.

THE "PERALTA" FAMILY GALLERY

The noble Spanish ancestors of his wife through whom James Reavis claimed his inheritance never existed, but to bolster his story, Reavis invented not only the ancestors and their names but also their portraits. In the flea market of Madrid he picked up a number of faded miniatures and paintings from discarded family collections, choosing those of aristocratic appearance and wearing costumes of the period desired. He then identified these as the various barons of Arizona, their wives, and other relatives. Some of the members of this invented family are pictured on this and the next four pages.

Reavis chose this distinguished face as that of "Don José Nemecio Gómez de Silva," whom he created to be the forebear of the barons de Peralta at the time of the Spanish conquistadors in the seventeenth century.

"Don Miguel Nemecio Silva de Peralta y de la Córdoba," who Reavis said received the land grant from King Ferdinand VI of Spain in 1748 and became the first "Baron of Arizona." He was supposed to have been the grandson of the gentleman on the preceding page and to have been portrayed as shown here at the age of three years and five months and again in 1738 at the age of thirty in the service of King Philip V.

At the age of seventy, "Don Miguel de Peralta" as "Baron of Arizona" and owner of large estates in Sonora and Jalisco in Mexico. With him is "Doña Sofía Ave María Sánchez Bonilla de Amaya y García de Orosco," whom he married in 1770 when he was sixty-two. She is shown at the age of sixty.

The "Initial Monument," a stone which Reavis faked to prove the demarcation of the land grant he claimed.

The "first baron" at the age of one hundred.

The "second Baron of Arizona, Don Miguel Silva Jesús de Peralta," said to have been born at Cumpas on the Yaqui River in 1781, when his father was seventy-three; pictured here at twenty and at forty.

Reavis created both a wife and parents-in-law for the "second baron." Below are her father, "Don José Juan Ibarra," and her mother, "Doña Ana Laura Escobedo de Ibarra." And above, the "second baroness, Doña Juana Laura Ibarra," at sixteen (left) and at the time of her marriage when she was twenty.

For the first time, the pictures are of people whose real identities we know. The woman is Reavis' wife, whom he, Pygmalion-like, converted into "the third Baroness of Arizona, Doña Sofía Loreta Micaela de Maso y de Peralta," and made the chief pawn in his great fraud. Through her he claimed his ancestry. The probable fact is that she was a half-breed American Indian, and she was brought up at the farm of a California prospector, John A. Treadway, shown here.

A share certificate of one of James Reavis' fraudulent companies, the Casa Grande Improvement Company, which had to have a capital of $50,000,000; among its directors was the famous lawyer Robert G. Ingersoll.

**THE ROMANCE
OF THE
PERALTA
GRANT**

will begin with a
later issue

PERALTA REAVIS

MRS. PERALTA REAVIS

What Peralta Reavis Knows About Arizona

TWENTY years ago I found this arid region a bower of wild, luxurious flowers of every hue and delicacy of tint—there were two springtimes then, at every swing of mother earth around the sun, beginning with each solstice. But the old adage that "seasons change" has been written indelibly upon the face of country and man during these too brief years.

similarity; and I note the ever-present oxidized iron, which gives a porous condition easily soluble in water, hence admirably adapted to irrigation processes in this torrid climate without baking irretrievably nor drying into hardpan with great fissures zigzagging the whole country. Apparently this is a mountainous country void of verdure, nevertheless

James Reavis at the height of his success, with his wife, the "third Baroness of Arizona." (Their pictures appeared in a newssheet issued by Reavis to attract investors for his companies in Arizona.)

The twin sons of James Reavis and the "third Baroness of Arizona." Clad in regal velvet, the two pretty boys appeared prominently at his trial and made great sympathy for his claim.

James Peraltareavis, deprived of his luxuriant whiskers, as prisoner No. 964 at the penitentiary in Santa Fe.

But it had little legal value, because the claim, rightful or fraudulent, could be decided only by the Government and Congress, in the last instance, not by a local judge.

On February 12, 1884, James Reavis, accompanied by two attorneys, appeared in the Phoenix courthouse. He made a long statement, insisting that the claim was valid and that he was entitled to sell quitclaims or gather rents in order to protect himself from depreciation of the value of the land which would soon become his legal property. One of his lawyers, Cox, submitted that all agreements made by settlers and property holders with Reavis had been "entirely voluntary" and that citizens had in many instances approached Reavis and offered payments themselves, in order to protect their interest and obtain security of tenure if Congress validated the claim and transferred the land to its rightful owner, James Addison Reavis. This, the attorney said, applied particularly to some of the largest companies, such as the Southern Pacific and the Silver King Mining companies, which regarded Reavis as the rightful owner.

Clark Churchill could hardly refute this. When he cross-examined Reavis, he concentrated on showing up the baron's sordid methods, to brand him as a crook and to expose his backers. In this way he may have hoped to appeal to the emotions of the citizens, to rouse them to fight Reavis and the financiers and promoters who had sided with the baron. The appeal to the minds could come later if, by some stroke of good fortune, a clue to the existence of fraud and conspiracy emerged.

"How many agents have you . . . at various places?" Churchill asked.

"I have a number of agents and attorneys at various places, but the exact number of them I do not recall," was Reavis' evasive answer.

He indignantly denied that he or his agents had ever used

intimidation. If any of them did, they did so without his connivance or encouragement, and they would be instantly dismissed.

"State how many conveyances you have made to different persons and to whom," Churchill asked.

"I do not know," Reavis replied.

"Have you received any money in payment for sales thus made?" Churchill insisted.

"I have, as I am informed by my attorneys."

"Do you know how much?"

"I do not."

At his trial in 1895 James Reavis revealed that he had received payments and promissory notes to the staggering total of $5,300,000 from Arizona settlers,* in addition to many other payments by companies and backers. But the great flood of money came to him only after 1887, and it must be assumed that at the time of the court case in Phoenix, in 1884, he had gathered not more than $100,000 to $150,000, which sum excluded the payments by the Southern Pacific and the mining companies. He had paid commissions to his agents and fees to his attorneys, but even so he must have kept a small fortune. He was, of course, not prepared to reveal details when Clark Churchill pressed him.

Churchill turned to the subject of Reavis' discreet backers. The ruthless methods employed by the Big Four of San Francisco in the construction of railroads were well known and widely resented. So Clark Churchill tried to bring out Reavis' connections with the railroad tycoons.

He asked him whether he had sold land or made a conveyance to the Southern Pacific Company.

"I did," Reavis replied firmly and with obvious satisfaction.

---

* Transcript of proceedings before the U.S. Court of Private Land Claims; also reported in Phoenix *Arizona Gazette*, June 13, 1895.

"State how much money you received," demanded Clark Churchill.

"The exact amount I do not recall."

"Was it five thousand dollars or more?"

"And more," Reavis replied proudly. "In accounting, I should count much more."

"Who did you make the bargain with to sell to the Southern Pacific Railroad Company originally? Who was the individual?"

"It was Mr. Charles Crocker."

"Did you receive any money from Colonel James M. Barney of the Silver King Mining Company?"

"I did, by a draft signed by him."

"State the amount of that draft."

"The amount of that draft I refer to, was five thousand dollars, which amount was paid by the bank."

"What was it paid for?" Churchill insisted.

"The money was in part payment for a deed from me to the property the Silver King Mine is operating."

Reavis proved to be such a slippery witness that Clark Churchill finally gave up in despair. The case was adjourned and dragged on for another year. Although Reavis may have believed that he had once more succeeded in bamboozling everybody, the case had greatly encouraged the resistance movement. While Reavis traveled to New York and San Francisco and lived on and off in his new palace at Arizola, and while his agents still roamed his realm and extorted money from gullible people, dark clouds had begun to gather on his horizon.

Several anti-Reavis committees were set up. At Phoenix the committee was headed by three respected citizens: Judge A. D. Lemon, John W. Crenshaw, and J. T. Alsap. At Florence, Tom Weedin took the chair, and other committees were formed at Globe and Tempe. Meetings were called and addressed by Attorney General Clark Churchill and Tom Weedin.

On April 11 the *Enterprise* could report:

In answer to our call the people of Florence held a mass meeting in Florence at the courthouse Tuesday evening. It was the largest assemblage of men ever seen at a public meeting. . . . [P]eople have at last realized the danger they are in and are ready to unite in a defense of their homes and rights.

Even larger meetings were held in Phoenix, and the *Enterprise* proclaimed, "The people of the Gila Valley begin the war against the Bean Pole Baron!" while the Phoenix *Herald* declared, "No More Fraud! Rascally Reavis Must Go!"

The new surveyor general, Royal A. Johnson, had been trying to disentangle the mass of documents which Reavis had filed in March, 1883, and to make sense of the report submitted by Rufus C. Hopkins after the latter's visit (together with Reavis) to Mexico. Johnson now became the object of fierce attacks in the newspapers. Reavis had been spreading rumors that Johnson could find no fault with his claim and that he was shortly to submit a report to the General Land Office in Washington recommending that the claim go through the lawful procedure of examination by the Government and Congress.

This was untrue, but Johnson refused to be harried. He insisted he must be allowed to conclude his examination, without fear and favor. This earned him the enmity of the citizens' committees, and he was openly accused of having been bribed by Reavis.

Surveyor General Johnson was a man of integrity, but he probably did not grasp the position into which Reavis had cunningly put him. He became involved in a mesh of political intrigues which Reavis and some of his influential friends had woven in Washington, as well as in Arizona.

In Tucson, Reavis had enlisted the help of the Republican nominee for Congress, Thomas Wilson. This politician not only was persuaded of the rightfulness of Reavis' claim, but also supported a cunning scheme which, if successful, would have made Reavis a multimillionaire. Reavis had renewed his proposal to renounce his claim to all the Peralta estates in Arizona and New Mexico for a down payment of $20,000,000 and annual payments to a total of $100,000,000, to be made by the United States Treasury. The Government would take over the estates as public lands and then lease or resell them to the present occupiers.

Reavis had engaged as his counsel in Washington the famous lawyer Roscoe Conkling, Republican Senator from New York, and soon he was able to pull strings at the seats of power. He might have indeed succeeded had the Republican party remained in power. But in 1884 the Democrats won the election, and the new members of President Grover Cleveland's administration listened to Marcus A. Smith, Democratic Representative from the Territory of Arizona and one of Reavis' unmitigated adversaries.

While the tug-of-war was going on in Washington, the fight continued in Arizona. Surveyor General Johnson found himself in a crossfire of a political campaign, subjected to accusations in newspapers—all embracing the Democratic party's cause—of being in alliance with Reavis. In a lament to William A. Sparks, commissioner of the General Land Office in Washington, Johnson wrote:

> It is characteristic of this man Reavis to presume upon receiving the ordinary courtesy . . . that he is on friendly social footing with me. I have complained bitterly to him . . . but without any avail whatever. He goes about the country posing as my friend and my champion, misrepresenting what the clerk or myself have told him officially in relation to his claim.*

He complained that the affair had resulted in political schemes "concocted by bad men to excite the people against my office . . . used as a lever of disappointed candidates for this

* Records of the General Land Office, Arizona Private Land Claim, Group 49, Docket No. 18 (in U.S. National Archives, Washington, D.C.).

office, expectant candidates, petty lawyers scheming for fees. . . ."

The Governor now switched the heat on Reavis and his Republican friends. The commissioner of the General Land Office ordered the surveyor general to halt further investigations and, in fact, made Johnson a scapegoat for all the trouble caused by Reavis. In May, 1885, he wrote to the surveyor general in Tucson:

> It is my opinion that the futile work in which you have been engaged for a year and a half . . . investigating an alleged claim which, from your own statement of its uncorroborated character had not been placed before you in a condition to be entitled to consideration, should forthwith be discontinued.
>
> The only effect of your action and proceedings has been to needlessly alarm citizens in lawful and peaceful possession of homes and property, to imperil valuable mining interests and to intimidate settlements upon public lands.*

Johnson, though hurt by this letter, was glad to comply with the order. There was jubilation in Phoenix and the other towns within Reavis' realm when the news broke.

Reavis was now openly called a con man, a land shyster; the *Herald* named him "the Duke of Arizona, Earl of the Iron Jaw, Count of Confidence, Lord of the Limber Tongue," and described his claim as "that bogus grant," while the Tucson *Citizen* announced that Reavis was "nailed up" and his "fraudulent claim punctured."

Almost overnight the baron's big business collapsed. Barratt and his agents did not dare show themselves in public. Some were badly beaten up, and in the saloons men talked of getting hold of Reavis and his bad men and stringing them up from convenient saguaro trees. Reavis had taken refuge at his fortress

---

* Records of the General Land Office, Arizona Private Land Claim, Group 49, Docket No. 18 (in U.S. National Archives, Washington, D.C.).

at Arizola. There he held a council of war with Barratt and Pedro Cuervo. The Mexican assured him that he and his henchmen could warrant his safety, with a gun, if need be, but Reavis realized he ought to leave the inhospitable valley as long as the going was good. Payments had in any case dried up; most of his agents, in fear of their lives, had gone.

The baron shuttered up his palace and, with Barratt and Cuervo, made an inglorious exit to California. He had amassed enough money to keep him in comfort for a long time, but he was determined to come back for more.

He was not a man to be daunted by a setback, however serious. His mind was full of new plans. If the source of money had dried up because of the settlers' campaign, he would find new funds from financiers in New York, prepared to take a gamble on the great Arizona development schemes which he was ready to propound.

But he realized that the adverse statements by the land commissioner—describing his documentary evidence as uncorroborated and undeserving of further consideration—were extremely damaging to his plans. He also realized that it was necessary to produce entirely new evidence to outwit his adversaries, who had become cocksure that they could destroy the Peralta Grant. He knew that the weakness of his case was the tortuous complexity of the various deeds and agreements and assignments: from the legendary old Mexican to Dr. Willing; from Dr. Willing as an inheritance to his wife, Mary Ann; from her in the form of an assignment to himself.

He decided to simplify the case. He had to find a "real heir" or, even better, a "real heiress" of the Peralta fortune, a direct descendant of the first baron.

He had nursed this idea for some years, ever since he had discovered in 1874 at Prescott that Willing's gunnysack contained but a few spurious documents. Only his subsequent forgeries had made it possible to file in 1883 the Willing claim with some prospect of success. Now he was going to find a Peralta descendant, a young woman whom he could marry and, by doing so, transform himself into a member of the great family he had ingeniously invented.

For a year after his exit from Arizona, James Reavis traveled widely. For some months he was in Mexico and California. Later he paid visits to New York, returned to San Francisco, and eventually, having found the "real heiress," was ready for the final dress rehearsal before reappearing in Arizona with the real heiress at his side.

Although for many months he was engaged in indefatigable activities, nothing had transpired of them into public knowledge. It was not until the late summer of 1885 that the citizens of Phoenix read with derision a brief note in the *Gazette*, reprinted from the Los Angeles *Express*: "Mr. J. A. Reavis, who has a land claim in Arizona, is visiting St. Elmo. He will start soon for Spain with the intention of searching the records of Madrid."

7

Reavis Creates an Heiress

Everything connected with the life story of Doña Carmelita Sofía Loreta Micaela de Maso y de Peralta, Baroness de Arizonac and de los Colorados, who became Mrs. James Addison Reavis, is shrouded in mystery and based on fraud.

Reavis was adept in creating human beings in historical records, but in Doña Carmelita he produced a woman made of flesh and blood, of the right age, of Spanish appearance, amenable or cunning enough to repeat the story which he had invented.

Carmelita's romantic story, which Reavis had devised and pondered over so assiduously that he himself virtually came to believe it, was not just a feat of imagination which would have done credit to an Alexandre Dumas or a Charles Dickens, but was also meticulously supported by forged documents at each stage. The result was a jumble of near facts and total fiction which later defeated the attempts of judges and lawyers to disentangle—and which still defeats the modern investigator.

So effectively had Reavis brainwashed this young woman that she, too, long after she had parted from her husband and to the end of her life, stubbornly maintained the legend of her noble origin from Spanish grandees. She changed the story of her life many times, made contradictory statements to newspaper reporters, when she first appeared as the great Peralta heiress, and gave an entirely different account when cross-examined at Reavis' trial; but she never admitted that she had been an accessory to the fraud and never budged from her claim that she was a real Peralta. All the documents presented on her behalf, including those concerning her parentage, birth, childhood, adolescence, betrothal, and marriage, were forgeries. Several witnesses, including a crooked notary who testified on her behalf and confirmed details she had given about her childhood, later admitted to having committed perjury. No records exist of lengthy periods of her real life, and her secret, so laboriously created by Reavis, was never completely unraveled by the Secret Service agents who for several years were occupied with the Peralta case.

Reavis may for some time have planned to produce a real heir or heiress to the Peralta Grant, a direct descendant of the first baron, but it is certain that the plan did not ripen into execution until he encountered the fierce resistance led by Clark Churchill, Tom Weedin, and the citizens' committees of Phoenix and Florence. Therefore, all the stories later produced by him and his wife that they had met almost ten years earlier, that he had discovered as early as 1877 or 1878 that she was a Peralta, and that he married her in 1882 could have been concocted only after he had despaired in 1884 of having his claim based on the Willing papers ever accepted.

Thus, it is almost impossible to provide an exact chronological sequence in the creation of the Peralta heiress, and one must begin by recounting Reavis' own story of discovery, which he announced after his return from Spain in 1887.

As will be remembered, the original story of the noble family of Peralta, told by the documents which Reavis filed with the surveyor general at Tucson in March, 1883, abruptly ended with the fading out of the second baron, who had sold his claim to Dr. Willing. The second baron, that old Mexican, had disappeared after this deal, and although Reavis tried to locate him in Wickenburg, nothing was mentioned of him thereafter in the submission Reavis made at Tucson in 1883.

When Reavis created the heiress, however, her grandfather reappeared in the story, which was as thrilling and melodramatic as it was well documented. The second baron, Don Miguel Silva Jesús de Peralta, had married Doña Juana Laura Ibarra at Guadalajara in 1822, two years before his father's death.

Like so many sons born to a life of leisure and luxury, Don Miguel Silva Jesús was an absolute wastrel. He soon spent his inheritance, had to sell the ancestral home, and retire to the estates in the province of Sonora, all that was left of the great Peralta possessions in Mexico. At forty—on a picture later produced by Reavis—he was a handsome man, with curly hair and a pale aristocratic face framed by a luxuriant black beard. His marriage to Doña Juana had remained childless for ten years, but in 1832, when he was fifty-one, a daughter was born and baptized Sofía Laura Micaela. A few years later Doña Juana died, and the motherless little girl lived with her widowed father. Through wars and revolutions the baron had fallen on bad times.

In 1860, when he was seventy-nine, a worried man pursued by creditors, a suitor appeared for Doña Sofía's hand. He was a young Spanish immigrant, extremely handsome and of a noble family of Cádiz in Spain. His name was Don José Ramón Carmen de Maso y Castilla. Only later did Don Miguel Silva Jesús de Peralta learn that he was a gentleman sport, who had lived as a professional gambler, idler, and ne'er-do-well in Los Angeles and San Francisco. However, the old man was not averse to the match of his daughter, considering that gentle sad-eyed Sofía was twenty-eight and that she could hardly expect to be provided with a dowry. The young lady was swept off her feet by the dashing Don José Ramón. This was not surprising inasmuch as she had spent her youth in the seclusion of the impoverished country house in Sonora and did not know young gentlemen of her standing.

For a year or two Don José—who for reasons known only to himself had shortened his noble name to José Maso—sponged on his father-in-law, until the old baron had nothing left with which to pay either his own creditors or the young man's gambling debts. He discussed with Don José a journey to Spain, in order to enlist help from their respective relatives, but at first, nothing was done about it.

Then, in 1862, they all set off for California. The old baron made this long and uncomfortable journey together with the young couple and Doña Carmelita de Maso, José's mother, who suddenly appeared out of the blue in some of Reavis' documents. José Maso intended to sail to Spain from San Francisco, in order to retrieve funds from his wealthy family in Cádiz. Doña Sofía was expecting a child, and at Agua Mansa, near San Bernardino in California, she was taken with labor pains. A midwife, La Generala, was quickly summoned, and that night at a lonely farm, Sofía Maso gave birth to twins, a boy and a girl.

Nearby was the old Mission of San Salvador. Established by Spanish priests, it remained a landmark when San Bernardino was founded in the middle of the nineteenth century by Mormons, who arrived in a train of 150 wagons and set up this outpost of Brigham Young's empire. The Mormon elders had their great vision to "open a gateway from the Pacific to the Mormon Commonwealth of Utah," a dream that was soon to bring them into conflict with the United States authorities. In those days San Bernadino was an almost uninhabited area, dotted with a few ranches, 100 miles from San Diego, 70 miles from the seaport of San Pedro, and 45 miles from the then small town of Los Angles. The Mormons purchased a few ranches and almost 100,000 acres of virgin land and began building without delay. In the course of a few years they laid out fine plantations, built a large irrigation system, and erected saw and flour mills. But San Bernardino flourished as a Mormon colony for only six years. After the Mountain Meadow Massacre and the conflict with Washington, Brigham Young recalled all the brethren to Utah. They left behind fine farms, several factories, and good canals and roads. Most of this property was purchased at a small fraction of its true value by Mexican and a few American newcomers. San Bernardino became a mainly Mexican town, and the Mormons were soon forgotten.

The Church of San Salvador was looked after by Spanish Franciscans. To this church the twins were hastily taken, in view of the boy's sickly condition. Father Fernando González baptized them; the girl was named Carmelita Sofía Loreta Micaela,* the boy José Ramón Carmen. Soon afterward the priest was called to administer the last rites to the desperately sick mother. Within twenty-four hours mother and son were dead, but the little girl was sturdy and survived. At the ranch the sorrow-stricken family found an Indian wet nurse, whose name was Tomasa.

José Maso, the young widower, faded out of the Peralta story with the rapidity with which he had arrived for his whirlwind romance and marriage. He was in a hurry to get to Spain. Before departing, however, he arranged that his mother, Doña Carmelita de Maso, and his newborn daughter would go to Sherwood Valley, where they were put up by his close friend, John A. Treadway. The baron and José Maso went to San

---

* The name Carmelita, which the later Mrs. Reavis used, did not appear on the forged birth certificate. It was probably given to her by her foster parents, the Sherwoods.

Francisco. The heartbroken old man remained there, too ill to accept his son-in-law's invitation to accompany him to Spain.

Two years went by. Maso had gone to Cádiz and sent a message to Don Miguel Silva Jesús, urging him to come to Spain because he needed his presence to recover certain old bequests of the Maso and the Peralta families. The old baron traveled to Sherwood Valley to see his granddaughter for the last time and then sailed for Europe. Neither he nor his son-in-law was ever seen again. That the old man died soon after his arrival in Cádiz was perhaps only natural. But that death also overtook the handsome Don José Ramón Carmen de Maso in the prime of his life was surprising. His death remained unexplained by Reavis.

Little Carmelita grew up with her grandmother (her father's mother) on Treadway's ranch. When she was five, both her grandmother and Mr. Treadway died,* and the little girl was taken to the house of Alfred Sherwood, the owner of a large ranch in the valley named after his family. When she was eight, she went to Knights Landing, to the house of Captain John Snowball, who offered to adopt her. She lived in his house until she was fifteen. Then it was decided she should be instructed in dressmaking. One day in the spring of 1877 Carmelita traveled alone on the train from San Bernardino to Los Angeles. In this train Reavis saw her and was struck by the girl's resemblance to the wife of the second baron. (He did not explain how he established this resemblance, as he did not claim that at the time he possessed portraits of members of the Peralta family.)

He spoke to the girl and found out who she was—she mentioned the name of Maso—and where she lived, and he briefly mentioned that he had reason to believe that she was the heiress to a great fortune. He was at that time working for the San

---

* After Reavis' trial it was proved that John Treadway had died in 1861, a year before the date given as Carmelita's birth. Thus, she could have hardly stayed at his house for several years.

Francisco *Examiner* and had to hurry to the city, parting from little Carmelita, but obtaining her promise that they would remain in touch by mail. Carmelita later returned to Knights Landing, where she worked as a domestic help and nurse for the Snowball family. Reavis and she exchanged letters, but he did not mention whether he ever visited her. He traveled to the Snowball home in the winter of 1882 and proposed marriage, and they were married on December 31, 1882, by civil contract by a San Francisco notary public.

Reavis was then still married to Ada Pope of St. Louis. He did not obtain his divorce until 1883 and therefore decided to keep the civil marriage secret. Carmelita received educational instruction at the Convent of San Luis de Rey and lived in a boardinghouse on Stockton Street. Reavis saw her frequently but assumed the role of her guardian rather than that of her husband.

When subsequently submitting documents relevant to these events, Reavis did not, of course, overlook introducing into this initial story of Carmelita's life documentary evidence according to which her grandfather, Don Miguel Silva Jesús de Peralta, had wisely remembered before his departure to Spain to make a deed in which he confirmed that she was his sole heiress and entitled to the Peralta estates in Arizona and New Mexico.

How did this story tally with the original Peralta claim filed in 1883, based on the Willing papers? It did, if only by a tortuous stretch of imagination. Having found the heiress, Reavis would have gladly forgotten the whole Willing business, but his original claim had been properly filed, and when in 1887 he submitted his second claim, on behalf of the real heiress, he could not very well discard all that he had elaborately tried to prove in 1883. Therefore, he later explained that the impoverished old baron, after the tragic loss of his daughter and the move of his little granddaughter to Treadway's farm, lived for about two years in San Francisco. Sometime during

1864, the baron, who was then eighty-three, must have made a last desperate attempt to recover something from his ancestral grant. He traveled to Arizona, met Dr. Willing, and sold him his rights. Only then did he sail to Europe to join his son-in-law in Cádiz or Madrid.

Throughout the Reavis campaign of fraud there were always drops of fact in the flood of fiction. Although he had undoubtedly constructed the melodramatic life history of the real heiress before he even set out to find a suitable girl to be fashioned into the living heroine of his story, one may surmise that he had restricted himself to the bare bones of the story, waiting to cover and embellish them with tasty tidbits, once the subject had been found.

How he found the girl whom he presented later with such a signal success as the only surviving scion of the Peraltas was never established with certainty. At his trial entirely new evidence was produced by secret agents of the U.S. Treasury, and this evidence is recounted elsewhere in this book.

Just who Carmelita really was will never be known with exactitude. She was probably a parentless child, one of many thousands of her day, the daughter of an Indian woman and an American settler or a Mexican ranch hand, born out of wedlock or bought and sold in something close to slavery, in the partially civilized lands of the South, on both sides of the American-Mexican border.

Then there is Carmelita's own story, on the whole corresponding to the "official" one composed by Reavis. She told it to a reporter in the autumn of 1887, after she had returned with her husband from their triumphant visit to Europe and appeared for the first time in public as Reavis' wife and the real heiress.

The interview was given at the Glenwood Hotel in Riverside to a reporter of the Los Angeles *Examiner*. The new Baroness de Peralta told the reporter:

My life story opens in a cloud of mystery. From the earliest period of my recollection I was aware that in some way my antecedents were a mystery which it was the interest of certain persons to weave into an impenetrable web. I can well recall an aged grandmother who bestowed upon me that affection which should have come from a mother's source but fate had destined that I should never enjoy a mother's love. She, my mother, was called away from the earth a few hours after she gave me birth, her first and only child.*

The scene of this opening of my life drama was laid in the northern part of California, about two or three hundred miles from Sacramento. I grew from a prattling chatterbox of a baby to be a happy, pleasure-loving girl. It was at that time in the year of 1868 or 1869 that Captain Snowball visited the beautiful valley which is treasured in my childhood's memory. I suppose I took Captain Snowball's fancy, for I went with him as his adopted child to his house at Knights Landing. My father, who you must know married a Peralta, at an early period of my childhood crossed the blue waters of the Atlantic on a visit to the home of his ancestors. While in Cádiz in Spain, he died, thousands of miles away from me, his daughter, who was thus left an orphan in the hands of strangers.

Summers came and went and from a little oval-faced girl of eight, I developed into a young woman and in the year of 1876 I decided to accept an offer made by a dressmaker, and in the busy toil of my new life passed the next few months of my existence. It was in the year 1877 when I determined to make a visit to Sacramento to some friends who had extended me an invitation. Taking the Central Pacific train I was soon carried to my destination. The car in which I was seated was entered by a prepossessing young man who, upon observing me, was struck with my resemblance to a family whose history was interwoven with his own. Obeying a sudden impulse, he approached me, and asked me earnestly if I knew any one by the name of Massol [sic!] in Sacramento.

That is my name, said I, astonished. My questioner was evidently as much surprised as myself, for he immediately seated himself beside me, and began to propound many questions, not only about myself but my relations. This young man was James

---

* She must have forgotten her twin brother.

Addison Reavis, the man who afterwards stood with me before the altar.

My visit was brief. I soon returned to Knights Landing where I remained until 1880, when I received an offer to enter the service of Mrs. Laughnour of Woodland. I had been there for about a year when an offer was made to me by a Mrs. Craig, which I thought advantageous and I accepted it. There I passed some of the most pleasant months of my life. Up to that time I was well treated and made many friends, and the world began to assume a pleasant aspect. I kept up a correspondence with Reavis, supplying him with the points and clues necessary for the further-ance of the work he was engaged in.

On the 31st December 1882 our acquaintance, which had by this time ripened into love, culminated in a marriage performed by civil contract in the presence of those only necessary to make the ceremony legally binding.

The months rolled on until 1885 when Reavis decided to make a trip to Spain, which had become absolutely necessary to fully establish the documentary evidence in his possession. Wel-comed warmly by the Peraltas [sic] we hurried to Madrid, where we at once presented ourselves to the head of the Peralta family, who knew the history of our family and how Don José Ramón Carmen Maso, my father, had gone home to Spain to die, and left his infant daughter in a strange land.

Apart from the evidence that Reavis produced, one and all were struck by my marked resemblance to so many of those who were members of the Peralta family.

In the meantime Reavis was busy searching among the archives and records of the courts, and slowly but surely amassed his evidence until, at last, he felt that his labors were completed.

It was during this visit that the contract of marriage was celebrated by a grand fiesta and the secret of our marriage, which had so long been kept, was open to the world.

It has been stated before, previous to this celebration, that Mr. Reavis appeared in the character of my guardian, and that it was thus he posed on his arrival in Spain.

This interview was written by a skilled reporter, and if he paraphrased the baroness' flow of words, one must assume that he faithfully stuck to the facts she supplied. She had obviously learned by heart the story of her make-believe life, a story which Reavis must have hammered into her brain morning, noon, and night. But in her excitement she made some silly mistakes, mixing up the name of Massol—the Sacramento merchant who had made a deal with Willing and assigned his rights to Reavis— with that of Maso, her imaginary father; she became confused about dates and was extremely vague about the places where she had spent her childhood and about her acquaintance with Reavis, which so suddenly "ripened into love," apparently by correspondence.

Poor woman, however cunning she was and greedy to protect her newly acquired wealth, she must have been going through hell, enmeshed in this gargantuan web of lies Reavis had woven.

Her story was, of course, a splendidly readable and romantic newspaper feature, although even a casual reader must have found it puzzling and implausible. She never mentioned by name John Treadway, with whom she lived in "the beautiful valley," for a very good reason, because she may have suspected that he was the man who had seduced her mother, a poor Indian woman, and was probably her natural father.

The alternative stories to Reavis' and Carmelita's accounts vary greatly. She was said to be pure Indian, picked up after a massacre at an Apache or Navajo camp. She was Mexican-Indian, a mestiza, rejected by her Indian mother when her lover jilted her, left at the steps of a mission church. She was the illegitimate daughter of a highborn Creole, an official in the government of Mexico, who had paid a California farmer to provide a home for her. One writer, Clarence Budington Kelland, stated that Reavis, in his quest for a girl who would fit the pattern of his story, had searched California and Arizona and at last found her on a lonely ranch at the foot of the Dragoon Mountains in southeastern Arizona, on John Slaughter's Six

Springs Ranch. Although Donald M. Powell, the chief reference librarian of the University of Arizona, who made a searching study of the Peralta Grant, rejected Kelland's surmise as not deserving further consideration, this possibility cannot be entirely dismissed.

If Reavis found Carmelita at Slaughter's ranch, he met one of the most remarkable men of his times in the Southwest. It was not until 1880 that Slaughter owned the great ranch, originally founded by the Mormons. He had previously ranched in Cochise County, had fought the Apaches from the early 1870's, had driven his cattle into the San Pedro Valley, and later purchased most of the 70,000 acres which reached into Mexican Sonora.

John Slaughter was a decent, upright man. He had adopted a tough policy for a tough environment. The depredations by rustlers cost him hundreds of head of cattle every season. He was accustomed to come across a body of many a bull calf killed just to provide a couple of steaks for an outlaw, and he knew what it was to have every stranger on his land an enemy: bronco Apaches who despised those Indians who had made peace with the white man; rustlers who hated the only obstacle to their trade for miles around; smugglers who knew that their capture would reap a good reward on either side of the border. Slaughter despised adventurers who ignored crops and cattle for the glitter of gold and silver. And he hated Tombstone, that Mecca of all the bad men, rustlers, smugglers, prospectors, outlaws, and bandits of Arizona and Mexico. Indicative of Slaughter's upright character was the fact that he eventually succeeded in cleaning up that town. Although wealthy from his own ranching activities, he took the job of sheriff of Tombstone after the famous gun battle at the O.K. Corral, which ultimately sent the surviving Earps fleeing for refuge in Colorado.

If little Carmelita had ever been a slavey at Slaughter's ranch, she would have been treated decently, and it is doubtful that the sheriff would have given her to a man such as Reavis.

Wherever Reavis found the girl, she had no reason to regret the change which had come to her life. At best she had been an orphan employed as a children's nurse or a domestic servant; at worst, a barefoot little drudge, slaving for a dish of food and a hard mattress. Many years later Reavis recounted, if only vaguely, his first meeting with Carmelita. When he first eyed her cautiously, he liked what he saw. She was tall and graceful; her young body was well formed; he liked her dark, shining, intelligent eyes, which belied her rather sulky mouth and her habit of cringing a little when she was spoken to. He must have known her in the late 1870's in California, when he was living in the south, before he became involved with the Southern Pacific tycoons and newspaper work. She was then only sixteen, perhaps a waitress in a Mexican tavern.

When he started to tell her about his plans, she understood quickly. He never told her the full truth, and if she knew it, she could have only guessed it. He impressed on her that she was of noble birth, and because she wanted to believe it, she did. When he met her, she could neither read nor write. She had little knowledge of behavior or of hygiene. Before he could risk introducing her into the limelight, he had to teach her many things. But she was a quick and intelligent girl, eager to learn so as not to lose the unbelievably comfortable way of living that Reavis had provided for her.

He took her to the school of the Convent of San Luis de Rey, and after a fairly generous donation, the mother superior was prepared to accept the little semisavage and turn Carmelita into an accomplished young lady of gentle birth and upbringing.

Periodically Reavis came to watch Carmelita's progress. And her progress delighted him. Soon she could read quite well and write with the beautiful calligraphy taught by the convent sisters. It may have been painful for him to watch her slowly form the letters, but in the role Reavis planned for her, there would be little writing for her to do. He could rely on his own excellent penmanship.

Once he was sure that he had found and created the Peralta heiress, Reavis embarked on the difficult job of building her imaginary life story. He had to invent her birthplace and decided on San Bernardino. The saints were on his side. At the mission house he found a kindly and, fortunately, not very clever priest. Reavis had not only to produce the appropriate documents proving the birth of the Maso twins and the death and burial of their mother, back in 1862, but also to provide proper entries in the church register of San Salvador.

The priest had given his permission to search through the records. Because the current church book was only thirty years old, the register was brief and in good order. It did not take Reavis long to find the baptismal records for the first six months of 1862. The page for March conveniently enumerated the births of seven children, mostly Indian.

The rector of San Salvador, Father P. J. Stockman, was at that time absent from his parish and had left it in charge of a young and an inexperienced priest, Father Joseph O'Reilly. Reavis talked him into lending him the old baptism and burial registers for a few days. In fact, he kept them for a month, going to San Francisco and completing in the privacy of his home the necessary "corrections." He removed the pages containing the original entries, together with a few blank sheets he found at the end of the books. Then he replaced the missing page in the births and baptism register. It still contained seven names. Five were the same as the original; two names had disappeared. In the places of the latter now appeared entries for the Maso twins: Sofía Loreta Micaela and José Ramón Carmen de Maso y Peralta. Likewise, in the burial register Reavis inserted a page recording the deaths of Doña Sofía Peralta de Maso and her newborn son, adding a note that they had received the holy sacrament. The pages he inserted were of the same paper; he had used the blank old pages to copy the five old and to add the two new baptism entries, and he applied a similar procedure to the burial register.

Father O'Reilly was glad when the books were at last returned by the local barber, to whom Reavis had given a few dollars and whom he had asked to request the priest to issue appropriate certificates. This Father O'Reilly did, duly copying the faked entries, signing the certificates with his name, and imprinting them with the mission's stamp.

Perhaps it is understandable that Reavis' habit of extreme caution, of forging right and left to make doubly sure, should have deserted him at this moment of a triumph so easily achieved. He had created an heiress out of a piece of paper, but for once he had omitted to make an important check. The priest did not tell him that there existed another register, an index ledger in which at the end of each year the names of those born and baptized, married, and buried within the parish of San Bernardino were listed alphabetically under their surnames, providing a cross-reference to all entries in the main registers.

Thus, when Reavis eventually returned the church books and got the certificates, he was unaware that his seemingly easy forgery had left a damning proof of his criminality in the sacristy of San Salvador. There were the books with the inserted pages and perfectly faked entries of the births of the Peralta twins and of their mother's death—open to anyone who wanted to inspect them. But there was also the index ledger which made no mention of these entries at all, but which listed the names of two Indian babies whose names now appeared nowhere else.

It was a mistake Reavis was later to brood on during his lonely years in jail. It came out into the daylight when Father Stockman and the Secret Service agents inspected all the books at the Church of San Salvador and compared the registers with the index ledger.

But for the time being, Reavis was in possession of an official and genuine certificate of the birth and baptism of Sofía Loreta Micaela Peralta de Maso, great-granddaughter of the first Baron of Arizona, the heiress to a royal grant of more than 12,000,000 acres of land in Arizona and New Mexico.

Reavis also decided to "discover" that famous Initial Monument, the rock with the engraved *diseño* of the Peralta Grant, of which Father Pauer had written so poetically in his report about the delineation of the estates in 1758. Reavis had gleaned from many ancient documents that Spanish surveyors had always set marking stones at salient points of territories apportioned to hidalgos or monasteries. Each such monument bore some kind of cipher or *diseño* chipped into the rock. A crucifix and initials were the simplest mark; more elaborate ones bore an outline of the estate, the arms of the king or the *caballero* who had been granted the estate, and sometimes the date of the grant.

Indian tribes always delighted in removing these stones, partly to register their protest against the palefaced invaders and partly to hold such stones with their magic signs as trophies or taboos. Comparatively few remained in their original positions when the areas came under the control of the United States, and most were weathered so that they did not appear to be artifacts. When they existed, firmly implanted in the ground, they were, of course, virtually irrefutable evidence of a claim to the land on which they stood.

Reavis intended to have such evidence. With Pedro Cuervo, and in great secrecy, he traveled to the Sierras Estrellas in search of a great rock which resembled the one mentioned by Father Pauer in the document which Reavis had so elaborately forged from various bits and pieces of genuine old documents. He found a suitable rock, jutting high above the valley, and on it he chipped vague marks very lightly, patiently filing away the freshly made edges and staining the grooves with vegetable juices.

The finished stone told little beyond the fact that a century and more earlier it had been subjected to human carving. The *diseño* was only faintly visible; but it was there, and above it even more faint but not altogether illegible was the crest of the noble family of Peralta. Here was the landmark—the vital *Monumento Inicial* which marked the western boundary of his realm.

When Reavis rode for many miles, following the boundary lines, he probably realized for the first time the immensity of the claim. It was food that fed his lust for possession. This lovely earth, with all the wealth below its soil and with its riches created by the men who toiled on its surface, had to be his.

8

Spanish Interlude

The protests against the Barony of Arizona, initiated by Churchill and Weedin, neither worried Reavis nor put a brake to his activities. The resounding success he had enjoyed with his first campaign to obtain tributes, royalties, and rents must have encouraged him to engage on even more ambitious schemes, but he was far too intelligent a man to believe that forces would not soon gather to challenge him more strongly. Having found the real heiress, he made plans to go to Spain and return with more documents in order to play out his master stroke—to file the claim by the direct descendant of the legendary Don Miguel de Peralta.

In the meantime he was determined to gather as much money as he could. In San Francisco in the spring of 1885 he was busily looking for new backers. Huntington had all but lost his interest in the Barony of Arizona, having come to an agreement with his rival Jay Gould, apportioning the spheres of operations for the Southern Pacific and the Texas Pacific. He had paid Reavis $50,000 and was still paying him regular, though small, royalties; but he realized that Reavis was now out for new fraudulent enterprises, and he was unwilling to get further involved.

Charles Crocker and Harvey S. Brown, the company lawyer of the Southern Pacific, were, however, still patronizing Reavis, and through them he met the San Francisco banker Maurice Herr, who was completely taken in by Reavis' self-assurance. They agreed to form the Arizona Development Corporation, with a capital of $25,000,000, and to float a huge issue of shares. Herr was to prepare the launching in San Francisco, while Reavis went to New York to explore the possibilities of floating the shares on the stock exchanges in the East. What obviously interested him most about the new corporation was that Herr agreed to pay him a monthly salary of $250 until the corporation was formed, and he was also to pay all his expenses.

Reavis traveled to New York with Carmelita. She had now assumed the role of his ward: the newly found young and beautiful Baroness Peralta de Maso, on her way with her protector, for a visit to Spain, the country of her great ancestors. He did not yet feel it safe to reveal that he had married Carmelita, in case his finely woven web of lies and pretense should be pierced.

He took with him Pedro Cuervo, the swarthy mestizo who had served him so devotedly as his bodyguard and who incongruously sported two huge silver-studded pistols in the belt of his Mexican costume and wore pristine white gloves on his massive fists. With them traveled a valet; Carmelita's chaperon, a matronly Mexican woman; and a maid, a pretty French girl from New Orleans. Barratt had been left behind at the Arizola office, in command of the few remaining agents and rent collectors, who were to continue their extortions during their master's absence, if this were at all possible.

From his friends in California, Reavis had obtained letters of introduction to several important people in New York. One of them was Roscoe Conkling, Senator from New York and one of the most astute and successful lawyers of his time. He was a real behind-the-scenes power in the Republican party; one of the Stalwarts, he had been responsible for the nomination of General Ulysses Grant for President in 1877, had worked for President James A. Garfield, and was an intimate friend of President Chester A. Arthur.

Conkling warmly welcomed Reavis as a man who appeared likely to become rich and politically influential in the emerging territories of the Southwest, and Reavis and his "ward" were soon Conkling's guests at various social functions. The cachet of personal friendship with the Senator, who had the ear of every important member of the administration in Washington and of New York financiers and businessmen, was sufficient to get Reavis accepted wherever he went.

Soon Reavis was on first-name terms with New York tycoons, such as Dwight Townsend and Henry Porter of the American Bank Note Company, and struck up a friendship with the banker Hector de Castro, a man of Spanish antecedents, who became enthusiastically interested in the Peralta Grant history. He also again met John W. Mackay, the mining engineer who ten years earlier had discovered some of the great silver deposits on the Comstock in Nevada, had become a millionaire, and had moved from San Francisco to New York. Reavis signed agreements with several of these tycoons, promising each a share in the Peralta Grant, but taking only Mackay into his confidence regarding the new claim on behalf of Carmelita.

So impressed was Mackay by the documents Reavis produced —and by Carmelita's personal charm and bearing that left no doubt about her noble ancestry—that he advanced a large sum (it is said $20,000 in cash) and also began to pay Reavis a monthly retainer of $500 as his contribution to the couple's journey to Europe.

After several weeks of an enjoyable and remunerative stay in New York, James Reavis, his "ward," and their retinue sailed for Cádiz in Spain. As in all his undertakings, Reavis had made elaborate plans for his trip, not ignoring the slightest detail. The former streetcar driver of St. Louis had long since adopted all the luxurious ways of a wealthy and important man. His friend Marcellus F. Berry, one of the vice-presidents of Wells Fargo and the American Express, provided him with an elaborate itinerary. Berry suggested that the party sail aboard the new Cunarder *Oregon*, the fastest steamship, which was making the New York to Queenstown run in only six days, but Reavis decided to go directly to Spain.

In Mexico, in 1883, when he was ransacking the archives with Rufus Hopkins, he had met a Spanish journalist, Carlos Santana, who later returned to Spain and became the editor of Madrid's most go-ahead newspaper, *La Correspondencia*. Reavis had kept in touch with Santana, who had promised to introduce him to political leaders and financiers interested in developing business between Spain and her former colonial territories in America. Santana had written:

> You will get a great welcome here by scheming courtiers and politicians, who are still dreaming of re-establishing Spanish influence in the Americas. Although we have been thrown out by the front door, we still hope to return by the back door. We are determined to hold on to Cuba, Puerto Rico and the Philippines. It would be wonderful if you could help to cock a snook at those damn *Yanquis*. And there would be honor and money for you.

The Spanish consul in San Francisco, a younger son of the Duke de Escalona, who was winning his diplomatic spurs, had also urged Reavis to go to Madrid without delay. These Spanish friends had accepted the Peralta legend on its face value. There were so many noble families in Spain, so many complex intermarriages which had over the centuries produced ever new and intricate titles and ranks, that even to the informed members of the aristocracy it was well nigh impossible to know whether the American Peraltas y Córdobas ever existed or were only a figment of imagination.

After a long passage across 3,200 miles of the southern route aboard a Spanish vessel, the baronial party landed in Cádiz shortly before Christmas, 1885. At the port the United

States consul, Antony J. Beneusen, greeted Reavis and Carmelita deferentially, having been informed by Daniel Manning, the Secretary of the Treasury and one of Conkling's cronies, of the impending arrival of the distinguished citizen from Arizona and the Baroness de Peralta.

A special coach was attached to the Madrid train, which began to make its tortuously slow progress through the green valleys of the Guadalquivir and the mountains of the Sierra Morena into the treeless calcined desert of southern Castile, through Seville, Córdoba, and Linares to the capital.

"This is the land of your ancestors. They were mighty kings and great warriors," Reavis explained solemnly to his wife. "Remember that in your veins flows the blood of proud *castelanos*. Look at those toiling peasants, there in the fields. They even toss manure with an air of dignity. To them Spain is the first kingdom in Christendom; Castile, its first province; and they themselves, the first of the Spanish people."

Carmelita obediently listened and looked with awe at her husband, who knew all these wonderful things about her homeland and her family, of whom she knew nothing. She eagerly watched the changing scenery from the train window: the ruined yellow castles, the pathetic tumbledown farms, and the men and women toiling in the fields and olive groves. The train moved at a speed of not more than fifteen miles an hour; there were many interminable stops, even at secondary halts. The American consul at Cádiz had warned them they would have to forage on the train. The station *fondas* would not provide the food the American travelers were accustomed to. Reavis had arranged that boxes with cold meat, fruit, and wine be delivered and stored in the luggage compartment. Carmelita's chaperon boiled milk on a small charcoal stove, and the women sipped cup after cup of hot chocolate, as thick as syrup, dipping into it slices of frothy *azucarillo,* the spongy sugar cake sold by eager attendants at every stop.

Armed railway guards patrolled the train corridors, assuring the distinguished passengers that everything was well and pocketing eagerly but with dignity a silver duro, their usual toll. It was by no means uncommon for gangs of robbers to hold up a train, but 1885 had started peacefully, after the revolutionary upheavals and lawlessness of the past few years. Thus, the baronial party reached Madrid safely after a long and exhausting journey across half of Spain.

At the capital a large suite had been reserved for them at Madrid's newest and most luxurious hotel, the great ornate pile of the Fonda de Paris, which had been raised upon the ruins of the Church of Buen Suceso, the scene of Murat's terrible massacre of 1808. From their windows they could watch the Puerta del Sol, the heart of Madrid, the rendezvous for all the newsmongers, scandalmongers, political agitators, place seekers, and every idle do-nothing Madrilenian. They stood in groups, discussing excitedly the daily gossip, until their throats were dry and they departed to one or more of the innumerable *tabernas* and *bodegas* of the side streets.

Life was pleasant and exciting in Madrid in the mid-1880's for those few thousands of the upper crust to whom money was no object. The country as a whole was exhausted and impoverished, not only by the loss of its empire, but also by a succession of revolutions which had shaken it almost incessantly for the past half century. But now Spain had, at last, the appearance of law and order and peace, although there were harebrained schemes and plots of ambitious politicians and generals to reassert the colonial rule, such as an attempt at restoring Spanish suzerainty over Peru and Chile, the short-lived reconquest of the Dominican Republic twenty years earlier, and the suppression of revolts in Cuba and the Philippines. If wars and revolutions had almost ruined the country, they had brought fortunes to some.

The great palaces, the beautiful patrician houses, the vast

estates were still unscathed, even though many had changed hands with the advent of a new aristocracy and an upper class consisting of war profiteers, venal politicians, and corrupt officials. "Money and honor," James Reavis repeated to himself. Yes, money and honor were here in Spain, even if honor as he saw it meant only titles and rank and power.

When he was introduced to some of the men in the seats of power, he was, at least for a moment, overawed and bewildered. How different it all was from the savage desert of Arizona, the rough cowboys, illiterate prospectors, wild Indians, and even wilder outlaws. Everyone here, even quite ordinary people, seemed to possess great culture and civility. They wore their top hats and frock coats with grave dignity, and those who did not sport shiny toppers and coats of fine cloth were attired in flowing *capas* and wide-brimmed sombreros. Everyone was a *caballero*. The women, whether great ladies in their Paris-fashioned silk crinolines or women of the lower classes in colorful costumes and black mantillas, were gentle, proud, and alluring.

Within days of his arrival, Reavis had made several influential and highly placed friends. Santana, the editor, had kept his word and had introduced him to many important people. Soon the doors were opening to the charming couple from faraway Arizona—the doors of the great houses of bearers of high-sounding names, around the royal palace and the ancient Plaza Major, as well as those of the new rich who had built themselves fine houses along the broad avenue of Castellana.

Santana had rattled off an interminable list of his titled friends, adding with the exactness of a good reporter that Spain had, at the moment, 243 grandees, 96 dukes, 920 *marqueses*, 717 counts, 110 viscounts, 36 barons, and uncountable numbers of hidalgos and nobles of lesser grades.

"Many of them were plain people as you and I, if I may say so with great respect to yourself, my *amigo*," he said with a smile, "and had been only ennobled in this century, by the various rulers with whom we have been cursed over the last fifty years. The old aristocracy, the nobles of Charlemagne and Charles and Philip, are dead, defunct, and forgotten; the few who aren't are as poor as church mice and count for nothing."

Santana proved an invaluable source of information for Reavis. What he could not provide, another and even more influential journalist did. He was the young and handsome Don Alfredo Escobar, who had taken a great fancy to pretty Carmelita. Don Alfredo's father was the proprietor of Spain's greatest newspaper *La Época* which he liked to compare with the London *Times*; indeed the influence his journal exercised in politics and business was even greater than that of the famous English newspaper. The elder Escobar, once a poor journalist, had amassed a great fortune, having sided with every subsequent ruler and government, and Alfonso XII had raised him to the exalted rank of the Marqués de Valdeiglesias. With sponsors like these, it was not difficult for Carmelita and her dignified American guardian who spoke Spanish so well and was himself partly of noble Spanish origin to be received at the royal court.

Reavis had written to several heads of families named Peralta, carefully selecting only those who occupied a high position or were wealthy. He had explained that his ward was an orphan of the great Peralta family, related to the *visitador del rey* of Guadalajara in Mexico and also, if remotely, to the famous governor of Santa Fe in the eighteenth century. He had received several replies and invitations. Spanish families are so large and have so many remote and unknown cousins that no one was surprised about a cousin from the New World desiring to renew family contacts, even after a century or two.

Cautiously, Reavis told these newfound relatives of Carmelita's the story of the Peralta Grant, and if some expressed more lively interest in a possible inheritance than was to his liking, he quickly discouraged them, saying that he was in the possession of documents showing that Carmelita was the sole rightful heiress.

When Reavis arrived in Spain, the court was in mourning. The king had died only a few weeks before; his widow, the former Austrain Archduchess Maria Christina, was expecting a child, who was immediately proclaimed king after his birth. Reavis decided to leave Madrid and start his searches in the archives in Seville and Cádiz.

One may surmise that he was determined to put his penmanship to good use. He knew that he could at last inspect and copy original ancient documents referring to land tenure and royal grants in the Spanish dominions overseas. In Seville he introduced himself to the curator of the *Archivos de Indias* as an American historian and was given full permission to search where and what he wished.

There were hundreds of cedulas and edicts dealing with such grants in New Spain, easily copied and almost as easily purloined, because he was often left alone in the reading room of the archives building. He was told that other such documents could be found in Madrid because priceless historical records, found in provincial museums, churches, monasteries, and missions in Spain and the former colonies, had been assembled by the government, since 1864, in the vast collection called *Colección de documentos relativos al descubrimiento, conquista y colonización de las posesiones españolas en América*. Heady with his discoveries and excited by the thought of the unending supply of everything he could need in the capital, he returned to Madrid, where he eluded the invitations of his new friends and their rather unnerving interest in his work by saying that he intended to take a brief holiday.

He traveled with Carmelita and the servants to San Sebastián on the invitation of General Carlos Ibarra, whom Reavis had persuaded that he was Carmelita's uncle. Reavis made the general believe that his father had been a first cousin of Carmelita's grandmother, Doña Juana Laura Ibarra, who had married the second Baron de Peralta in 1822. That neither the second baron nor his wife ever existed was another matter.

Carmelita stayed with her new relatives, and Reavis returned to Madrid. He took comfortable rooms in the Calle de la Concepción, near the Cathedral of San Isidro in the Old Town and for a time remained hidden from his friends. He wished to have a quiet place in which to work on his forgeries each evening after his visits to the archives.

He now had to devise the final and most important part of the second baron's life. He had to produce new documents of the marriage of Carmelita's parents, the gentle and sickly Doña Sofía de Peralta and the handsome young Spanish immigrant José Ramón Carmen de Maso y Castilla, who called himself José Maso, and to prove Carmelita's legitimacy. He did so, and the most important of these documents was a codicil to the last will and testament of the second baron (originally made in California), appointing his granddaughter, Carmelita, his sole heiress. The codicil conveniently contained a clause referring to the Peralta Grant and prevailing upon the heiress to pursue the rights granted to her great-grandfather.

Well satisfied with his work, Reavis packed his treasures into a stout ironclad box and deposited it in the vaults of the Banca d'España. Then he traveled to San Sebastián to join Carmelita. A most pleasant summer passed, during which the couple, in fact married for at least two and probably three years, became betrothed. General Ibarra, as the bride's senior relative, was asked for and gave his permission, and the wedding was celebrated in the bosom of the newfound family, General Ibarra giving the bride away. Reavis made sure that the marriage was also recorded later before the United States chargé d'affaires in Madrid, thus making it legal in regard to the United States authorities.

Following Spanish custom, Reavis was now entitled to call himself Baron de Peralta y Córdoba, for the wife's noble title can and, indeed, should be assumed by the husband. Later, after their return to America, Reavis called himself James Peralta-reavis, expressly not using the baronial title in deference to American democracy.

The honeymoon was spent aboard General Ibarra's yacht. The couple made a pleasant cruise along the coast of Biscay and in the Mediterranean, arriving in Málaga and continuing the journey to Madrid.

In the autumn the capital was the scene of great festivities. The new king, Alfonso XIII, was born in May and his mother, Queen Maria Christina, was proclaimed regent by the Cortes. One evening in September the baron and baroness, in a great equipage, with outriders and liveried flunkeys, rode through the Calle Major to the palace. They were conducted with a number of other carefully selected foreign visitors and a throng of dignitaries and courtiers and their ladies into the presence of Her Majesty. Anybody who has visited Madrid knows the lofty marble halls of the royal palace, the immense hall of the ambassadors, the throne room, and the priceless furnishings and pictures and chandeliers, which are the same today as they were eighty years ago, on that warm autumn evening, with the breeze gently blowing from the Guadarrama Mountains.

Carmelita was attired in a wonderful creation of brocade, silk, and lace. On her head was a costly diamond tiara, which Reavis had ordered the court jeweler, Joacquín García, to design and make in only a week, paying for it, without a murmur, a price almost double that which García would have charged any of his usual customers. Carmelita looked radiant, her jet-black hair coiffured into a mass of curls and ringlets, falling onto her bare shoulders. However outwardly prudish and pious the Spanish court pretended to be, the fashion of the day decreed that the bodice must be low and the décolleté deep.

The eyes of all the male guests were on the young Baroness de Arizonac.

Reavis wore court dress, with breeches and silk stockings. He also wore the star of the Order of Carlos III, knowing from his assiduous studies of Spanish customs that he was entitled to display it as a hereditary honor bestowed on the grandfather of his wife.

With the other guests, they passed the long suite of marble-walled halls and antechambers, hung with priceless tapestries, flanked by cuirass-clad *alabarderos* and armored arquebusiers in plumed helmets, Catalan pikemen, and a host of major-domos, *ujieres,* and *caballerizos.* Gentlemen of the Queen's Chamber escorted them toward the throne.

The great chamberlain, knocking the marble floor with his staff, announced the names of those privileged to be presented. The queen mother stretched out two fingers of her gloved hand for a hand kiss by the men, while the ladies remained seemingly petrified in a deep and long curtsy. Maria Christina looked approvingly at Carmelita and said graciously, *"Bienvenida,* Baroness, to my court and our country. I hear that you are Spanish. I hope to meet you again in private audience." With a slight nod Carmelita was dismissed. Next morning every news-paper in Madrid carried in its *últimas noticias,* or gossip columns, the story of the Baroness de Arizonac's great success at court and Her Majesty's gracious invitation to a private audience.*

A week or so after the gala reception, the baroness was commanded to appear at the palace. Carmelita had changed beyond recognition into a young lady not only of charm, which was her nature, but also of refinement and amazing self-assurance. Maria Christina, after that visit, during which Carmelita answered her questions about life in the American West, Indians, and outlaws, must have taken a real liking to her. She probably found her much more natural, intelligent, and amus-

* Madrid *La Época,* September, 1886.

ing than the ladies of her entourage. Another invitation followed to the splendid palace of La Granja, near Segovia, where
Carmelita received the great honor of being shown the royal
baby, a rather pale and sickly-looking child. Reavis received no
further royal invitations. However courteously he was treated
by the officials, he was, of course, looked down upon as just *el
americano*, whereas his wife was regarded as a noble woman, the
descendant of a grandee of Spain, even if her ancestral history
had been somewhat lost.

Queen Maria Christina had, of course, been briefed by her
prime minister, Antonio Cánovas del Castillo, the leader of the
Conservative party, who intended to use the seemingly so pro-
Spanish *el americano* in one of his involved political and
financial plots. From that day on, there was no end to invitations to the great houses. Many noblemen arrived in their
carriages at the entrance of the Fonda de Paris and sent up their
flunkeys to leave their visiting cards, as a token of respect.

James Reavis, though enormously pleased and flattered, was
at a loss about how to exploit all these new friends, who showed
a truly Spanish hospitality that knew no limit or restraint. If,
attending a soiree or a gala dinner at one of the great houses, he
admired some costly ornament, an ormolu clock, a porcelain
statuette, a Toledo sword, or a piece of Eibar work of inlaid
gold, silver, and ivory, he inevitably found it wrapped in his
carriage on leaving the home of his host. Reavis, always ready to
be generous when there was profit in it, reciprocated no less
lavishly. The exchange of presents cost him at least $10,000. He
consoled himself with the thought that this was money easily
gained and well invested.

The Baron de Arizonac now had not only friends in the
highest society, men such as the Marqués de Alcanices, son of
the Duke de Sexto and known as "Beau Pepe" (whose interest
was, in fact, more centered on the beautiful Carmelita than on
her businesslike husband) , the Duke de Tamanes, Count Bena-

lua, and the old Duke de Frías, who also pursued Carmelita with his gallant attentions, but also men of far greater power and importance, though not endowed with melodious titles.

Instinctively, and with his experience of business negotiations with New York tycoons and Washington politicians, James Reavis knew that the real power rested with the men who controlled Spain's finances. He was—again with his experience of New York—not particularly surprised to discover that they were neither dukes nor even Spaniards. The man who operated the Madrid and Barcelona stock exchanges, the banks, and state finances, was a small corpulent man with the prosaic name of Ignace Bauer.

Like many of the great captains of finance of the nineteenth century, Ignace Bauer had been a poor Jewish boy born in western Germany, which had also produced the Rothschilds, whose representative he was in Spain. Bauer had arrived in the Paris of Louis Philippe with a little bundle containing a change of linen and a spare pair of stockings. One decade and the reign of Napoleon III sufficed to make him a millionaire. He then moved the sphere of his activities to Spain, where he first doubled, then trebled and quadrupled his fortune as a financier of Marshal Francisco Serrano, the republic, King Amadeo, and the Bourbon restoration. Now he was the intimate friend of the Marqués de Albaredo, the minister of finance. Some cynics said that Bauer was the real finance minister of Spain. His palace at the Calle Ancha de San Bernardo was one of the most sumptuous in the capital. His collections of Velásquez, El Greco, and other old masters could almost vie with those of the Prado and Louvre. His wife, Ida, a tiny fat motherly Jewess, had become a patron of the arts, collecting innumerable lame ducks among Madrid's poets, writers, painters, and musicians. Bauer built a splendid theater in Madrid and gave it as a present to his wife, naming it El Teatro Ida and carrying its annual deficits.

One of Bauer's equally powerful associates was his coreligionist Georges Polak, whose antecedents were shrouded in even greater mystery than Bauer's. Polak had come from eastern Europe by the way of Germany and France. He had financed the building of railways in northern Spain, which he now controlled, as he did the new electricity undertakings and tramways companies in Madrid, Barcelona, and Valencia.

His wife, Mathilde, a close friend of Señora Bauer, took a great fancy to Carmelita. She showered presents on her and, with truly Jewish concern for health, warned her of Madrid's treacherous climate.

"My dear child, this *Madrith* is a terrible place," she told Carmelita. "You should go to the coast. The autumn wind can be fatal, particularly for your delicate skin." She told Carmelita of a proverb, which she misquoted and mispronounced, but which runs like this:

> *El aire de Madrid es tan sutil*
> *Que mala a un hombre y no apaga a un candil.*

This means: the air of Madrid seems so subtle that it could not extinguish a candle, but it will put out a man's life.

While the women chatted, Señores Bauer and Polak were closeted after interminable dinners, which did not end until long after midnight, in the great library, with the Baron de Arizonac. James Reavis had arrived in Europe well equipped with documents and balance sheets of his various enterprises, such as the great Arizona Development Corporation, and companies he had discussed in New York. There was no need for Reavis to embark on any new business plans; his income had reached more than $100,000 in 1885, and with his trunk full of his Peralta documents, it was now only a question of time to gather a few millions. He could spend $200 a day without the need to mortgage as much as an acre of his future domain or ask a banker for an advance, although a loan would have been granted without question.

It seems that Reavis was much more fascinated by the social possibilities which were now open to him than by new business propositions. He was more intoxicated than ever by his incredible story, which apparently everybody completely believed. The whiff of glory was as pleasant and elating as the feel of money in his pocket. At those conferences late at night—nobody went to bed before dawn in Madrid, and nobody who was anybody rose before eleven or midday—Bauer, or Polak, or both invited other influential businessmen. There was the Marqués de Campo, who controlled the entire tobacco trade in the Philippines and Cuba, headed the Valencia Railroad Company, and owned the largest silver mines in Spain and a third of Spain's merchant fleet. Another tycoon was the Marqués del Cayo del Rey, who had started his life as plain Señor Miguel of unknown antecedents and who now dictated to the stock exchange at Madrid as successfully as to the bourses of Paris and Brussels.

Great plans for the exploitations of mineral resources in Mexico, tin mines of Bolivia, and the newly discovered petroleum fields of Venezuela were hammered out at these nightly conferences at the *palacio* Bauer or at the no less sumptuous mansion of the Marqués de Campo, in Madrid's exclusive Paseo de Recoletos. The financiers assured Reavis that he would have carte blanche as their representative in their South American enterprises. It would be up to him to organize and build up a promising business empire, a renewed and much more profitable conquest than those of Cortez and Pizarro over the Incas and Mayas 300 years before.

The Baron of Arizona, however cunning and intelligent a fraudsman, was neither a merchant adventurer nor an empire builder. He had not the great vision of these men who greatly overestimated his worth. Nor did he have their dedication to Mammon. Deep down he was a crook, a con man of the kind which the pioneer days of the West had produced in consider-

able numbers; otherwise he would have become another Huntington, Vanderbilt, Gould, Hearst, or Rockefeller. In some
ways he was an artist, a forger par excellence, a genius in
counterfeiting, but this, perhaps, was his only real talent, fired
by an imagination which found satisfaction in fooling people
and raising himself above the lowly status his mother had
taught him was shameful. He was flattered by the attention
which the serious businessmen paid him, but he listened with
only one ear to their complex plans. He was the sort of man of
whom it was once said that he was happier to make a penny out
of a petty fraud than to earn a piece of gold by an honest deal,
even if the fraud might be more difficult.

Although he did not need the money, Reavis accepted the
bankers' drafts, which the Spanish businessmen almost forced
on him, as advances for his future expenses and fees for recon-
noitering potentialities in Mexico and South America. When he
came to grief, seven or eight years later, none of his Spanish
partners-to-be came forward to accuse him. They wanted to
forget that they had ever known him. They shared this desire
with many of the tycoons in New York and San Francisco.
These astute businessmen glibly denied that they had ever paid
anything to him or had associated with him as a partner.

Even more fantastic proposals were put before him than the
exploitation of South American resources. The Spanish prime
minister's younger brother, Don Serafín Cánovas, introduced
him to a number of high-ranking officers. The most distinguished of them was General José López Domínguez, leader of
the Monarchist party and nephew of the great Marshal Serrano.
As a young lieutenant, he had fought in all his uncle's battles;
he was with the Austrian army at Solferino, with the British in
the Crimean War. He had distinguished himself against the
wild Kabyles of Morocco, become minister of war, and suppressed the Catalan rising and the workers' revolt in Barcelona.
A political soldier of almost Churchillian character, he had

served the republic which he hated, had been a Liberal, a Conservative, a Monarchist, all this for the greatness of Spain. Now, in 1886, he had not abandoned his dream of a rejuvenated Spanish empire in America. He had been part of the driving power behind that ridiculous war against Peru and Chile in 1866, when a Spanish fleet, in a Gilbert and Sullivan attempt, had tried to seize the two republics and restore Spanish rule after more than half a century of their independence.

What General López Domínguez and his brother generals discussed with James Reavis has been lost to the records of history. The only pointers preserved are paragraphs in contemporary newspaper columns, which mysteriously alluded to "important and highly confidential talks of His Excellency General Don José López Domínguez with the distinguished visitor from the Colorados, the Baron James Peralta, a Spanish-American and a devoted friend of the kingdom," inaccurately describing Reavis' nationality and incorrectly speculating on the missions entrusted to him.*

However, even though one can only apply conjecture, it can be assumed that General López Domínguez had some highfaluting schemes, perhaps the landing of Spanish troops in Lower California, a heroic march on Los Angeles, a bombardment of San Diego, the hoisting of Spain's yellow and red flag with the spread eagle where the Stars and Stripes were at the time flying not too securely. These secret talks were conducted at the Madrid *palacios* only twelve years before the outbreak of the Spanish-American War. When the war came, Reavis, whatever had been his promise to General López Domínguez, was unable to carry it out; he was serving his prison sentence for fraud at the Santa Fe Penitentiary.

Maybe James Addison Reavis, the third Baron de Peralta by his own grace, missed his hour of greatness in Madrid. Maybe he could have gone down in history books as one of the great

* Madrid, *La Época* and *La Correspondencia*, August and September, 1886.

pioneers, empire builders, or manipulators of international intrigue, instead of being remembered only as the prince of con men. Perhaps it was the warning he received in Madrid from an old and wise woman which stopped him from taking the plunge into fame and instead pushed him into notoriety and eventual disaster.

Señora Bauer had introduced Reavis and Carmelita to Madame Buschental, one of the few hostesses in Madrid in whose salons politicians, financiers, and men of letters and the arts mixed in the fashion of the famous Parisian salons of the late eighteenth century. Maria Buschental, née Baroness de Pereira, of Rio de Janeiro, and reputed to be the natural daughter of Emperor Pedro I of Brazil and thus the half sister of the reigning queen of Portugal, was a remarkable woman. Her late husband had been Jacques Buschental, a Jew from Strasbourg, whose career had been one of the fantastic stories of the era. Emerging from poverty after the Napoleonic Wars, he made his first fortune in France and went to Spain, where he lost his money during the revolution of 1822. He then took himself to South America, where he became the financial ruler of Uruguay, Paraguay, and La Plata. He was involved in every political and financial intrigue which periodically rocked South America after the liberation from Spanish rule.

In 1830 he married the beautiful Maria, thus gaining every desirable contact with the Brazilian court and business world. Involved in vast business enterprises with the United States and the City of London, he amassed an enormous fortune. Buschental, a friend of Baron Hirsch, the Rothschilds, and Bischoffsheim of London, controlled for many years the great undertakings upon which London financiers in Brazil, Argentina, and the rest of South America embarked. When he died in London in 1870, he left his widow a huge fortune.

Madame Buschental, or, as she liked to call herself, la Baronesse de Buschental-Pereira, established her private court in

Madrid. When James Reavis met her, she was seventy-two years old, an imposing matron, with all her faculties as active and sharp as or more so than those of the politicians and businessmen who frequented her salons. Nothing which went on in the great world of politics and finance remained secret from her.

"Young man," she told Reavis, "you're playing a dangerous game. You're clever and talented, but you're inexperienced in the ways of leaders of nations and international finance. I made certain enquiries with my friends in America, and I believe that I know more about you than most of the people you have met in Madrid. You've a beautiful wife, you're rich, and you should be happy. If you want to accept the advice of an old woman who knows something about the world and its ways, then keep away from the schemes you are now pursuing. Your secret is too fragile to bear exposure."

Reavis must have been petrified by these words, spoken gently and with a smile. It seemed that the old lady knew more than was good for him. It was obvious that she did not believe his elaborate story of the Peralta Grant. How much she knew, or whether she only guessed, by subtle intuition and from her great experience, that he was a fraud, he never discovered. But he promptly accepted her advice. He decided to cut short his stay in Madrid, and after that meeting with Madame Buschental, he became extremely cautious and vague in his negotiations with the Spanish politicians and financiers.

Not that his sojourn in Madrid was just a series of secret conferences. The Baron de Arizonac and his wife took part in almost every event of the great spring season. They were regular guests in Madame Buschental's huge box at the Royal Opera House, a box that could accommodate thirty guests and was twice the size of the royal box. There they heard Adelina Patti, Lucca, Albani, and the other prima donnas and great tenors of the Italian opera. Reavis and Carmelita, neither of whom could boast much education, even sat through the interminable Spanish classic dramas of Calderón or López de Ayala. Fortunately for them, there was also entertainment in a lighter vein—masked balls, soirees, great fiestas, and above all the bullfights performed by the most famous *toreros* of the kingdom.

Reavis was greatly impressed by the *corridas* at the newly built great Plaza de Toros on the Venta del Espíritu Santo, which cost $250,000 to erect and furnish and which could accommodate more than 13,000 persons. He admired the great matadors of the day, Ángel Pastor or Hermosilla, but for himself, he thought that a proper wild rodeo, such as that which the cowboys back in Arizona performed, was a much more exciting entertainment.

There were great nights at the exclusive clubs, at the Casino and the Gran Pena, and morning rides at the Retiro and Campo. On such occasions Reavis met members of the diplomatic staff of the British ambassador, Sir Robert Morier. He informed them that he intended to visit London and was told that he must hurry: the London season was beginning, and it would be one of particular brilliance and excitement because of Queen Victoria's golden jubilee the next June. Some of the members of the embassy were young diplomats from great English families. Reavis had hoped to get introductions from them, but they seemed somewhat reserved and did not offer to give him letters of introduction.

However, Madame Buschental had introduced him to the Portuguese ambassador, Dom José da Silva Mendes Leal, who some years before had served in London. His wife, Donha Rosina, who was as fat and gay as he was cadaverous and grave, had taken a great liking to Carmelita. In any case, Madame Buschental's word was sufficient for Mendes Leal to give Reavis a letter to a Portuguese diplomat in London, the Marqués de Soveral, a member of the Marlborough House set and an intimate friend of the Prince of Wales (later King Edward VII). Mendes Leal assured Reavis that Soveral would have no difficulty in opening all the doors of England's stately homes for him. "Particularly when the marqués, whom everybody in London calls the Blue Monkey, meets your charming and beautiful lady," he added with a wink.

A few weeks after his arrival in Madrid, Reavis had bought a fine mansion outside the capital, on the road to Escorial. It belonged to the family of the Duke de Fernán Núñez, and although it needed repairs, it was full of exquisite furniture. The baronial couple gave several receptions there, and shortly before his departure, Reavis ordered the caretaker to restore and redecorate everything, as he wanted to occupy the place, either on his return from Paris and London or on his next visit to Spain, which he intended to pay during the following year.

As things turned out, he never returned to Spain. Driven by a desire to see once again some of the documents at Seville, he went to the *Archivos de Indias*. Perusing the documents, he decided on the spur of the moment to pocket or insert a few which attracted his special interest. This time he was watched by a conscientious clerk, Antonio Juárez. The man noticed that Reavis covered a document with his handkerchief and then adroitly pushed it into an envelope. Confronted by the clerk, Reavis became very indignant and, when Juárez called the curator, declared that he had only intended to borrow the document for a few days. The curator notified the police, and criminal proceedings were started.

The case was hushed up with the help of Reavis' high-placed friends, who were inclined to regard the incident as the indiscretion of an overeager historian and collector. Several years later, at his trial, this incident at the Seville archives was used as a damning evidence of his fraudulent schemes.

During the last week of April, 1877, equipped with Mendes Leal's introduction and letters from Spanish aristocrats to Lord Derby and Lord Granville, the Baron and Baroness of Arizona set off for London by the way of Paris. During the journey, as

Reavis later recounted,* he was shadowed by some sinister people. He believed they were either secret agents or hired assassins bent on robbing him of his documents. Reavis never disclosed for whom, in his opinion, these agents had been working. Pedro Cuervo kept watch, and nothing untoward occurred during the journey, although one of the trunks with the documents was missed for several days, until it was safely restored to its owner.

The baronial couple interrupted their journey in Paris for only a brief respite, deciding to return to the gay capital on a later occasion. They arrived in London when the city was in the throes of great preparations for Queen Victoria's jubilee festivities.

* See Reavis' testimony before the U.S. Court of Private Land Claims at Santa Fe in June, 1895.

9

High Life

London made an immediate and deep impression on the Baron and Baroness of Arizona, an impact they shared with many other American visitors who had arrived for the queen's jubilee. When the train from Dover threaded its way through the capital's suburbs toward the new Victoria Station, they were impressed by the vastness of the capital. Madrid, which they had learned to know well, now seemed just a glorified and bigger "Frisco," which was still a large pueblo.

"It's the capital of the great British Empire," Reavis explained to Carmelita, who could not take her eyes from the scene that slipped rapidly by the windows of the train. There were poverty and squalor, too, when the train passed the outer districts populated by the artisan class, but many houses were neat, with little front gardens.

"Look, all the houses are built of brick, and it seems that many are homesteads of one family only," exclaimed Carmelita, remembering the adobe dwellings of faraway Arizona.

Senator Conkling had written to James Russell Lowell, the United States ambassador in London, and asked him to provide every assistance to James Reavis. He informed the ambassador that Mrs. Reavis was of noble Spanish birth and that her husband was an important businessman who held interest in railroads and silver mines in the Southwest. Ambassador Lowell, who had already achieved fame as a poet, satirist, and political essayist, cared little for visiting tycoons. But he did not want to annoy the politically influential Conkling. He therefore sent a young attaché to welcome the visitors at Victoria Station.

Some of his New York associates had recommended Claridge's Hotel to Reavis, but Marcellus F. Berry of the American Express had sent his profuse apologies to Madrid, informing Reavis that no suite was available in that famous London hotel. Instead, a reservation had been made for the baronial couple and their servants at London's newest and largest hotel, the Metropole. Reavis would have been annoyed had he known the real reason for Berry's failure to secure a reservation at Claridge's. Berry had received a courteous letter from the management, saying that after perusal of their records, they were unable to confirm that Mr. J. A. Reavis and his wife, the Baroness de Arizonac, figured among the names of personages whom Claridge's would be honored to entertain. In simple language this meant that the couple were not welcome at the hotel which accepted only the patronage of foreign princes and well-known millionaires.

As it happened, Reavis and his wife found the Hotel Metropole much to their liking. This newest "monster luxury hotel," which Frederick Gordon, one of the most go-ahead hoteliers of his time, had added to his Grand Hotel and Victoria Hotel, was certainly the most modern caravanserai in Europe. English comfort was blended with American luxury; to the French cuisine had been added such innovations from across the Atlantic as iced water, clam chowder, soft-shell crabs, terrapin, porterhouse steaks, and rye and bourbon whiskeys, in an effort to make American guests feel at home.

During the first few days Mr. Lowell's attaché acted as guide, and the baronial couple embarked on a shopping spree through London's West End. Carmelita was overwhelmed by the display and selection the stores of Regent Street, Piccadilly, and Bond Street had to offer. Many of them displayed signs adorned with royal crests, announcing that among their customers were Her Majesty the Queen, His Royal Highness the Prince of Wales, the Empress of Russia, the King of Spain, the Shah of Persia, and so forth. The sight of these plaques prompted James Reavis to remark, "Just the right store for you, honey," even though he found the bills a little surprising.

Reavis accompanied Carmelita to various evening entertainments, to the opera at Covent Garden and Drury Lane, to pianoforte recitals by Charles Hallé, to the concerts of the Philharmonic and the Sacred Harmonic societies at Albert Hall, even though these highbrow events bored him. He thought they would assist Carmelita's further education.

Because of the imminence of the jubilee festivities, there were only drawing-room receptions at Buckingham Palace at the end of May, and the baronial couple nearly missed being presented to the queen.

But the letters of introduction which the Duke de Frías had given Reavis in Madrid to English aristocrats surmounted all difficulties. Lord Granville, a former foreign secretary, had no doubt about the Baron de Arizonac's worthiness and arranged with the queen's lord chamberlain, the Earl of Kenmare, that the baronial couple be given priority on the reception list.

While levees, held at St. James's Palace, were limited to men, attendance at a drawing room conferred a sort of diploma of high moral respectability on ladies of unimpeachable character. The ladies were permitted to be accompanied by their husbands or, if unmarried, by a close male relative. The etiquette observed in obtaining an invitation was highly elaborate. A letter of the people who made the presentation—in this case Lord and

Lady Granville—had to be sent several days in advance to the lord chamberlain, with an application which contained all required data on those to be presented.

Reavis boldly included in the application details of his wife's ancestry, mentioning the dozen or so titles and orders held by her great-grandfather and grandfather. Three days later a messenger from Buckingham Palace brought the royal invitation to the Hotel Metropole. Two large gilt-edged cards bore the names of the Baron James Addison Peraltareavis and the Baroness de Peraltareavis y de la Córdoba, written in beautiful copperplate, and a printed set of rules was enclosed.

The rules included detailed commands for dress and demeanor: "The lady to be presented shall appear in full Court dress, that is in a dress with a low bodice, short sleeves, train and lappets, and in a head dress with ostrich plumes." It was added that while the train, lappets, and plumes were indispensable, the regulations on the low bodice would not be enforced in the case of a lady of delicate health. The plumes had to be white, black being permitted only if the lady was in mourning. They were to be worn in such a manner that the face of the lady was fully visible in the royal presence, and no more than two plumes could curl toward the face. In lieu of lace lappets, a tulle veil of two widths, a yard long, might fall at the back. Accompanying gentlemen had to wear court dress—either in velvet or in cloth, with white waistcoats and tie—or uniform.

Lady Granville took Carmelita to her court dressmaker and supervised all the details of the new wardrobe. Reavis decided to wear a silk tailcoat he had had made for himself in Madrid. On the advice of his English mentors, gold buttons and gold embroidery were added. He looked like a foreign ambassador, sporting also a cocked feathered hat and wearing on his chest the star of the Order of Carlos III, which he had bought in Madrid.

When the great day came, they drove to Buckingham Palace

in a huge hired landau with two liveried flunkeys standing on the platform behind the seats. The Baron and Baroness de Arizonac surely arrived in state. The guests were admitted at two o'clock, but long before that hour a line of carriages formed in the Mall, lined by crowds of staring and cheering sightseers. When the carriages were driven into the quadrangle in front of the palace, the company alighted, and a procession formed through the large hall and across the sculpture gallery. Passing the great staircase, Reavis and Carmelita glanced at the Yeomen of the Guard standing rigidly at attention. The procession traversed the picture gallery to enter the long suite of reception rooms, guarded by gentlemen-at-arms with their halberds. Carmelita looked anxiously at the other ladies in front of her, imitating their elaborate method of keeping their trains over their left arms, only letting them fall and trail on the ground when they approached the queen.

The drawing rooms had been redecorated for the jubilee and looked magnificent. These suites and the throne room were the only really elegant ones at Buckingham Palace, which at that time had only two bathrooms and a maze of dark and rather dilapidated corridors and nooks, while sanitary arrangements caused exasperation to visiting foreign royalty.

Half an hour passed before the baron and baroness entered the presence chamber, where Queen Victoria stood in the center of a semicircle of members of the royal family and court officials.

"How tiny she is!" whispered Carmelita to her husband, who squeezed her arm and murmured, "For Lord's sake don't forget to curtsy."

Carmelita had rehearsed her curtsy for several days, in front of a mirror in the hotel room. She managed well, although it was not easy, for she had to curtsy not only to the queen but also to each royal personage. The queen extended her hand for the kiss, and Carmelita remembered to walk off sideways. In a few moments the ordeal was over. All the women and their companions went to a drawing room, where refreshments were served. Within minutes the beautiful baroness was surrounded by many male guests, eager to be introduced.

James Reavis was full of pride as he watched his wife. He felt it was a personal triumph that he had transformed a little half-breed, who only a year or two earlier had been sweeping floors and nursing children at a ranch in California, into a lady who was now the center of attention at the English queen's court.

The reception at Buckingham Palace was only the beginning of a fantastic round of state balls, garden parties, and soirees in the houses of the aristocracy which preceded and followed the great day of the queen's jubilee. No day passed without some engraved invitations with the crests of ancient and newly ennobled families being delivered at the Hotel Metropole for the baronial couple from America.

Reavis had written letters to several of the important people whose names had been given to him by his friends in New York and Madrid. Among them were Baron Ferdinand de Rothschild and Alfred Rothschild, brother of the first Lord Rothschild, grandson of the great Nathan, who had established the English branch of the dynasty and had ruled from New Court in the City of London. Reavis had enclosed copies of his letters of recommendation from Ignace Bauer, the Rothschilds' associate and representative in Madrid, and recieved by return invitations to the houses of the famous bankers. He had also sent a note to the Marqués de Soveral, at the Portuguese legation, because Dom Mendes Leal in Madrid had told him that Soveral was a close friend of the Prince of Wales.

The Baron de Arizonac was determined to enjoy London, and he was confident that he and certainly his wife would make a mark in English society, as they had done in Spain. No one in the English capital in the late 1880's, not even the richest and most eccentric members of the great noble families, could outdo the lavish hospitality of the Rothschilds. The brood of old

Mayer Amschel Rothschild had built for themselves palaces and mansions all over Europe, but the most gorgeous were in England, where Nathaniel—who had two years before at last achieved his most coveted desire and had become a lord—exercised unlimited influence in the City, the world's financial heart, whose pulse controlled the destinies and prosperity of nations.

The Rothschilds had built themselves a string of palaces in Piccadilly and around Hyde Park, in Hamilton Place, in Seamore Place—so that the district had been nicknamed Rothschild's Row, or more vulgarly Jews' Row. At 143 Piccadilly, Ferdinand had built a Louis XIV palace, a showpiece of the capital, with a white marble ballroom that vied with that of Buckingham Palace. Alfred, the most extravagant of them all, who had remained a bachelor against all the family's tradition, had his palace at Seamore Place, crammed to the roof with old masters, eighteenth-century gold and silver plate, Sèvres porcelain, Beauvais tapestries, and an enormous collection of gems, jade, and objets d'art of every period and every country of the world. At his musical soirees, famous conductors, virtuosos, and singers appeared more often than at any opera house or concert hall in Europe or America. Liszt, Verdi, Gounod, Sullivan, Rubinstein, Johann Strauss, Offenbach, Patti, Melba, and a host of other famous stars were only too eager to perform in his music room, pocketing fantastic fees. The music room was so huge that its owner could arrange a rendering of Tschaikovsky's famous *1812 Overture* by the massed bands of the queen's Brigade of Guards, complete with pyrotechnic effects and the pealing of bells, effects which normally provided a problem to the managers of even the largest concert halls in London.

However sumptuous the London palaces of the Rothschilds, they were dwarfed by the country mansions which, among other members of the family, Ferdinand and Alfred had built for themselves. Alfred's Halten Hall, near Wendover, which was finished in 1884, after many years of building, rebuilding, and decorating, was described by a contemporary critic as "a nightmare of gorgeousness and senseless magnificence." A. J. Balfour called it "the most vulgar and fantastic edifice in England, a combination between the Palace of Versailles and the Casino of Monte Carlo." To his housewarming party Alfred Rothschild invited more than 3,000 guests; each was given a jewel-encrusted present: lockets or perfume flasks for the ladies, tobacco boxes or watches for the men.

Ten miles away, at Ferdinand's Waddesdon Manor, the Prince of Wales was a frequent guest, going there several times each year for the pheasant shoots. On each occasion 5,000 to 8,000 pheasants were massacred, and at least once as many as 12,000 were shot. Not knowing what to do with them, after all the guests and friends had been sent a few dozen brace, Ferdinand ordered the rest to be carried to London; then, at the door of his Piccadilly palace, footmen presented a brace or two to every passerby, the birds' necks tied with the blue and amber silk ribbon in the racing colors of the donor.

It was to this circle that the former streetcar conductor from Missouri found himself introduced almost overnight. The baronial couple were graciously received, even if the kindness shown to them was mixed with some condescension. The great English aristocrats sometimes regarded wealthy visitors from America with ill-concealed amusement. But they followed the example of the Prince of Wales and his Marlborough House set by being outwardly kind to the visitors from across the Atlantic. Indeed, James Reavis and his wife were treated more considerately than many of their countrymen whose only claim to being received into London society was that they had amassed great fortunes out of dubious speculations in real estate, railroads, or gold rushes and who had no aristocratic ancestry, such as that of the Peraltareavis.

The Rothschilds had, of course, no qualms about welcoming

a man who had done well in business. When Reavis presented himself to Baron Alfred Rothschild, his host stretched out his hand in warm welcome.

"So you are a friend and business partner of Mr. Collis P. Huntington?" he asked. "He is a great man, a great pioneer, I met him through Baron Hirsch, who, as you know, also has an interest in American railways. Mr. Huntington told me about his fascinating adventures in his younger days in California during the gold rush. I am enchanted to meet a friend of his. And how is dear Mr. Huntington at present? What great enterprise occupies his lively mind and talents?" he added with a smile which did not conceal the slight irony of his question.

Reavis was able to assure him that Huntington was doing very well; he mentioned the rapid expansion of railroad construction all over the West and Southwest of the United States, and he also remarked that Huntington had not lost his interest in mining, even if Eldorado was now a thing of the past. Then Reavis said, "For myself, I have great plans for the development of Arizona, where my wife owns great estates, more than twelve million acres. A New York finance consortium partners me in these schemes, which will include large irrigation developments. We have already set up several corporations."

"Quite so," Alfred Rothschild replied, apparently suddenly bored with discussing business. Although he attended board meetings of his banking house and was a director of the Bank of England and of man scores of companies, he considered business an unpleasant, if necessary, drudge. At heart he was an art connoisseur and collector; he despised money for its own sake. He turned to Carmelita and contemplated her beauty with obvious pleasure.

"Madame, would you bestow upon me the great honor and render the greatest of pleasures by attending one of my little adoration parties? That is, if your husband is good enough to give his kind permission?" he asked her.

"Adoration party?" Carmelita was astonished, "What is that, sir?"

"Oh, I arrange little intimate parties in honor of beautiful ladies—that is, ahem . . . one lady only at a time. Five or six of my friends attend them, sometimes including the Prince of Wales, and we call these little dinners adoration parties."

James Reavis did not like the idea, but he decided that annoying a Rothschild and perhaps the Prince of Wales himself would be bad policy.

"The baroness will be greatly pleased to attend," he said. He had already heard of that strange institution of London's professional beauties. Some of them were American women, who had become the toasts of London and graced with their presence the soirees and dinners at the great houses. He was confident that Carmelita would know how to keep the men at arm's length, even at an adoration party. He realized that this would be another step on the slippery ladder to social success and, no doubt, to even greater successes in the business world, which seemed now to open its doors widely and invitingly to him.

There is no record of Carmelita's debut at Alfred Rothschild's adoration party; even the columns of contemporary London newspapers devoted to sensationalism, such as the *Globe* and the *Echo*, which usually published all the scandalous gossip about the Prince of Wales, had to refrain from reporting all the promiscuous affairs of the heir to the throne. His name was constantly linked with those of his ladyfriends, such as Catherine Walters, better known as "Skittles," Lily Langtry, and Miss Chamberlayne, from Cleveland, Ohio, nicknamed "Chamberpot." It was in deference to the queen, in the year of her golden jubilee, that even the sensational journals observed some restraint.

The Baroness de Arizonac, at least for a short while, was now listed among the professional beauties, ranking with such famous society ladies as Lady Randolph Churchill, Mrs. Cornwallis-West, Lady Dudley, the Duchess of Manchester, and Lady Helen Vincent, whose photographs were collected by everybody in the same way as those of Hollywood pinup girls half a century later. For a few weeks Carmelita's pictures adorned the pages of the glossy journals, from *Funny Folks* to *Vanity Fair*, and including a new mass-circulation paper, aptly named *Tit-Bits*.

It was probably because of the reflected glory of his beautiful wife rather than because of his own importance as an American millionaire that Reavis was invited by Thomas Bowles, the editor of *Vanity Fair* to sit for a portrait by Leslie Ward, the celebrated "Spy," whose caricatures could make or break a politician or a leader of society. He was duly drawn by "Spy."

Before embarking on his European tour, James Reavis had grown a beard, having read in American journals that all the gentlemen of distinction sported beards or sideburns. In Arizona, mainly trappers, grimy gold prospectors, and elderly cattle ranchers were bewhiskered, and he had made the decision to adorn his well-cut features with a growth rather reluctantly. However, it certainly suited him, and he looked very distinguished with his temples beginning to be peppered with silver.

An Italian barber in New York had cut his beard *en pointe*. When in London one of the ladies exclaimed, "Oh, Baron, I declare you have Vandyke's beard," Reavis, naïvely and slightly embarrassed, replied, "No, madame, begging your pardon, it's a veritable one and all my own," thus immediately acquiring the reputation of a wit.

The official introduction of the baronial couple to the Prince of Wales—apart from Carmelita's more discreet meeting at Alfred Rothschild's adoration party—was effected by the good service of the Marqués de Soveral. This diplomat occupied for many years a singular position in the Marlborough House set. Rich and independent, he was much less concerned with his diplomatic duties to King Louis I of Portugal than with his own pleasures and extravagant foibles; the prodigal and libertine ruler of Portugal was apparently quite satisfied to be represented at the Court of St. James's by a man of the same feather. The success in London of the Marqués de Soveral was based entirely on his exuberant sense of humor, which endeared him to the Prince of Wales, himself an unrepentant practical joker. The marqués was extremely ugly, and his swarthy, toothy, lean face, his gangling gait, and his jerky movements gained him the very appropriate sobriquet of the Blue Monkey. Hardly anybody called him by his title or even knew his Christian name.

Reavis and Carmelita were bewildered by some of the things they witnessed at soirees or weekend stays in the stately homes of England or even on their two visits at Marlborough House. Although Reavis had been told that he must not expect any of the formality which pervaded Buckingham Palace, he was staggered and shocked by the foolery which was going on in the presence of the Prince of Wales and with his active participation and obvious enjoyment.

The Blue Monkey, abetted by Christopher Sykes, a young and rich Member of Parliament, and vivacious Lady Jane de Grey, was the stage manager of elaborate larks which never failed to amuse the prince, while they deeply grieved Queen Victoria. At one of the Marlborough House dinners, Lady de Grey arranged that a set of cheap china be smuggled in, and she bribed two footmen to drop it to the floor of the antechamber, making the prince believe for a few moments that all his priceless porcelain had been smashed.

At house parties in the country there were apple-pie beds, leaking hot-water bottles, weak tea served in whiskey decanters, and roasts, simulated of cardboard by well-known artists to look like the real article. On one occasion, Reavis was told, the Prince of Wales, in cloth cap and rags, had accompanied Lily Langtry, disguised as a flower girl, to sell violets in Piccadilly Circus. The prince liked American visitors and was not particu-

larly selective. Many Americans addressing the prince in broad
Midwestern dialects, new-rich speculators, and Jewish financiers
from New York, who would have been spurned by the Boston-
ian upper crust, were welcomed to the prince's parties. He was a
great admirer of Consuelo Vanderbilt, the Duchess of Marlborough, who invented for his amusement ever more silly larks,
such as serving canapés with grated soap instead of cheese.

The Baron and Baroness de Arizonac were bewildered when
a ball at Marlborough House was opened by a jet-black Negro
and the Princess of Wales. The Negro was King Kalakua of the
Cannibal Islands, one of Her Britannic Majesty's lesser colonies
in the Caribbean Sea, who had come to the jubilee celebrations.
The Prince of Wales had insisted that he be given precedence
over his nephew, the German crown prince (the later Kaiser
William), whom he hated. "The black brute is a king, isn't
he?" he told his chamberlain. "And if he is a king, then he ranks
higher than a crown prince!"

The future king of England, apart from pursuing his many
love affairs, also had a mania for strange superstitions: there was
a strict order at Marlborough House that mattresses must not be
turned on a Friday, knives not crossed on the tables, and
thirteen guests never be invited.

Reavis gained the impression that all the upper-class English
were eccentrics, indeed half-demented. But he changed his
opinion when the great day of the queen's jubilee arrived. At
the great state ball in the presence of the queen, during the
interminable procession through London's streets to Westmin-
ster Abbey, and inside the ancient abbey itself, those gay
promiscuous cavaliers and their frivolous giggling ladies, usually only bent on gossip and scandals, appeared in startlingly
different roles. The men in resplendent uniforms of the court
and the royal navy and army, many of them bearers of ancient
hereditary offices, observed great decorum and superb dignity.
The women in their gorgeous bustle gowns walked along the

nave of the abbey with their eyes downcast and looking very chaste.

Carmelita found the great pageantry almost breathtaking. Thirty rulers and princes had come to pay homage to the "Grandmother of Europe." They included the kings of Denmark, Belgium, Portugal, Greece, and Saxony; the crown princes of Germany, Austria-Hungary, Persia, Japan, and Siam; princes and rajahs from India, laden with jewels; the queen of Hawaii; the thakur of Morvi, mounted on a horse covered with a mail cover made of pure gold; and the maharajah of Kuch Behar, hung with carved rubies, each the size of a plum. The streets were crowded with such masses of people that Reavis thought they must exceed the whole population of California. Carmelita whispered to him, "Surely there can't be so many flags in the whole world as are flying today."

The huge crowd along the pavement, behind soldiers in crimson uniforms and gold braid, never stopped waving, cheering, and calling the queen's name. Around the abbey stood hundreds upon hundreds of the queen's subjects, warriors and tribesmen from every corner of the great empire. Sepoys from India, Mounties from Canada, Kaffirs and Bushmen, slit-eyed Malays, turbaned Arabs, Chinese from Hong Kong, wild-looking savages from Guinea, almost naked and painted and tattooed, Maoris from New Zealand, Fuzzy-Wuzzies from Fiji—all acclaimed their queen in every tongue of Babel.

On that June 21, 1887, a bright and beautiful morning, the queen drove in a gilt landau, drawn by six horses, flanked by her Life Guards and twelve Indian Lancers officers, with three of her sons, five sons-in-law, and nine grandsons, all mounted and in glittering uniforms and helmets, preceding her carriage, and with a long procession of equipages with her daughters, daughters-in-law, nieces, and cousins and ladies of the court following. When she entered the abbey, the solemn chords of Handel's *Occasion Overture* began, and everybody rose and bowed or curtsied when the small figure, led by her son, that most elegant "first gentleman of Europe," passed slowly toward her throne near the altar.

At night Reavis and Carmelita admired the great fireworks display in Hyde Park and other public parks and finally attended three of the many great balls given by noble familes. The festivities continued for many days, in the great mansions of the rich and in the gin palaces and taverns of ordinary people.

Slowly the festive turmoil subsided, but there were still many shows to see. At the great new exhibition halls of Earl's Court was the famous Buffalo Bill's *Wild West Show*. Queen Victoria would normally have hardly visited this sort of entertainment, but she graciously consented to attend a gala performance, at which the Prince of Wales was presented with an Indian chieftain's magnificent feathered headdress. Reavis and Carmelita were hugely amused by the antics of the well-groomed and very civilized Red Indians, who were very different from the savage Apaches of Arizona, but whom the English believed to be genuine.

Enchanted by London, Reavis decided to spend the summer in England and rented a fine country mansion, near Guildford in Surrey, belonging to some impoverished aristocrat. It was full of antique furniture and Georgian silver, with a resident "ghost" and a perfect butler, whom the owner hired out with his home. The baronial couple made arrangements for several house parties and prepared invitations for many of their high-born friends. But unexpectedly, at least for Carmelita, all these plans had to be abandoned. In quick succession Reavis had received several cables from his attorneys, urging him to return home.

He had been absent from Arizona for more than two years, ever since Churchill and Weedin had driven him out. The excitement in the towns and settlements had long since quieted down. Apart from occasional letters from his attorneys in San Francisco, the citizens had heard nothing more of the baron and had begun to assume he had given up his claim. However, their interest was suddenly stirred up by the appearance of a new claimant.

George Willing, Sr., the father of the late Dr. Willing, announced that he was staking his own claim to the Peralta Grant based on his son's documents.

Backed by a financial syndicate in Philadelphia, Willing had opened an office in Phoenix and, having engaged several agents, began to hawk quitclaims in the same fashion as, though much less efficiently than, Reavis and Barratt had done in 1883 and 1884. He informed the newspapers of the legal basis of his enterprise:

> My son, Dr. George M. Willing junior, had made a will which is placed with my attorneys in Philadelphia. His widow has interest in all his property during her life. Thus Mrs. Mary Ann Willing is entitled only to a life estate. A James Addison Reavis had obtained from the widow a general warranty deed for her late husband's estate. Under that title Reavis was seeking to claim a fee simple and warranty estate. Mrs. Willing's deed issued to Reavis is invalid, for her life estate holds good only. She could not convey a greater estate than she owned.

Emulating Reavis, Willing also issued a "Notice to all persons locating in Arizona, or opening mines, that 300 square leagues of land was granted by the King of Spain to Señor Don Miguel Peralta, and purchased by Dr. George M. Willing. . . . All now located on the grant will be dealt with in a just and liberal manner . . . and shall have no cause to complain." And very much in the Reavis manner, he added: "Persons locating advisedly cannot, however, expect such lenity."

Old Mr. Willing was a mere greenhorn, He bungled everything right from the start, and his attorneys were of not much use either. He did not have even the few spurious deeds of his son's, not to speak of such an elaborate and vast collection of impressive documents as was in Reavis' possession. His amateurish attempt at mulcting the settlers misfired after a few months; his financiers backed out, and his Phoenix office was closed. This was the last Arizona heard of Mr. Willing.

But Barratt reported that the incident, though short-lived, resulted in a strong revival of the citizens' committees. Meetings were again convened in Phoenix, Florence, and Globe, and newspapers began to publish editorials demanding that the U.S. Government declare once and for all that the Peralta Grant was a fraud and that criminal proceedings should be taken if James Addison Reavis ever dared come forward again.

Mary Ann Willing, apparently incited by some smart lawyer, had also tried to stir up trouble. Having found out that Reavis had received considerable payments from the Southern Pacific, the Silver King, and other companies, she began threatening legal action if she was not paid the promised $30,000 for the assignment of her late husband's agreement with Miguel Peralta. Harvey S. Brown, the San Francisco attorney, cabled Reavis, advising him to return home and deal with all this unpleasant business. Other cables had already arrived from Reavis' financiers, Mackay and Herr, as well as from some of the New York tycoons, who had advanced money for his great development schemes and had not heard from Reavis for many months.

So the baron packed his trunks and, with Carmelita and his retinue, sailed by the fastest Cunarder to New York. He was not particularly worried. He dismissed the Willing affair with a snap of his fingers. In his coffers were scores of documents he had gathered in the archives of Seville and Madrid. At his side was the real heiress of the Peralta Grant, a polished young lady with the experience of high life and great society, who could now be trusted to behave in public like the scion of the ancient Spanish family.

In the junk shops of Madrid's Rastro, Reavis had picked up some useful pieces of new evidence, which tallied in a satisfactory way with various documents. They were portraits of two men and a woman, faded, poorly painted miniatures and a few blurred daguerreotype pictures. Several were in identical frames, probably mementos of some long-dead parents and grandparents of a noble Spanish family that had fallen into poverty and had sold all their effects.

It was not difficult for Reavis to see in the faces depicted in the portraits of the men, the first and the second barons de Peralta y de la Córdoba. He showed some of the pictures to Carmelita, pretending that they had been given to him by General Ibarra. Pointing to one of the miniatures, he told her, "This is your grandmother, the noble Doña Juana Laura," and gingerly fingering a brittle early photograph of a young sad-eyed woman, he added, "And this, my dear child, is your lamented mother, Doña Sofía, photographed in 1860, after her marriage. It was your father, Don José Ramón, who gave this old photograph to your Uncle Ibarra."

Reavis was confident that he had little to fear when he submitted his new and decisive claim. This time the evidence was not merely a concoction of dubious and spurious documents, such as those he had used to prop up the Willing claim. This time he not only had acquired "irrefutable evidence" on paper but also had a living witness to the claim.

Nor had he in Madrid only forged new documents or taken genuine ones out of the archives and altered them appropriately. To reap his golden harvest, he had sown the seeds of his evidence on both sides of the Atlantic. What he had done at the Mission of San Salvador in San Bernardino, when he inserted Carmelita's birth into the church register, he had repeated, with much greater risk but successfully, almost under the noses of the archives' curators in Spain.

In the *Archivos de Indias* in Seville and in the *Colección* in

Madrid now reposed documents, ready to be discovered and examined by experts, which proved beyond doubt that the Peralta Grant had existed. Reavis had made several preambles, beautifully written on old vellum. Combining them with genuine documents relating to other old grants, he inserted them into dockets relating to reports of the viceroy and governors of New Spain to King Ferdinand. Several such viceregal notes, informing the king of the execution of his command and describing the settlement and delineation of the Peralta estates, now reposed in the Spanish archives.

He was raring for the fight. This time, he knew, he would make short work of the twaddling little officials at Tucson or Phoenix, the hillbilly journalists and backwoods lawyers. This time he was sure that he could challenge the Government in Washington and Congress, and succeed. Victory was, at last, in his grasp. Soon he would be richer and more powerful than any of those Spanish grandees and English aristocrats who politely looked down their noses at him in Madrid and London.

Like a Spanish conquistador setting foot on American soil, determined to conquer an empire, James Addison Reavis landed in New York.

10

The Baron Develops Arizona

It was a very different James Reavis who returned to America. If during the years of his assiduous study before his visit to Europe he had acquired knowledge of the methods of the viceroys who had ruled Mexico and of the legal paraphernalia with which the Jesuits and Franciscans had controlled the administration of New Spain in past centuries, he had added to it the knowledge of the machinery of government in the royal capital of Spain and of the archives of Seville. If he had, before his departure, merely dabbled in big business, aiming at extracting comparatively small contributions from a few credulous financiers in New York, he now appeared in the business metropolis of the United States as an eager promoter.

In Madrid and London he had rubbed shoulders with such captains of finance and industry as the Rothschilds, the Bauers, and the Polaks, men whose native intelligence and acumen for business were superior even to the qualities Reavis had admired and envied in his early mentors Huntington and Crocker.

These men had amassed great fortunes by seeing openings where others were blind, by applying rapid calculation and transforming it into swift decisions. They were men who framed vast and bold projects against seemingly insuperable difficulties, who were unconcerned by officialdom and legal conventions.

James Reavis was determined to emulate these men. If hitherto his glib talk of "opening up Arizona to civilization" had been but one of the confidence tricks in his armory, he now decided to become a tycoon in his own right. The Peralta Grant, this compelling vision of a misguided genius, to which he had devoted more than ten years of his life, had become a stepping-stone to more ambitious enterprises.

In one way or another the ideas behind the bill which Senator Barry Goldwater and Senator Carl Hayden jointly submitted in 1956 to Congress for a dam at The Buttes, a bill which eventually resulted in utilizing the Gila for the irrigation of hundreds of thousands of acres of agricultural land, and earlier projects, such as the Roosevelt Dam on the Salt River (on which the U.S. Reclamation Service spent $20,000,000), may be traced back to schemes Reavis propounded for water conservation in Arizona more than half a century before.

The tragedy of James Reavis was that he invariably channeled his energy into schemes which were fraudulent, because he was a crook, a cheat, a mountebank, and a charlatan at heart, a dreamer so enchanted by his vision of the Peralta Grant that he could not grasp the opportunities which reality offered. It was notable at his trial that he stuck to his claim that his wife and he were the rightful heirs to the ancient grant, even when he had to admit the criminality of his actions and to accept the evidence proving his fantastic forgeries.

If James Reavis were on trial today, there can be little doubt that the defense would be able to bring forward psychiatric evidence that he was a schizophrenic. The dreamworld which becomes a reality is, of course, a familiar symptom of this mental disease. But few sufferers also retain a semblance of ice-cold sanity so that they contrive well-nigh perfect proof for the benefit of others that the dream is real and the practical work-aday world a baleful deception.

After his return from Europe, Reavis stayed for only a brief while in New York. He rented a whole story of the Fifth Avenue Hotel, where he conducted negotiations with the financiers and tycoons, such as John W. Mackay, Hector de Castro, Dwight Townsend, and Henry Porter, who had advanced money to him before, and he presided over conferences with many others.

Senator Conkling introduced him to men prepared to float companies for the exploitation of Arizona's natural resources, and they accepted Reavis' claim almost without question. At such conferences the table was thickly laden with the documents Reavis had brought from Madrid and Seville, added to those he had forged earlier: his irrefutable proof of his new claim on behalf of his wife, the real heiress.

One after another companies with huge nominal capitals were formed: the Casa Grande Land and Improvement Company of Arizona; the Casa Grande Land and Improvement Company of New Jersey; companies for the construction of roads, irrigation dams and canals, railroads and tunnels, telephone and telegraph communications, gold, silver, copper, and coal mines; companies for the erection of factories and mills in Phoenix, for breeding, buying, and selling livestock, for curing and canning meats, and for growing and canning fruit and vegetables.

One of the Casa Grande companies—soon there were to be a score of companies, all prefixed "Casa Grande"—was to build water reservoirs, and water rights were to be leased and sold. These water rights were valued by serious and experienced surveyors at at least $2,000,000. The main company, the Casa

Grande Corporation, was to have a capital of $50,000,000, divided into 500,000 shares at $100 each.

Reavis became the director of all these companies, but to serve as presidents and vice-presidents, he succeeded in enlisting some of the most reputable figures in New York and San Francisco. The San Francisco *Examiner* could correctly state: "No scheme of modern times had been supported by such an array of eminent public men and no undertaking has had such a vast amount of capital centralized for its success." The only flaw was that only a few of these eminent men subscribed substantial amounts; like Reavis, they were waiting for the general public to bring in the millions. Even so money began to roll in from many sources. Down payments on signature of agreements were made quickly. Ten, twenty, thirty thousand dollars seemed unimportant to Reavis' backers in view of the potentialities of his vast schemes. Reavis pursued his policy of conning greedy men with a virtuosity that surely deserved a better purpose.

Senator Conkling, a man of probity, must have been completely taken in, at least during the first year of this great hustle. He devoted his attention to the Peralta Grant side of Reavis' affairs and looked after political contacts in Washington, where Reavis had taken a fine house near Pennsylvania Avenue and lavishly entertained his influential friends. For the business development matters the Senator turned his client over to another great lawyer, with whom he regularly appeared as associate counsel in important cases. This lawyer was Robert Green Ingersoll, and Reavis gained in him the most important ally of all.

Ingersoll was approaching fifty years of age when Reavis first met him. He was then at the peak of his reputation: as a lawyer, as a leader of antireligious campaigns, and as a champion of many lost causes. Freethinkers, liberals, advocates of women's suffrage, fighters against corruption in administration, and clever confidence tricksters—all such people, honest and crooked alike, could be assured of Ingersoll's support and help. Although he mixed with extremists and cranks, he did not neglect worldly matters and was making an income of more than $150,000 a year from his legal practice. Many people considered him the devil's advocate, but important companies retained him as their attorney because he was a brilliant lawyer.

In many ways Ingersoll and Reavis were birds of the same feather, although the lawyer never consciously did anything dishonest. He had become involved in a variety of the most bizarre commercial enterprises initiated by outright crooks—such as a process for maturing whiskey in a day or two so that it tasted as if it were six years old, as if it were the finest Scotch, and the manufacture of "indestructible and fire-resisting" wooden utensils.

Ingersoll was a man who loved good living; he weighed 220 pounds and was constantly nagged in vain by his devoted family to diet. Although he made a large income at the bar, money was always a problem. He had invested big money—and had lost most of it—in various spurious enterprises in the Southwest long before he met Reavis. Some of his enterprises concerned old Spanish grants in New Mexico, and Ingersoll had become a legal expert on the kind of grant typified by the claim Reavis professed to hold. Indeed, Ingersoll had used methods which were kindred to those employed by Reavis, although they were short of forgery.

In one case Ingersoll had acquired mining rights in the mountains of northern New Mexico. Under a retroactive law, the mining company which he had formed had to spend at least $1,000 on development annually to validate the claim. Preoccupied with legal cases in New York and his agnostic lectures and anticlerical activities, Ingersoll had done nothing for a time to develop the mine. When other prospectors walked in and staked their claims, Ingersoll recruited some Mexican toughs to recapture his mine by armed force. Simultaneously he took up the issue with the commissioner of the General Land Office in Washington—and, for the first time, lost a legal case of his own. He thereupon bribed various claimants and floated shares in a company, making a large profit. Some gold was dug, but by 1883 it had become evident that the placers were exhausted and not worth mining. Thus, Ingersoll lost not only all his profit but also money he had invested at the final stage of this enterprise.

Hardly more profitable was Ingersoll's ranching enterprise in New Mexico. The great lawyer had been chief counsel for the defense in one of the most notable trials in American history. The plaintiff was the Government of the United States, and the charge was one of fraud in connection with contracts for the Star Mail Routes, a network of mail deliveries in areas without railroads. When President Garfield took office and investigations into graft began, several senior Post Office officials hurriedly resigned. The corruption had been cleverly hidden and complicated. Investigations were protracted and intensified, after Garfield's assassination, under President Arthur. The upshot was an indictment which charged the Assistant Postmaster General, a former Senator from Arkansas, and a group of contractors of the Star Mail Routes with corruption. Briefly, the graft had been to increase payments out of all proportion to the original contract figure, and a typical example cited in court was the mail service in the Dakota Territory, where one route was to be subsidized by the Post Office at a mere $398 a year, but where the contractors had, by means of allegedly false accounts and false affidavits, netted more than $6,000. Since there were hundreds of such routes, the graft total was considerable.

Ingersoll had a tough job contriving a defense. He did so mainly on technicalities, plus his flair for spellbinding speeches. After being out for three days and nights, the jury returned a guilty verdict only against two minor conspirators, whose guilt was beyond doubt, but reported disagreement in regard to all the chief accused, and the jurors were eventually discharged. Ingersoll left the courthouse and drove down Pennsylvania Avenue like a conquering hero.

Soon afterward he went into a strange partnership with one of the defendants in the Star Mail Routes trial, the former Senator, Stephen Dowsey, who owned ranches in New Mexico. Ingersoll borrowed money, added some of his own, and became part owner of 24,000 acres of arable land, with claims to 4,500,000 acres of water rights, 45,000 head of cattle, and 800 horses. He and his partner floated the Paolo Blanco Company with a nominal capital of $2,000,000 and, in theory, stood to make an easy killing of $1,000,000, if the public took up the shares. But as soon as the news spread of the financial transaction, trouble arose among the settlers. Claimants appeared with documents, indicating that they owned the area. One claim was even for the land on which the main ranch, barns, and cattle pens stood.

Ingersoll and his partner were involved in costly litigations, and although most of the claims were proved fraudulent, they had to settle with the genuine claimants, and Ingersoll eventually lost a large amount of money instead of making a million. "I have a positive genius for losing money," he used to say. "Well, no matter. It is better to give than to receive."

It was, however, not only this philosophical outlook that prompted him to feel considerable sympathy for James Reavis and his Arizona schemes, but also to Ingersoll's way of thinking, here was a man who had patiently amassed a mountain of evidence to prove that he was the rightful owner of a vast estate, which made the Paolo Blanco ranch look like a pocket handkerchief. Ingersoll could readily understand how galling it was for a man like Reavis, a man with a great vision of civilizing the wild Southwest, to be thwarted at every turn by a horde of trespassers and squatters, specious officials, and backwoods journalists, who were hindering not only Carmelita's rightful inheritance, but also the development of a great country. Ingersoll had come to love the great open spaces of the Southwest, after his few short visits to New Mexico. "The country is a poem by Shakespeare set to music by Wagner," he wrote with rather lyrical bombast.

Moreover, it was probably enough for him to know that Reavis had encountered the hostility of petty officials, such as the surveyor general, or county and state judges. He had always fought officialdom—even when officialdom was justified. He had gained both fame and notoriety in his campaign against the laws prohibiting the passage of obscene material through the U. S. mails; he had successfully defended the freethinker De Robigne M. Bennett, arrested for mailing his violently blasphemous tract "An Open Letter to Jesus Christ."

Even if Reavis had been merely a Don Quixote fighting official windmills, Ingersoll would have sided with him. But he saw in Reavis a man genuinely aggrieved, a man who had quietly worked for many years to prove the validity of his just claim, a man whom he considered, in an almost insanely wrong assessment of character, to be an honest and almost diffident person, who deserved assistance. If a man of Ingersoll's legal knowledge and mundane experience came to such a conclusion, nothing shows better what a superb actor Reavis was.

The great lawyer had carefully examined all the Peralta documents put before him. This pile of cedulas, edicts, deeds, and reports, extending over the centuries and embracing the legalistic ritual of bygone regimes and judicial bodies, fascinated Ingersoll's legal mind. His great success as a lawyer was based on his grip of the facts in a case. In court he could speak for hours on end, hardly referring to his notes and spreading out the tangled facts in a plain, easily understood survey, comprehensible to the most bewildered juror. This grip came from his meticulous preparation of every case he handled and from the marshaling of every fact. When, after long study, he closed a file, every minute detail was clear and fixed in his mind. Ingersoll's defect in the case of the Peralta Grant was that he did not expect forgeries. If he had some doubt about one or another of the documents, Reavis took good care to dispel such doubt at once. Reavis was a man, though without formal training in legal matters, who had a similarly orderly mind. Not a statement, not a note, and certainly not a single document which looked even remotely spurious were laid before Ingersoll and the experts on Spanish grants whom the lawyer had called in. Not a single statement of claim lacked its supporting document, either the original or a legally endorsed or certified copy.

Very few people ever duped the greatest American lawyer of the nineteenth century by feeding him with forged documents. Reavis did. Ingersoll had seen hundreds of claims based on Spanish grants; none had been so irrefutably documented as was the Peralta Grant. When Ingersoll became the leading champion of the Baron of Arizona and reaffirmed again and again that the claim was genuine, it was not the colored view of a lawyer receiving a fee; it was the opinion of a lawyer who had been fully convinced that he represented a just cause.

Thus, Ingersoll became not only Reavis' main attorney in his subsequent litigation against the United States Government, but also an enthusiastic partner in the many fatuous business enterprises. Soon Reavis could announce that Robert Green Ingersoll had signed the articles of the Casa Grande Corporation as one of the incorporators and had become its first president.

It mattered little that Reavis' old adversaries in Arizona now once again mounted the barricades. A few weeks after the formation of the first company, the Tucson *Citizen* found a local merchant who had accepted a draft of the Casa Grande Land and Improvement Company to the amount of $398. The draft, because of some technical fault, was returned dishonored. The *Citizen* wrote:

> How many others the grand Peralta fraud has imposed on has yet to be determined as the victims seldom squeal. This Casa Grande Land and Improvement Company was represented by the broken nosed Baron to have in bank $5,000,000 which they proposed to pour into the lap of Arizona just as soon as the people living on their 40,000 square miles of territory can be educated to accept it. Probably the Baron's friends were short of small change when the little $400 draft arrived. . . .

The sarcasm was misplaced. At that time $400 meant nothing to Reavis. From New York he had hurried to San Francisco. There he inveigled several bankers and moneyed people into signing agreements for financing the Casa Grande companies. Among them was John H. Benson, a banker to whom Reavis had been recommended by Senator Conkling. Later a syndicate was formed in California; it was headed by Samuel H. Collins, San Francisco's biggest jeweler, and Moses Rosenkrantz, a wealthy and respected bullion broker. Each member of the syndicate agreed with Reavis to invest $30,000, and in addition, the syndicate paid Reavis $2,500 a month "towards the payment of the expenses of prosecuting the suit of the Peralta Grant for which members of the syndicate were to receive a conveyance from Reavis and his wife in proportion to the amounts supplied."

Reavis made promises left and right, but he was careful not to make proper assignments. All conveyances were conditioned on the success of the claim, and the businessmen who willingly paid money in return for a mere promise did so because of a pronouncement made by James O. Broadhead, the famous St. Louis attorney, Congressman, and, later, the U.S. minister to Switzerland. Invited by Reavis to New York and Washington, Broadhead held conferences with Ingersoll and Conkling. The outcome was that, in the autumn of 1887, he made the following announcement:

> The Peralta Claim has been submitted to Senator Roscoe Conkling, Mr. Robert Green Ingersoll and Mr. A. Hurd, who have pronounced it good. I have been associated with them in the case and my opinion coincides with theirs. Mr. James Addison Reavis is the gentleman who is pushing the claim and he is a man of remarkable energy and persistence.

A declaration of such a significance, made under the signature of a lawyer and politician of Broadhead's standing and mentioning three other legal luminaries, was a triumph which James Reavis had hardly dared to expect within such a short time after he had presented his new documents and his real heiress. The time was now ripe to reenter Arizona and present the new claim on behalf of Carmelita Sofía Loreta Micaela de Maso y de Peralta, Mrs. James Reavis, the Baroness de Arizonac and de los Colorados.

Reavis arrived in Tucson with a large party, in which was his wife; an elderly gentleman, whom he introduced as his uncle, John Reavis; a pretty young lady, described as Señorita María de Pilar Peralta, a young cousin of the baroness'; his personal secretary, Cyril Barratt, now looking much more respectable and well groomed than before; the inevitable Pedro Cuervo, still sporting silver-studded pistols in his cummerbund; two dark-skinned servants or bodyguards; and a lady's maid. They installed themselves at the Hotel San Xavier, taking over half of the building.

The baron had altered his pointed Vandyke beard, which he had worn during his visit in Europe, to a pair of luxuriant side whiskers. His hair was almost white, and he looked extremely dignified. The entry in the hotel register read: "James Addison Peraltareavis and the Baroness Peraltareavis." His wife was described by a reporter:

She appears to be about 24 to 26 years of age. Though of medium height, she has a dignified carriage, and her general bearing certainly gives one the impression of a Spanish lady of no means antecedents. Her face is oval, with large dark eyes and dark hair. Her nose is a little inclined to broadness, but her complexion is very clear. She speaks English fluently, and her general manner is cordial and agreeable. She is accompanied by Miss Peralta of San Francisco, a third cousin, and there are two colored attendants in the party.*

Accompanied by his secretary and his bodyguards, Reavis went to the surveyor general's office. Royal A. Johnson, his unwilling ally, who had been unjustly accused of having been biased in the baron's favor after the filing of the first claim in 1883, was there no longer. Johnson was a Republican, and when—for the first time since Abraham Lincoln and after a quarter of a century of power—the Republicans had been defeated in the election of 1884, the Democratic President, Grover Cleveland, had replaced Johnson by a Democrat, John Hise.

Reavis knew that he could expect even less assistance from Hise than from his predecessor. Hise was a friend of the Democratic Representative Marcus A. Smith, who during the congressional campaign of 1887 was reelected as Arizona's delegate to Congress largely on the basis of his opposition to everything Reavis stood for.

But Surveyor General Hise could do nothing but dutifully accept the bulky file which Reavis handed over. It was a volume bound in black leather and embossed on the front cover with the ancient crest of the Peraltas, the barons of Arizona. It contained a whole array of photographs and certified copies of the last will and testament of Don Miguel de Peralta, the testament and codicil of Don Miguel Silva Jesús, the second baron, in favor of his granddaughter, and all the supporting documents going back to the report by Father Francisco Pauer about the

* Los Angeles *Examiner*, October 5, 1887.

ceremony of the location and delineation of the estates. There were legalized copies of Carmelita's birth certificate from the Mission of San Salvador, the civil contract of her marriage to Reavis, and many other documents proving her direct descent.

With the submission of the new claim, Reavis also filed an application for an immediate survey of the boundaries of the estates, "so as to fully ascertain the area to which the claimant expects his rights to be validated." The attorneys and surveyors had obliged by transforming the ancient and cumbersome measurements contained in the original document of 1758 into more comprehensible American measures of surface:

> Beginning at the west end of the Initial Monumental Stone, with a map about 12 by 36 inches upon the south face, thence north crossing the Gila and Salt rivers a distance of 24.83 miles to a point, thence east 149.3 miles to a point, and from the west end of the Initial Monumental Stone, the place of beginning, thence south a distance 24.885 miles to a point, and thence east a distance of 149.3 miles to a point, described as the eastern extension of the northern point of the western boundary of said Concession of Peralta or the Peralta Grant.*

Reavis put a special emphasis on the Initial Monument. Since he had so carefully planted the *desiño,* mentioned by Father Pauer, on that old rock, it had remained undiscovered and unmentioned until it suddenly appeared in his application. The baron was confident that this additional and visible historical proof of the genuineness of the claim would perplex his enemies. With his retinue and a photographer, he traveled from Tucson to the Gila, and there, in front of the Initial Monument, photographs were taken of the baroness, attired in a black velvet coat and a beribboned hat and wearing a gold chain with a gold plaque embossed with the Peralta coat of arms

---

* Records of the General Land Office (in U.S. National Archives, Washington, D.C.).

around her neck. The photographs were then sent to all journals in Arizona and to many newspapers in New York, Washington, San Francisco, Sacramento, Los Angeles, and Santa Fe.

Although Surveyor General Hise was obliged to file the new
claim, he was empowered to turn down the application for the
survey of the claimed land, even though Reavis offered him
$10,000 "to defray the cost." Hise and the Democratic politi-
cians were determined to hinder Reavis wherever they could.
When Ingersoll appealed against Hise's decision to the commissioner of the General Land Office in Washington, he got
short shrift. The commissioner ruled that "the effect of such a
survey would be too segregate the surveyed land from the
public domain and to give the claimants the power of eviction
under local laws, and to vest [in the claimants] such presump-
tive rights as will enable them to cajole or force occupants to
compromise with [the claimants] for . . . remaining in possession of homes and property."*

This was just what Reavis and his attorneys had hoped for,
but the Cleveland administration was not prepared to play their
game.

The reaction of the people of Arizona to the baron's reap-
pearance after two years of absence was of a very different kind
from the half-panicky and half-resigned attitude which had prevailed during his initial extortion campaign in 1883 and 1884.
This time the settlers had been forewarned by many news
stories heralding the great development schemes which the Casa
Granda Corporation and its subsidiaries were planning and by
the startling opinions expressed by Senator Conkling, Ingersoll,
Broadhead, and others.

The Arizonans were ready to take up the fight. Their newspapers proclaimed a holy war against the baron. The Tucson
Citizen warned:

* General Land Office, *Annual Report of 1888* (U.S. National Archives, Washington, D.C.) .

If Reavis will put an appearance in the Salt River Valley and press his suit with the same brazen effrontery as he does on the outside, he will get a decision in his favor mighty quick—if Judge Lynch can be induced to hold court . . . there is but little doubt that in this particular instance he will gladly preside!

This was a direct incitement to violence, and since it appeared in a paper in Tucson, where people had nothing to fear from the baron's claim, the temper of the settlers within his now clearly delineated realm could easily be imagined. Reavis understood the warning and decided it would be unwise to visit Phoenix or the Gila Valley.

In any case he had more urgent business to attend to elsewhere. With the backing of his famous attorneys and partners he felt that, short of physical assault, he had nothing to fear. The validation of his claim seemed now only a matter of time and formalities. Traveling with his wife and his retinue across the continent, between San Francisco, New York, and Washington, he reappeared in Arizona only from time to time and usually for only brief visits.

His demands for comfort had long since exceeded what his modest palace at Arizola could offer. He had acquired a large hacienda in Chihuahua in Mexico, where he spent vacations in a really baronial style. Although Arizona rejected him, he was certainly made welcome in Mexico, and he reciprocated by generous donations to charities. At Guadalajara he gave $1,000 for new altar cloths for the Cathedral of Santiago and was the patron of the hospital and of a home for the blind. On the plaza at Monterrey, in the province of Nuevo León, he set up a monument and a drinking fountain, which cost him $2,000, in honor of the memory of Don Miguel de Peralta, who was supposed to have lived there at one time. At his trial it was said that he spent $60,000 each year on travels, always staying in luxury hotels, retaining large suites, and entertaining his friends and business associates.

He visited Mary Ann Willing in St. Louis and signed a new agreement with her, giving her $600 on account of the promised $30,000, although by then he must have cared little whether Mrs. Willing would cause trouble or not. His claim was now based not on her dead husband's dubious agreement, but on the claim of the real heiress. But Reavis, it seemed, gratefully remembered the kindness Mary Ann had shown him many years earlier at St. Louis, and in later years he sent her presents, including elegant dresses discarded by his wife, and from time to time gifts of money, of $100 or so.

There were also some discreet matters to attend to. With Carmelita he went to Sherwood Valley to find people who would remember the little orphan, abandoned by her father and grandfather, those legendary noble Spaniards, José Maso and Don Miguel Silva Jesús de Peralta. They visited Alfred Sherwood who was a little bewildered at seeing Carmelita so elegant, well spoken, and prosperous. What happened between Reavis and Sherwood was only much later revealed at his trial, but Reavis left with an affidavit signed by Sherwood and duly certified by a notary, in which the baroness' former foster father confirmed that he "well remembered her grandfather, that she had been brought to him a babe, when about twelve months of age, that he knew she had been christened at the mission in San Diego County, that he knew she had a twin brother who with her mother had died soon after his birth, and that her father was Don José Ramón Carmen Maso who had left for Spain, where he was said to have died." This was another very useful little document, which was duly filed with the surveyor general at Tucson.

Other people in San Bernardino and Sherwood Valley, in Sacramento and Knights Landing, were approached, and Reavis found three men—Miguel Noe, Andrés Sandoval, and José Ramón Valencia—prepared to testify that they had known Don Miguel Silva Jesús de Peralta and his family and everything about Carmelita's antecedents and birth. Although Reavis was conducting these additional researches rather as a hobby—he could never tear himself away for any length of time from the Peralta mystery—this additional evidence (which was eventually to lead to several prosecutions for perjury) was not unimportant in the pursuit of the claim. It certainly contributed to the confusion which the baron cunningly spread about, later to make investigations of the attorneys and special agents employed by the Government into a prolonged ordeal.

Most of his time, however, was occupied with the launching of ever new development schemes, which, at least on paper, were now in full swing. In addition to floating shares of the many corporations and companies, he was bent upon offering "land and mining concessions" to new dupes. The following is an excerpt from one of the flamboyantly phrased prospectuses which, well printed and illustrated, might put modern public relations experts to shame:

One of the largest and best portions of the Territory is the immense tract known as the Barony of Arizona, the property of Mr. J. A. Peralatareavis, which is now to be colonized on a large scale. The tract contains 12,500,000 acres and is known as the Peralta Grant, and is an old feudal property dating back to the time of King Philip V of Spain, who granted it to Don Miguel Nemecio Silva de Peralta de la Córdoba in 1742. The grantee was a lineal ancestor of Mrs. Peraltareavis, a resident of California, into whose possession it has fallen by the Spanish law of primogeniture succession. The property has been in litigation for some years, but in November last the United States Court of Private Land Claims finally determined the exact boundaries of the estate, and thereby practically sealed Mrs. Peraltareavis' claims.

A clear title to any or all of the property is thereby assured. There are few individual properties in New Mexico or Arizona so vast in extent and so admirably located for colonization purposes.

The estates embrace the Gila, Salt, San Pedro and San Carlos rivers as water-courses. It is impossible to estimate the value of this immense property, blessed as it is in mineral and agricultural resources. It contains the most famous mineral belt in Arizona, that of the Pinal Range, with the adjacent mountains in close proximity to these abundant streams; also the renowned Deer Creek coal fields, the largest coal measure yet discovered in America, and an anthracite deposit near the Gila Buttes which promises to surpass anything yet developed.

Within the boundaries of the Peralta Grant many important mining camps have sprung up, notably Silver King, Clinton, Silver City, and Old Dominion. The Town of Phoenix lies within the border, as do also Florence, Globe, Solomonville, and Silver City. The Southern Pacific Railroads cuts across the southwest corner. Numerous branch lines which are to traverse the very heart of this great property have already been surveyed and their projection is the question of only a short time.*

Other prospectuses and advertisements in newspapers in California and the great cities of the East described "the wonderful fertility of the valleys of the Salt and Gila, which it is proposed to irrigate by storing the waters of these two rivers." One storage dam, "nearing construction, will be at the Little Tonto Basin, with a reservoir capacity of 989,600,000,000 cubic feet." Another reservoir, with an area of 32 square miles and with a capacity of 67,540,432,425 cubic feet, was to be located at The Buttes, about 10 miles from Florence on the Gila. From the latter was to be built a canal, 200 feet wide and 25 feet deep, to extend to a point on the Southern Pacific Railroad near Red Rock, and thence westward to cover the Maricopa Plains, "designed to supply 6,000,000 acres with abundant waters at all times of the year."

The companies headed by Ingersoll and managed by Reavis employed several engineers and surveyors who produced quite sensible and feasible plans, although Reavis insisted that every estimate concerning water supply be doubled or trebled in the

* James H. McClintock, *Arizona* (Chicago, Clarke Co., 1916), Vol. II.

prospectus. Although he thus purposely overcalculated the amount of water available, he did envisage irrigation programs that were the forerunners of the great Salt River, Gila Valley, and San Carlos projects.

A project for the Toto Basin envisaged vertical walls 2,000 feet high, within which a dam 450 feet high was to be built, with sixty-three discharge pipes carrying water into the box canyon; "an impregnable chasm as dark as night," Reavis poetically described it in a prospectus. The water was to be taken over a distance of 8 miles by means of several tunnels leading out to the plains. One tunnel to the south, through the Superstition Mountains, was to be 44,000 feet in length with a 50-mile waterway at its end, connecting with the proposed Gila—Buttes Reservoir.

These were grandiose plans, devised by some able engineers, though Reavis enhanced and glamorized them almost into fantasy. The cost of these projects was estimated at more than $12,000,000—the money to be raised by selling shares of the companies. In all this Reavis was a prophet, but one without honor.

In these and other, even more fraudulent prospectuses, Reavis always insisted that the Court of Private Land Claims had "determined the boundaries of the Peralta Grant and thereby practically sealed . . . the claim."

Exactly the opposite was the case. After the election in 1888, when the Republican party with President Benjamin Harrison returned to power, Reavis was confident that his friends would be able to expedite the validation of his claim. But his main supporter in Washington, Senator Roscoe Conkling, ailing for some time, died in the winter after the Republican victory for which he had worked hard, in the blizzard which swept New York.

In Tucson Surveyor General Hise was dismissed, and Royal A. Johnson returned to his office. He found in the desk of his predecessor a half-finished report which was destructive to the Reavis' claim. Johnson had worked on the tangled affairs of the Peralta Grant for many years, ever since it had been first filed in 1883. He had considered in a dispassionate manner all the arguments in its favor, as well as all objections and doubts, in spite of political pressure. Reavis' attempts to influence and even to bribe him, and the newspapers' attacks against his person and position.

After he had returned to his office, Johnson was determined to finish this affair. He began to write the final report for the General Land Office in Washington, using to a large extent the evidence collected by John Hise.

At last on October 12, 1889, Johnson sent to Washington his report, which became known as the *Adverse Report of the Surveyor General of Arizona, upon the Peralta Grant, a Complete Exposé of Its Fraudulent Character.**

Of course, Reavis did not take it lying down. He immediately instructed Robert Green Ingersoll and James O. Broadhead to file a suit against the United States Government.

* Published as a pamphlet by Arizona Gazette Book and Job Office, Phoenix, 1890.

11

Secret Agents in a Battle of Wits

Five years were to elapse before the case of James Addison Peraltareavis and others against the United States of America was tried by the Court of Private Land Claims at Santa Fe. The decision, taken by Reavis on the advice of his attorneys, Robert Green Ingersoll and Harvey S. Brown, proved fatal. Had Reavis, in spite of the surveyor general's report, continued his financial maneuvers, as he had done successfully for many years, justice might never have caught up with him. Although payments for quitclaims and rents had dried up and the citizens of Arizona had manned their defenses, the prince of con men might have been able to carry on and, for years, inveigle credulous people into advancing money for his schemes, to float new companies, and, finally, to transfer his activities to other spheres and other regions.

But his lawyers—particularly Ingersoll, so enthusiastically convinced that the claim was genuine and must succeed and relying on his proved ability to sway judges and jurors—encouraged Reavis to go to the offensive. This, his final challenge, was taken up by a man who not only proved to be the toughest opponent Reavis had ever encountered, but also could match any of the legal tricks the baron's lawyers began to employ when the fight became more desperate and more hopeless as time went on. This man was Matthew Given Reynolds, the special attorney appointed by the court which was to try the action against the Government.

In his report of October 12, 1889—the so-called *Adverse Report*—Surveyor General Royal A. Johnson pointed to a number of highly suspicious details which he had found during the protracted examination of the documents. Johnson stressed in his report that he had only inadequate means to carry out a thorough examination, and he admitted that the technicalities of the task had nearly defeated him. "The furnishing of triplicate copies of all the papers on file here to accompany this report," he wrote to the commissioner of the General Land Office in Washington, "is a tremendous undertaking and will be next to impossible within a reasonable time." He said that he required Spanish copyists and translators, more clerks, and more funds to make a proper job of it.

Nevertheless, his report contained many observations which were extremely damaging to the claim. He did not mince his words when, in the conclusion, he called the claim "an attempt at a gigantic fraud and nothing more."

Johnson made a detailed description of the most important documents. His immediate suspicion was aroused by the title sheet of the original grant. This was a brittle yellowed sheet of thin parchment, obviously a genuine eighteenth-century deed, but it was badly tattered and consisted of several parchment pieces stuck together. On only one of the strips, pasted onto the document, was there any mention of the name of Peralta. The inscription read: "In relation to the Concession given to Don Miguel de Peralta, Baron of the Colorados." The following leaves, containing the actual details of a grant of lands, were printed. It was the royal cedula, the edict of King Ferdinand VI, commanding the viceroy in Mexico "to grant and concede" the estates.*

In addition to mentioning discrepancies in the various texts, Johnson pointed to two startling discoveries he had made: some of the writing on the old parchments was done with a steel pen, and the printed documents were set in a type which, in the opinion of an expert, was of much more recent design than any type possibly used in 1776, the date of the document in question. Johnson did not claim credit for these discoveries, nor did he mention the expert who told him about that typographical puzzle.

Many years later, when the Peralta Grant had become a legend and the bad baron had become the hero of tales published in magazines and even in an official guidebook of Arizona, writers told of a young printer who had unmasked Reavis as a forger by having found out that some of the documents were written on paper which "plainly bore the watermark of a Wisconsin paper mill that had only been in existence ten or twelve years." Now Reavis was not the kind of small-time crook who would have made such a silly mistake. His forgeries were excellent, and if he made mistakes—and quite a few were discovered—they were much more involved. But as in most tales, there was a drop of truth in the story about the young printer who contributed to Reavis' downfall.

Tom Weedin, the editor of the Florence *Enterprise,* who had for years fought Reavis so bravely, had been doing some sleuthing together with Clark Churchill, the attorney general, who had challenged the Peralta Grant back in 1884. Weedin was a pious man, a devout Christian. He detested Ingersoll's blasphemous activities as much as or even more than Reavis' conduct. When Ingersoll became the president and chief exponent

* See page 76.

of the baron's various development companies, Weedin published scathing attacks on the famous lawyer. The editor resented the judgment on secular and business matters of a man who rejected spiritual truths. Ingersoll's antireligious excesses only redoubled Weedin's determination "to destroy the whole Peralta gang." When he heard that Churchill was helping Johnson prepare his report, he sent his assistant, Bill Truman, to Tucson, being himself unable to leave his newpaper office.

Truman was known in Florence as Stammering Bill because of a speech defect. He was a fair-haired youth, as shy and quiet as most people afflicted by an impediment, but he had brains and was a first-class printer, greatly interested in typography. Catalogues of typefaces sent by foundries in the East to the little Florence printing shop were his favorite reading. He had carved out letters from wood blocks to provide type for bigger headlines than his boss could afford to buy. Although Weedin had no particular reason to suspect that there were flaws in the printing on the ancient documents, he told Bill to have a good look at them.

Stammering Bill went to the surveyor general's office and, known as Weedin's assistant, was permitted to inspect some of the documents, especially the printed cedula. He gingerly smoothed the fragile brittle parchment. Its whiteness had long since turned to the brownish yellow of age, and the printing ink had the dull sepia hue which occurs through partial exposure to light. Bill had a long look at the document. At first he may have disbelieved his eyes, but his mind surged with excitement.

"Lord help me," he murmured, "I know that type."

He remembered that at his workshop back in Florence there was a catalogue from the firm of Brownlie & Son, typefounders in San Francisco. "The fine ornamental face designed by the country's foremost typographers, available in eight sizes from Brevier and Pica upwards to 36 points," said the proud announcement in the caption. It was not an attractive type in the aesthetic opinion of Stammering Bill, who had advanced tastes in typography. The capitals had the flowery romanticism of mid-nineteenth-century art and a regard for Gothic pseudoornamentation. The letters had too many squiggles and serifs. Not all the subscribers to the Florence *Enterprise* were fluent readers, and Weedin knew that they might find it difficult to cope with such an ornate type. He had ordered only a small quantity, and it was used infrequently for the job printing of posters and official announcements.

Bill was positive that it was exactly the same type in which the ancient document of the Peralta Grant was printed—allegedly in 1776, when not only Brownlie & Son but also the city of San Francisco were not even dreamed of.

It was not evidence but intuition that made Johnson, Churchill, and Weedin decide that further investigations would be worthwhile. Stammering Bill* was sent home posthaste, printed a few samples from the type, and hurried with them back to Tucson. The San Francisco foundry was approached and sent a whole selection. Soon there was little doubt that the ancient Spanish and the recent American types were identical. Still, there was a possibility that the San Francisco designer had copied the old Spanish type. But this was more farfetched than the simple assumption that Reavis had used a type, cut in 1885 by Brownlie & Son, because it greatly resembled one he had seen on genuine documents of the Spanish viceroyalty of Mexico in the archives of Guadalajara.

Clark Churchill, who had perfect mastery of the Spanish language, had become intrigued by other startling puzzles in some of the documents. In a passage above the rubrica, with which King Ferdinand had approved the grant, there occurred the following text:

---

* The name of Stammering Bill does not occur in the trial reports and transcripts, but Mulford Winsor, director of the Arizona Department of Library and Archives, identified him as Bill Truman.

> *Passo ante mi*
> *fecha en Madrid*
> *A dos de Decembre de Mill Setecientos y Setenta y Dos*
> *Yo el Rey.*

In plain English this meant: "Passed by me—Dated in Madrid on the second December One Thousand Seven Hundred Seventy-two."

Not only was this poor Spanish, but what struck Churchill were the many spelling mistakes which the king's chancellor, the Duke of Taranco, had made in these few lines of a simple endorsement. Double consonants, such as *nn, mm, rr, ss,* and *tt,* so often used in English spelling, hardly ever occur in the Spanish language, and the double *l* has a very different pronunciation from *l.* Churchill made a comment about these spelling mistakes which Johnson appended to his report:

> The unfortunate Taranco wrote *passo* instead of *paso* with one "s"; he wrote *Decembre* when the word is properly *Diciembre* in Spanish; he wrote *mill,* when it should be *mil* with a single "l." One would not have expected this at the king's court!
>
> By looking at the very bottom of Exhibit A [the acknowledgment of the receipt of the cedula] the Viceroy of New Spain is also afflicted with weak knowledge of Spanish: *"Passo mi"*— translated into English would be "it passed me," but as a Spanish phrase, the word *passo* should be *paso;* that is, one "s," and there should be an accent on the "o"; the preposition *"por"* should be between the two words, that is *"paso por mi"* (and not *"passo ante mi"*), though even such an expression was improper for the case. For this reason I say that the author of this document was an American who spoke bad Spanish. . . .

Johnson and his helpers laboriously compared some of the documents with other old Spanish deeds at the surveyor general's office, deeds whose genuineness was beyond doubt, and they came to the conclusion that on at least a few the writing was done with a steel nib. They knew that the steel pen was not in use before 1800. It may be that each of these discoveries was trivial and insufficient to brand Reavis as a forger. But putting them together and adding various other dubious details, such as the fact that some documents consisted of pasted-on pieces of parchment and that others omitted references to the Peralta family but spoke of anonymous land grants, heightened Johnson's long-standing suspicion. He must have been longing to be done with Reavis and the Peralta Grant, and even though he may have been uncertain that some documents were faked, he described in his final report the claim as a "brazen fraud."

It took four months before the commissioner of the General Land Office, Lewis H. Groff, replied. By then some of Reavis' Republican friends in Washington had been busily at work on his behalf. Wires were pulled with President Harrison's Secretary of the Interior, John W. Noble, a Missouri politician. Reavis had appealed for help to Senator Francis Cockrell of Missouri, whom he had known in St. Louis.

The commissioner's letter, dated February 20, 1890, was somewhat strangely worded. It referred only briefly to the suspected forgeries which Johnson had pointed out and it ticked off the Arizonan surveyor general for spending so much time and trouble on the examination of the documents. Commissioner Groff wrote:

The call for information was not intended as a direction to you to make up a report, complete or incomplete, from the evidence before you, with the view to the submission of the same to Congress; neither was it intended that any step, whatever, should be taken to clothe the case with any additional dignity, or cause alarm to the inhabitants of Arizona Territory. . . .

Were this a case, which *prima facie,* involved some legal or equitable rights, and ought therefore, be laid before Congress . . . the consideration of it in your office should have been exhaustive; and the record prepared in as complete a manner as possible, after

full investigation, before your report and recommendation were
submitted; but the correspondence had shown that there is no
fund available for more thoroughly investigating and exposing
the alleged claim.

On the outside it looked as if Groff wanted to pigeonhole the
whole matter. Perhaps this was also the desire of Reavis' friends
who had used their influence in Washington. The commissioner
concentrated on the legal aspects and arrived at the conclusion
that three principal questions should be considered:

> First:—was there ever a grant to one Peralta in the manner,
> and for the lands alleged? Second:—If there was such a grant, can
> the lines of concession be laid down on the earth's surface with
> such certainty as to avoid interference with the legal rights of
> others? Third:—Supposing such a claim once existing, are there
> now any heirs or successors in interest of the original grantee . . .
> whose claims demand recognition?

The commissioner left it in some doubt whether the answers
to these questions were in the affirmative or the negative. He
stated that "originally good titles, under Spanish and French
grants, have been frequently lost on account of vagueness, and
have been pronounced void for uncertainty, as will be seen by
the decisions of the Courts in Louisiana, Florida and Missouri."
Describing the proofs submitted as "of too dubious character,"
the commissioner declared that "the heirship of Mrs. Reavis is
not proven, even allowing the papers produced to be genuine."
His letter, nine pages in length, ran hot and cold. Although he
apparently accepted Johnson's findings that the claim was
fraudulent, Groff put all these accusations in quotation marks,
thus leaving it open whether Reavis was a forger or not. He
reminded Johnson of the direction issued on May 2, 1885,
relating to the first claim based on the Willing papers, by which
Johnson had been ordered that further consideration of the

claim "should be forthwith discontinued" and he said that "a full discussion of the various points . . . that here is a no valid claim . . . is deemed unnecessary," but he added "unless required in the future by higher authority."

Finally, the commissioner ordered Johnson "to strike the case from your docket, and notify Mr. Reavis of the action, allowing the usual time for an appeal to the Hon. Secretary of the Interior."

Although most people saw in this direction the death knell of the Peralta Grant, it was also open to different interpretation; Reavis could lodge an appeal and reopen the whole tedious affair once more. However, when Surveyor General Johnson released his report to the public, there was great jubilation in Arizona. The newspapers, hitherto critical of Johnson's handling of the claim, now fell over one another to congratulate him. Governor N. O. Murphy invited Johnson to Phoenix, where a great reception awaited the surveyor general at the governor's mansion, decorated with flags, bunting, and flowers.

The people of Phoenix and the Salt River Valley came out in crowds to acclaim him. The *Herald** wrote:

> Nearly every man and woman in the city came forward to express their friendship to Mr. Johnson. Mayor Coast escorted Johnson and his accomplished wife to the executive chambers where they were introduced to the ladies and gentlemen who called to pay their compliments. . . . The reception proved truly that Surveyor General Johnson held the high place that he so well deserved in the hearts of Salt River Valley's populace.

Tom Weedin was less optimistic. In his *Enterprise* he warned that "Reavis and his backers are now concentrating their efforts to the establishment of a Land Court, which they hope to control. . . .The present ruling is the first blood for the

* March 23, 1890.

settlers, but there are several hard rounds yet to be contested before the claimants are ready to throw up the sponge."*

In this Weedin was right. Reavis, his wife, and, amazingly, the Southern Pacific Company joined in filing a suit, at first before the Court of Claims. Their submission stated that the surveyor general had made "some sort of report" on their claim, of which they were unable to obtain a copy and of whose contents they were ignorant. They charged that the Government had denied them guarantees under the Constitution in respect to their property, had thrown the same property open to settlers and trespassers, had disposed of a large amount of land, had collected payments from sales, had reserved 1,500,000 acres for its own use, and had appropriated waters from the Gila River for irrigation purposes—all this in disregard of the fact that the land was justly claimed by the heirs to the Peralta Grant.

Therefore, the claimants demanded an initial judgment for $6,000,000 in damages for losses already suffered, an injunction forbidding the Government to continue any actions which would cause further damage, and a judgment for a further sum of $5,000,000 in damages suffered by the claimants by preventing them to develop water and mineral rights. Altogether the demand was for $11,000,000, but it was made clear that claims for "further relief and costs" would be filed. Leading counsel for the claimants was Harvey S. Brown, the Southern Pacific attorney, assisted by a San Francisco lawyer, Philip B. Thompson, while Ingersoll, who remaining the legal brain behind the case, delegated John H. Knabel as his assistant. James O. Broadhead, until he became U.S. minister to Switzerland, also took part in the preparation of the case. Several of the lawyers were politicians, sitting in Congress or in state legislatures. The United States Court of Claims was represented by H. S. Biggs, a Treasury attorney.

* March 1, 1890.

At the time when Reavis and his lawyers were busily preparing new evidence, Congress decided to institute a new tribunal to deal with the many claims which had been filed by other people to land in the Southwest, particularly in New Mexico, Arizona, and Texas. In March, 1891, a law established the Court of Private Land Claims. While the existing Court of Claims adjudicated upon any claims a citizen might raise against the Government, the new court's judicature was to be concerned exclusively with land claims originating from old Spanish, Mexican, and French grants. The institution of such a court was strongly opposed by Congressmen from the Southwest because they regarded it as a forum for land-grabbers like Reavis to reassert themselves.

Reavis and his attorneys jubilantly welcomed the establishment of this new court. The Globe *Arizona Silver Belt* sadly recorded that "the evil effect of the new Land Claims Court can be seen in the revival of the alleged Peralta Grant." However, neither the optimism of the claimants nor the fears of their opponents were justified. The litigation upon which Reavis embarked led to his ruin, and the new court proved a mighty protector of genuine rights of the citizens.

The first presiding judge of the new Court of Private Land Claims, Chief Justice Joseph R. Reed, appointed Matthew Given Reynolds as its special attorney and charged him with conducting preliminary investigations and taking testimony in the cases of a number of minor land claims and, above all, in the case of the Peralta Grant.

Matthew Reynolds, a Missouri man like Reavis, had been a naval officer before he turned to law studies and established a law practice, during which time he acquired a good knowledge of Spanish and French grants in Missouri and Louisiana. While in his early thirties, he was elected to the Missouri legislature and, as both a lawyer and a legislator, gained the reputation of a shrewd, honest, and energetic man.

Reynolds was eager to cross swords with such famous lawyers as Ingersoll, Broadhead, and Brown, and he took up the challenge with gusto and diligence. He was fortunate to find an assistant, a New York attorney named Severo Mallet-Prevost, who had been born in Zacatecas, Mexico, and who had a mastery not only of the Spanish language but also of old Spanish and Mexican laws. The two men decided to retrace the investigations and searches by which the baron claimed to have assembled his putative evidence. Reynolds went about his assignment with meticulous care. He engaged an expert graphologist, William N. Tipton, to examine every document copy and photograph submitted by Reavis, including entries in the archives in Mexico and Spain and in the church missions and courthouse registries in California and Arizona.

Two special agents—Levi A. Hughes and Peter Grady—were borrowed from the Secret Service of the Treasury Department (it was not until 1908 that Attorney General Charles J. Bonaparte set up the Federal Bureau of Investigation to assist Theodore Roosevelt in his drive against corruption), and they proved to be extremely clever detectives.

The attorneys representing Reavis had requested the court for a continuance so that new evidence could be collected and appended to the claim. The formal filing of the case at the Court of Private Land Claims' office at Santa Fe was thus delayed until February, 1893. But for many previous months Reavis had been preparing his case. Although he was much earlier off the mark than Reynolds, Mallet-Prevost, and the detectives, soon a fantastic race ensued, with Reynolds and his assistants traveling the width of the United States, collecting evidence and taking testimony from everybody and at every place Reavis had ever mentioned.

One thing which apparently had begun to worry Reavis was the proof of his wife's birth and baptism at San Bernardino. Upon this proof depended, of course, her descendance from the

Peralta family and her claim of being the real heiress. Reavis asked James O. Broadhead to accompany him to California; but the famous lawyer was unable to oblige immediately, and the trip had to be postponed until the spring of 1893.

In the meantime, Reavis went to Mexico, trying to bolster his ancient documents by some new discoveries at the Ayuntamiento archives in Guadalajara. Once again, as in 1883, he was lucky. He had to be. He badly needed some new documents because those he had produced with his first claim had been declared "entirely spurious" in the *Adverse Report* of Surveyor General Johnson.

When he left Guadalajara, Reavis had in his possession certified copies of two documents of extreme importance. In a dusty file of records, bearing a label with the date of 1824, he found—or so he declared when the papers were eventually filed at the Santa Fe office of the court—a probate document of the first baron's testament, endorsed with the signature of the notary Ballesteros. In the same file, it seemed, were also several other documents, some of minor importance, such as the commission of Don Miguel de Peralta as a captain of the royal dragoons, and also a cherry-colored folder containing four cedulas and a genealogical table of the Peralta family, including detailed data on the second baron and his wife and of their marriage in 1822.

That the ancient documents had become mixed up with more recent ones and had been filed in a folder marked 1824, thus escaping earlier detection, could be explained without much difficulty. Apparently the second baron, possibly after the death of his father in 1824, had been anxious to examine his family papers, and thus they were filed together. All Reavis now needed was some additional corroboration of the circumstances of Carmelita's birth at San Bernardino and the testimony of people who had met her grandfather, father, and mother.

The Court of Private Land Claims had its offices at Santa Fe, but because claims concerned land all over the Southwest, ambulatory counsel were employed for taking testimony from claimants, counterclaimants, and witnesses. Although the Peralta Grant was of course, the biggest, most complex, and most important case the court had to deal with, there were a number of other claims, concerning alleged Spanish and Mexican grants. Among them were that of Robert F. Hunter, a Washington, D.C., banker, who had acquired rights in a title claimed by the Papago chief Ochoa to 3,284 square miles in Pima County, and claims based on Spanish grants known as Baca, San Rafael, Sonoita, Bobocomari, and Nogales de Elias.

In order to save witnesses—some of them Indians, miners and prospectors—long journeys to Santa Fe and to avoid heavy costs to the Government, because witnesses would have to be recompensed for loss of time and traveling and subsistence expenses, the ambulatory counsel and special agents of the court visited the witnesses and recorded their testimony under oath. These testimony-taking sessions were often held at very unlikely places, in saloons, town halls, mining camps, and even in the open air, or, as a contemporary chronicler poetically said, "under the light of the moon."

Claimants were entitled to be present or be represented by their lawyers at these sessions, could question witnesses, and could challenge their depositions. Claimants could also collect evidence from witnesses in the form of affidavits and submit it to the court, although in such cases the witnesses would be interrogated by the court's counsel or would be required to appear in person at the final trial of the case.

After his return from Mexico, Reavis took advantage of this arrangement and, in 1890 and 1891, traveled widely in California, accompanied by his attorney, Harvey S. Brown, collecting affidavits from people prepared to testify that they had known the old baron and his family back in the 1860's, particularly when he, his daughter, his son-in-law, José Maso, and the latter's mother had made that famous halt in 1862 at San

Bernardino, on their journey to San Francisco, when the twins were born and Doña Sofía died in childbirth.

At these initial testimony takings Brown acted on behalf of the claimant, and the court was represented by H. S. Biggs, a mild-mannered attorney from whom Reavis encountered little opposition. Reavis had hoped that James O. Broadhead, the famous St. Louis lawyer, would come to California, but Broadhead was at that time deeply involved in politics as a Congressman in Washington and had informed Reavis that he could not attend until the spring of 1893.

This was not altogether disagreeable to Reavis. Not only had he been busy trying to tap new sources of money, but his wife was also expecting a child. The couple traveled with several servants to New York, where Reavis wanted to confer with Ingersoll and meet his business associates. As always, the baron and baroness lived in state, occupying a large suite at the Fifth Avenue Hotel, even though funds were now low. Reavis was spending a fortune on traveling, hotel bills, his retinue, and, above all, legal expenses. He employed at that time at least ten attorneys, all of them leading lawyers who commanded very high fees.

On March 8, 1893 the baroness gave birth to twins, two boys who were fittingly named Miguel and Carlos Jesús, after their great-grandfather and grandfather, the first and second barons of Arizona. The confinement took place at the hotel, where Reavis ordered a large room to be transformed into a delivery room. Several doctors attended the baroness and nurses were on duty day and night. After all, this was the birth of Peralta heirs, and to Reavis, money was no object.

His hopes in New York did not materialize; the financiers who had advanced substantial sums for the floating of the many Casa Grande companies were keeping their pockets buttoned up. The stock exchange committee had refused to admit the dubious stock for quotation on the bourse, and the general public was far from eager to invest money in the shares, until the Peralta case, which had attracted the attention of New York and Washington newspapers—an attention which was not favorable—reached a more hopeful stage. Ingersoll, preoccupied with some great legal cases, showed only perfunctory interest.

Reavis was now rapidly running out of money, although he succeeded in forming yet another syndicate headed by a Washington financier, John McMurren. This time his backers insisted on funds to be held by trustees. Reavis nominated Broadhead, hoping to lay his hands on at least a part of the money, but Broadhead kept to the letter of the agreement and told Reavis he would have to wait until the Peralta Grant was validated.

Nevertheless, Reavis was in high spirits. He gave interviews to New York papers, expatiating on the fact that his wife had given birth to twins: another proof of her Peralta ancestry. Was she not herself one of twins born to Doña Sofía, the daughter of the second baron? Obviously, twins ran in the Peralta family!

At last James O. Broadhead could tear himself away from his duties at the Capitol and went with Reavis to California. This journey proved very expensive, but Reavis was prepared to risk his last dime. He knew that Broadhead's mere presence at the testimony takings would create an aura of probity or, at least, of verisimilitude, and he direly needed to restore his tattered reputation.

For the first time, at these testimony recordings in California, Matthew Reynolds appeared as ambulatory counsel for the Government. He treated Broadhead with utmost politeness and the respect due to a top sawyer of the legal profession and Reavis with a cold formality which discouraged the baron's attempts at friendliness. Reynolds asked the witnesses few questions but made copious notes. While the depositions continued, the Secret Service agents were briefed by Reynolds to check up on every witness, his background and his stories.

The most important witnesses were Miguel Noe senior, his

son Miguel junior, Andrés Sandoval, José Ramón Valencia, Alfred Sherwood, Captain John Snowball, and a surprising figure who appeared from nowhere, Don Miguel Lauro Peralta y Vásquez, described as a newly discovered third cousin of the second baron.

Miguel Noe was an elderly Mexican merchant residing in San Francisco. He testified that he had been a close friend of Don José Ramón Carmen de Maso y Castilla, that gentleman sport who had married Doña Sofía de Peralta. Through Maso he met the old baron, whom he recalled vividly as a dignified and charming old gentleman, in full possession of his faculties in spite of his great age. He also remembered little Carmelita Sofía Loreta Micaela—none other than the present Mrs. Reavis—whom he had first held in his arms when she was only two and a half weeks old. The baby had been brought to San Francisco by her grandmother, Señora Maso, and John A. Treadway, the kindly farmer who had provided hospitality for the grief-stricken family after Doña Sofía's death.

Miguel Noe's memory about all the events of some twenty years before proved prodigious. He stated that José Maso sailed to Cádiz in August, 1863, while the old baron remained in San Francisco for another ten months before following his son-in-law. Little Carmelita had been taken for a brief visit to San Francisco to be kissed good-bye by her father. Later Noe had accompanied the old baron to Sherwood Valley to see that the child and her grandmother were well cared for. After the baron's departure for Spain, Noe received several communications from him and also from his friend José Maso, but he was unfortunately unable to produce the letters after all these years.

The witness said he had heard of Don Miguel's demise in the country of his ancestors and, about 1866, of the untimely death of his friend José Maso. Regarding it as his duty, he traveled in that year to Sherwood Valley and found Carmelita a bouncing and healthy little toddler. Again, in 1872, he visited her when she was staying with Captain Snowball at Knights Landing, and he had been glad to see that the child, by then a beautiful ten-year-old girl, was treated by the Snowball family as their own daughter.

Noe's son, Miguel junior, was able to bear out his father's testimony. He recalled that, as a lad of nine, he had accompanied the old baron on several hunting expeditions into the Coast Ranges; this only showed that at eighty Don Miguel Silva Jesús must have been a very fit old gentleman. The younger Noe stated that the baron several times mentioned a great fortune into which his granddaughter would come one day and said that he had made provisions for rewarding the Noes for all their kindness.

Andrés Sandoval obliged Reavis with a deposition of great usefulness. Reavis had met him through Noe, who remembered that Sandoval kept the boardinghouse in Monterey Boulevard, near Balboa Park, where the baron and Maso stayed for a time. Sandoval corrected Noe on this: it was the grandmother and the baby who had been his guests, while the two men stayed at the Balboa Hotel nearby. He well remembered the dignified figure of the Baron de Peralta, and dapper and voluble José Maso, whose gaiety, alas, was damped by his grief for his young wife and by the knowledge that soon he would be parted from his little daughter.

José Ramón Valencia had been a waiter at Sandoval's restaurant, and he, too, recalled the Peralta family, who used to take their meals at the guesthouse in Monterey Boulevard; he well remembered the baby girl.

Alfred Sherwood, the owner of the big ranch, signed an affidavit, testifying that in July, 1862, an American settler, John A. Treadway, who had a small farm in Sherwood Valley, brought to his house a Mexican or Indian woman and a newborn child. Treadway asked him to put up the woman and the baby girl, her granddaughter.

Asked by Broadhead to recall the event as well as he could, Sherwood stated: "Treadway said that the woman and the child would remain for a time, but he didn't know for how long."

"Did Treadway give you further information?" Broadhead asked.

"He said something that the child would probably come into a big fortune one day, that he was promised remuneration for his trouble and, as he had to go away, I should take good care of the child, and that I would be paid for my trouble and expenses."

"Did you ask him about the child's history?"

"Treadway several times intimated that there were certain secrets connected with the history of the case and that the safety of the child would not admit of his giving me the whole history of the case . . . and I did not press him for any further answer at that time."

Treadway never came back and left the valley soon after. Sherwood never received any payment; but his wife grew to love the child, and Carmelita was brought up with their children. When she was eight years old, Captain John W. Snowball, a wealthy rancher, got in touch with Sherwood. Snowball desired to adopt a girl and had heard of the little orphan living at Sherwood's farm.

In his affidavit Captain Snowball could only confirm that he collected the girl from Sherwood Farm and that she lived in his family until she was about fifteen. That was in 1876, when she wanted to learn dressmaking. She then lived with a Mrs. Bradshaw who kept a millinery and dressmaking shop in Sacramento, returned in 1880 to Knights Landing, where, for a time, she looked after the Snowball family, and finally left to take a domestic job with a Mrs. Laughnour at Woodland.

Reavis had taken good care that these depositions were published in newspapers. Articles appeared in the San Francisco *Call* and in the *Examiner*. Reavis had filed his suit at Santa Fe and had kept the clerk of the court, William Strover, busy for days with the unpacking and sorting of the mass of documents.

Strover later told reporters that the baron and several lawyers or secretaries "drove up in an express wagon and an array of boxes and packages, all marked 'Peralta Grant,' were unloaded." Three long tables, placed end to end, were covered with documents, ancient books, pictures, including a large oil painting of the Baron de Peralta, in his robes as a grandee of Spain. "There were documents with large leaden seals attached and signed by the king of Spain. There was a complete history of the marquis, letters to him and from him."*

In the autumn of 1893, Reavis believed the time had come to take up residence once again within his realm. The loyal Pedro Cuervo with four or five tough-looking Mexicans preceded the baronial family, but it seems that he found the palace at Arizola not in the condition of comfort expected by his master. When Reavis, his wife, the twins, and their servants arrived, they took, therefore, accommodations at the Sanitarium Hotel, built only shortly before, when a small settlement sprang up near the baron's palace and a Southern Pacific Railroad station was established in 1892 at Arizola. Cuervo hired a team of Papago workmen; they cleaned and painted the house, tended the overgrown gardens, and restored the baronial palace to its previous glory.

Reavis had brought with him a Stockton civil engineer, James B. Whitney, who had had experience of the San Joaquin Valley irrigations. Accompanied by Cuervo and Mexican bodyguards, Reavis and Whitney rode for many days over the valleys of the Gila and the Santa Cruz. New great irrigation projects were soon after announced by the Casa Grande Corporation in illustrated leaflets, and in the spring of 1894 the San Francisco *Examiner* published a series of articles, probably written by Reavis, expounding the new schemes.

* *Arizona Magazine*, September, 1910, Vol. X, p. 5.

Many new settlers, who had no experience of the baron's agents and their extortion campaign in the mid-1880's, looked with interest and even with approval at these projects, which could bring great prosperity to the new Gila Valley settlements. Some of them received Reavis with friendliness and deference, and he could move about without fear. The reception was, however, a mixed one. Those who recalled his previous activities were hostile, and on some occasions the baron's party had to move on quickly to escape rough handling.

Tom Weedin at Florence had gone into action again and repeated his warnings in the *Enterprise*. Undaunted, Reavis proclaimed that he was "to undertake the colonization of the Peralta estates and . . . while not wishing to appear in the light of a man who praises his own property . . . [he] could say that all who had traveled over the Barony admit that its resources are superb."

Driven by curiosity, rather than by hope of any tangible results, Tom Weedin went to Arizola to see Reavis. They had not met since that memorable day, nearly ten years earlier, when Reavis had tried to bribe the editor and only succeeded in fanning up the great resistance movement. But this time the baron was not eager to revive his acquaintance with his old adversary. When Weedin arrived at Arizola, the baron was away on one of his surveying tours. Weedin never got past the front gate, where two wild-looking Mexicans, incongruously dressed in knee breeches and coats with gilt epaulets and brass buttons, like some Spanish bullfighters, and armed to the teeth, turned him away.

The only glimpse Weedin had of the baronial family was of the twins, escorted by an Indian nurse and two bodyguards. The babies were sheathed in gold embroidered frocks of heavy purple velvet. He also spotted the baroness, clad in regal black, as she strolled in the garden. She spoiled the effect by lifting her skirts and running pell-mell for the house, when Weedin called across the stockade to ask her permission to enter. Reavis apparently had forbidden his wife to talk to any strangers in his absence.

While the baron and his family were enjoying the last sojourn within the frontiers of their estates, Matthew Reynolds was completing his plans for the great exposure. After Christmas, 1893, he sent Severo Mallet-Prevost and William Tipton, the handwriting expert, to Tucson to make an examination of the documents filed there with the first claim in 1883, based on the Willing papers. They had already made a thorough study of the documents which Reavis had filed at Santa Fe.

Then Mallet-Prevost went to Mexico. He spent several weeks at Mexico City and Guadalajara. Before he left for Santa Fe in April, 1894, he sent a preliminary report to Reynolds saying that he was "entirely convinced of the spurious character of every paper there filed," but he suggested that a search was needed in the *Archives de Indias* in Seville and the royal archives in Madrid in order to prove that the Peralta Grant had never existed.

It took some effort to persuade the Government to approve the appropriation for Mallet-Prevost's journey to Spain. After some delay, the Spanish expert sailed early in June, arrived in Madrid on June 12, and received all necessary assistance from the U.S. minister, J. F. Taylor. Although he reported to Reynolds that he "found the Spanish officials bound down by a far greater amount of red tape than their Mexican brethren, and that to obtain the orders necessary to examine the archives great patience had to be exercised," he concluded his investigations with startling results and returned to New York on August 15, 1894.

At the *Archivos de Indias* at Seville, Mallet-Prevost interviewed the curator José Quintano, who well remembered Reavis' visit in 1886. He told the special investigator that Reavis had searched for several weeks for documents of which he, Quintano, had never heard before. The visitor came with letters of introduction from high-placed people in Madrid. He was so amiable and knowledgeable about the history of Spanish possessions in America that Quintano gave him a free run of the archives, assuming that Reavis was just a cranky American enchanted with ancient history. The winter of 1886 was severe, and Quintano, suffering from influenza, had to stay for some days in bed at his home. When he returned to his office, Reavis triumphantly led him to one of the shelves.

"Look at this, Señor Quintano," he exclaimed. "Here, in case seventy-seven, in drawer number three, I found the *legajo* [file] which contains most of the documents I was trying to find. It's a wonderful discovery, you must admit. I have found documents of whose existence you and the other archivists had no knowledge, and I claim some credit for having thus enriched the research into the history of Nueva España in the eighteenth century."

Quintano looked at the documents and was not particularly impressed. They referred to the Peralta Grant, but they consisted mainly of single leaves, stuck to other documents which contained no reference at all to the Peralta case. The archivist grew a little suspicious and ordered one of his clerks, Antonio Juárez, to watch *el americano* at his further searches.

After a few days Juárez came to his chief in a perturbed state. He reported that "Mr. Addison" (he got a little mixed up about Reavis' names) had tried to put into one of the files a document which he apparently had brought in from outside. Quintano took a written deposition from his clerk, which he showed to Mallet-Prevost. This was what Antonio Juárez had stated in 1886:

> Mr. Addison began to examine the *legajo* No. 72, which he continued to study at great length on the 14th, 16th and 17th, and on the 18th he continued to examine a bulky *expediente*

[dossier]. Having completed his examination, he did not ask for another file, but I noticed that he began turning back through the file, from the end to the beginning, constantly stopping in an extraordinary manner. A short time before the closing of the reading room the only *legajo* upon the table [was] to his left and . . . in front of him [was] only the *expediente* . . . his notes and a glass of water. Then, in an instant, I saw [Mr. Addison taking] with [his] right hand . . . an envelope from his coat pocket, holding his handkerchief in his left. He then called me to the table, showed me the document saying simply that he needed a certified copy of that document.*

This document was folded lengthwise. No other documents were thus folded, and moreover, all the documents but that which Reavis asked to be copied bore rubber stamps and numbers of the archives. Quintano examined the document and had strong suspicions that it was not authentic. He assumed that Reavis had tried to insert it into the *legajo,* having brought it into the room in the white envelope which the clerk had noticed.

The director of the archives withdrew Reavis' permit to search the archives. Then it was discovered that during Quintano's illness the American had asked for and been supplied with a number of certified copies of documents which he said were extracted from other *legajos.* The archivist now suspected that these documents or parts of them had also have been brought into the building by Reavis, inserted into the files, and then "discovered." This, in fact, was exactly what did happen.

Reavis was asked to return all the certified copies for examination. When he refused, Quintano reported the matter to the *juez de paz* of the criminal court in Seville, and criminal proceedings were begun by the police. By then Reavis had left Seville, and when the case was transferred to the Madrid police,

* Written testimony (in English translation) presented by the Government at trial of the case, Santa Fe, June, 1895.

some of his high-placed friends succeeded in quashing the investigations.

Mallet-Prevost went to Madrid and retraced Reavis' steps in the capital in 1886. He discovered his discreet quarters near the Cathedral of San Isidro and interviewed the landlady, who told him how Reavis had spent many an evening and night writing on ancient-looking documents and how he ordered her not to disturb the collection of little jars and bowls, containing inks and chemicals, brushes, and quill pens, which stood on his table.

The incidents at Seville tallied with the results of certain inquiries Mallet-Prevost had made in Mexico before his trip to Spain. There, too, suspicion was expressed by the archivists about some of the documents which Reavis had so luckily "discovered" in some unexpected places and among files quite unrelated to land grants. This was established after the investigators made a second visit to Guadalajara in the autumn of 1894.

In the meantime, Reynolds and his two Secret Service agents, Levi A. Hughes and Peter Brady, were as busy in California as Mallet-Prevost had been in Spain. Reynolds decided to re-examine several of the California witnesses. As it was his duty, he notified Reavis of these new sessions, but strangely, neither Reavis nor any of his lawyers put in an appearance. The main reason for this was that Reavis was running out of money to pay his attorneys' fees. Indeed, several of them, either because they had become suspicious of the case or, more likely, because Reavis already owed them their honoraria, withdrew from the case; among them were Philip B. Thompson and John H. Knabel. Reavis had also lost the help of James O. Broadhead, whom President Cleveland had appointed minister to Switzerland.

Before Reynolds began taking depositions in the winter of 1894, he sent Tipton to interview Surveyor General Johnson at Tucson, while Special Agent Brady visited Phoenix and talked

to many citizens, including James Monihon—the man who had
stood at the cradle of the Peralta Grant, when he first met Dr.
Willing in 1866 at Prescott—who had since become mayor of
Phoenix. Special Agent Hughes traveled to the Mission of San
Salvador—the birthplace of the baroness—and discovered that
Reavis had paid another visit there in 1892. Hughes also talked
to Father P. J. Stockman and Father Joseph O'Reilly. During
Reavis' first visit Father Stockman had been absent from the
mission house, and Father O'Reilly had, in good faith, given the
visitor certified copies of some birth and death certificates.
When Father Stockman returned and was told about it, he
examined the book and discovered with dismay that somebody
had doctored the church register by removing leaves and sub-
stituting others. Some entries, referring to the birth of twins
named Peralta Maso and to the death of a woman of the same
name, had been forged.

During his inquiries into the background of the San Francisco witnesses, Special Agent Tipton accomplished a remarkable piece of detection. He found an attorney of doubtful
repute, named William W. Allen, who some years earlier had
defended Miguel Noe on a charge of some petty crime.

Anxious not to become involved in what looked like a serious
case, Allen volunteered startling information to Tipton. He
said that shortly before the first testimony takings, he had drawn
up an agreement between Mr. James Peraltareavis, the Baroness
de Peralta, and a Mrs. Elena Campbell. This agreement provided for a payment of $50,000 to Mrs. Campbell for certain
unspecified services. As it happened, Mrs. Campbell was a
daughter-in-law of Miguel Noe senior, the star witness who had
testified of his friendship with the second baron and José Maso.

At first Allen pretended to know nothing of the services
required of Noe by Mr. Peraltareavis. He said he had mislaid
the draft of the agreement. But cautioned by the special agent
that he would be an accessory to a criminal act if he did not tell

the full truth, Allen repented and made a clean breast of his secret.

He had been approached by Reavis with the suggestion of finding for him some people, preferably Spaniards or Mexicans, who, for a generous payment, would be prepared to testify in a litigation. In short, Reavis was trying to buy witnesses ready to perjure themselves, and Allen in return for a good fee supplied them.

He found Noe, and Noe found Sandoval and José Ramón Valencia. It was just a bunch of little crooks, ready to sell their own grandmothers. There were many meetings between Reavis and these men, and the conspiracy was cunningly staged and well rehearsed. Eventually Allen signed the following statement:

> Reavis spent a great deal of time instructing Miguel Noe as to the appearance, personal customs, habits and manners of José Maso and the old Baron, and to instruct them where and how they appeared in San Francisco, and where and how they disappeared.
>
> Noe's testimony concerning the Peralta case was prepared in my office by Reavis, some written by his own hand. Noe and the other men were instructed to memorize all these details and to swear that the events were true.

Allen eventually became worried about his own ignominious part, and he told the special agent that when he realized that Reavis wanted to use these false witnesses not in some civil litigation but in a claim against the United States Government involving many millions of dollars, his patriotic sentiments were aroused, and he "drove Reavis from the office, denounced him, and warned Mr. Noe to proceed no further in such a transaction."

This was, of course, only after Allen had pocketed his fee. Noe did not follow the attorney's advice and, indeed, did

proceed, presenting himself as a very plausible witness endowed
with an enviable memory. Allen threw himself on the mercy of
the Government investigators, but he still had some odd notions
about the administration of justice. He wrote to Reynolds: "I
will work for you and produce all witnesses . . . who will
discredit Reavis's evidence . . . for a fee of $15,000 and Gov-
ernment transportation for myself and a stenographer."

Reynolds could have asked for warrants and put the whole
gang behind lock and bars on charges of perjury and conspiracy,
but he may have been deriving some amusement from playing a
cat-and-mouse game with the Baron of Arizona. He decided to
leave the perjurers at large and produce them at the trial.

In October, 1894, a commission of the Santa Fe court, headed
by Judge Thomas C. Fuller and including Severo Mallet-
Prevost and Special Agent William Tipton, traveled to Guadalajara to take the official testimony, corroborating Mallet-
Prevost's earlier findings. The investigations centered on the
famous royal cedula of December 20, 1748, the document which
first mentioned the grant of the estates to Don Miguel de
Peralta. The chief archivist of the Ayuntamiento, Emitirio
Robles Gil, was asked whether he had searched for that original
document, and he stated that he had searched the archives with
the greatest of care; but he never found it. But, surprisingly, Gil
did find a *legajo* containing certain documents of a public
notary, Diego de la Sierra y Dueñes, which went back to the late
seventeenth century, more than fifty years before the legendary
Miguel de Peralta arrived in America from Spain and some
twenty years before he was born. Among these documents
which dealt with land grants, there were two mentioning the
Peralta Grant, but after closer examination they were found
"notoriously not genuine."

Gil recalled Reavis' visit in the company of Rufus Hopkins,
the clerk at the Tucson office of the late Arizona Surveyor
General Joseph W. Robbins. It became obvious that, as later in

Madrid, Reavis had produced by a sleight of hand a few prepared forgeries, inserted them into a convenient file, discovered
them, shown them to Hopkins, and obtained certified copies.
Apart from being a master forger, Reavis had excelled in
seeding and planting forged documents wherever he wanted to
discover them afterward.

Reynolds, in the meantime, continued the reexamination of
witnesses. In December he went to San Francisco. He questioned Miguel Noe again, and the old man staunchly stuck to
his original story: yes, he had known the baron; yes, he had
been a friend of José Maso; yes, he did visit the little orphan
girl; yes, he knew she had great expectations as an heiress— He
may have feared that if he had admitted his lies, he would be
taken in custody, so he played for time. In the end he succeeded
in outwitting Reynolds and the police. When the perjurers'
gang was eventually rounded up, Miguel Noe was found to have
disappeared; he escaped to Mexico and was never apprehended.

Asked about the $50,000 deal with Reavis, Noe had tried to
furnish a plausible explanation: "Mr. Reavis appointed me his
agent. I was to try to raise money amongst my friends in San
Francisco to be invested in the Peralta Grant schemes; my own
son, Luis, was to invest five thousand dollars. The payments Mr.
Reavis made to my daughter-in-law were to induce my son and
his business associates to become investors."

It did not make much sense, but Reynolds left it at that. He
turned to Noe's visits to Sherwood Valley.

"Do you remember when you visited Mr. Sherwood and saw
the child, now Reavis' wife, in charge of her grandmother,
Carmelita Maso?" Reynolds asked.

"Yes, it was in 1864. That was the first time."

"And when was the second time?"

"I believe in 1868, but it might have been later."

"You knew that this child had an interest in a large tract of
land in Arizona and that she was of noble Spanish birth?"

"Yes, sir," was Miguel Noe's firm reply.

"You knew that fact at that time?"

"Yes, sir. Don Miguel de Peralta, Mr. Maso, and Mrs. Carmelita Maso told me about it, and also that the child was born at Agua Mansa, near San Bernardino, the place now called Riverside."

There was little that Reynolds could do with the stubborn old man.

Reynolds summoned Alfred Sherwood. But before he questioned Carmelita's former foster father, he heard two other witnesses, of whom James Reavis had no previous knowledge at all. They had been found by Secret Service Agent Levi Hughes.

One was Hiram Hatch, an elderly farmer from Sherwood Valley, who for many years had known both Alfred Sherwood and John Treadway, the man who had brought the baby to Sherwood's home. Reynolds first asked him about Treadway.

"Yes, I have known him. I saw him at Sherwood's house; for a time they lived together," Hatch replied.

"Was Treadway a man of family?" Reynolds asked.

"Yes, sir, certainly he was."

"Who constituted his family?"

"An Indian squaw and one child."

"It is said Treadway left the valley and returned with a small child and her grandmother and a Mexican nurse. If the women and the child had stayed at Treadway's house, would you have known it?"

"I should think I would."

"Can you say whether there was a woman at Sherwood's house by the name of Carmelita Maso, the grandmother of the child?"

"I never heard of her," said Hatch.

The other witness was an Indian woman, called Jennie Mack, who had been a domestic servant with the Sherwoods for many years. Reynolds asked her whether she remembered a little girl and her grandmother staying at Sherwood's. She remembered the little girl well but did not know anything about a grand-mother.

"Do you remember Mr. John Snowball coming to Mr. Sher-wood's house and taking away the little girl?"

"Yes, sir."

"What was the girl's name?"

"Sofía, but we also called her Carmelita."

"Whose child was she? Treadway's?"

"Yes, sir."

"Who was her mother?"

"She had no mother, sir. Her mother left her."

"Do you know who her mother was, and what was this woman's name?"

"Yes, sir, she was Mr. Treadway's squaw, and her name was Kate."

There were several other witnesses from Sherwood Valley, who had known Treadway, his squaw, Kate, and the little girl. Some, like a man named Tom Williams, described Treadway as a ne'er-do-well and said that Treadway was ostracized by Ameri-can settlers because he lived in sin with an Indian woman. They remembered that the woman Kate had run away one day and had left her baby girl behind. Treadway took the child to Sherwood's. None of the witnesses had ever heard of the Peralta family or of the birth of twins and the death of a woman journeying in the district. Nobody had ever seen a grandmother of the child, supposed to be a Spanish or Mexican lady.

Reynolds then called Alfred Sherwood. The rancher was visibly embarrassed. He had heard that several witnesses from his valley had been summoned, and this time his testimony was very different from that taken in the presence of Reavis and Broadhead. Then he had answered leading questions cleverly put to him. This time he was entirely frank.

"Mr. Sherwood, do you know a man by the name of John W. Snowball?" Reynolds asked.

"Yes, sir, I do."

"Do you remember the occasion when he obtained from you a young girl?"

"I do."

"Did you know that child from its infancy?"

"Yes, sir, nearly since her infancy. I was away from home when she was brought by Treadway, but I knew her when she was about two months old."

"Who was the child's reputed father?"

"John A. Treadway."

"Do you know who was the reputed mother of that child?"

"She was an Indian woman, who lived with Treadway."

"Do you remember the year in which the child was said to be born?"

"She was said to be born in March, 1863."

"Now, Mr. Sherwood, were there any Spanish women, or one woman, living in your house in 1862 or 1863? A woman who might have been the child's grandmother?"

"No, sir."

"Was there during that time, or at any later time, a man by the name of Miguel Noe at your house, as a visitor for three or four days, who came to inquire for the child that you let Snowball have?"

"I do not recollect it. If he had, I think I would have remembered it."

"Well, if such a man had been at your house, in 1864, inquiring after the child and had told you that she was an heiress to a very large fortune, you would probably have remembered it?"

"I would, certainly. It was after Treadway's death, and such an inquiry would have caused me to make a mental note of it, certainly."

"Mr. Sherwood," said Reynolds with emphasis, "I ask you again, was there a woman said to be Spanish, by the name of Carmelita Maso, and said to be the grandmother of this girl, living in your house from the summer of 1862 continuously until 1865 or 1866?"

"No, sir. Never."

"Is it not a fact that along about 1877 this girl Sofía, or Carmelita, came back to your place with a man by the name of James Addison Reavis, whom she represented to be either her guardian or her husband, and asked you to let her have the picture of her father, that she wanted to have it enlarged and would return the original to you?"

"I do not recollect the circumstances. I believe Reavis came along and took a picture away."

"Mr. Sherwood, will you please state fully the statements that were made to you in 1887 or thereafter, by the man J. A. Reavis, as to the title to the property known as the Peralta Grant in Arizona, and how this girl became interested in it. Please state it in your own way," Reynolds demanded.

Alfred Sherwood thought hard for a few moments and then said, "Reavis and his wife came in 1887 to my house. I believe they had returned from a trip to Europe. He told me that the Baron of Arizona had made a deed to benefit this girl, of this tract of land in Arizona and New Mexico, it was all deeded to her, and he exhibited some Spanish documents, told me they were genuine."

Sherwood paused and, with disarming honesty, added, "Sir, the only plea I have for doing what I have was my solicitude for the girl, and I told him anything I could do I would, and he said all he desired was a short statement. . . . Two or three times he exhibited those documents coming from Spain and one purporting to be a deed from the Baron of Arizona."

"What did he say about identifying his wife with Carmelita Maso?"

"I think he said that some formal steps would be necessary. He asked me to make an affidavit in the first place in 1887."

"Later on he came back and prepared a statement, did he not, so that the connection [between his wife and Carmelita Maso] could be made?" asked Reynolds.

"Yes, sir. He prepared such a statement."

"Do you remember the date of your first testimony?"

"It was on the sixteenth of October, 1890."

"Now, the memoranda of your statements that were made at that time were made up by Reavis, as to the mother, father, etc., of that girl, were they not?"

"Yes, sir. Reavis outlined it."

Sherwood again assured the Government attorney that all he wanted to do, when he signed the affidavit and made the statements, was to help the girl whom he had known almost from birth.

Although the evidence Mallet-Prevost had brought from Spain showed beyond question Reavis' machinations at the archives at Seville and Madrid, the law required that testimony be given by the Spanish officials before a judicial commission. Thus, after a conference with the U.S. Attorney General Richard Olney in Washington and an exchange of diplomatic notes between the State Department and the Spanish Foreign Ministry, Judge Wilbur F. Stone, accompanied by Mallet-Prevost, left New York on January 5, 1895. They returned from Spain at the beginning of March.

The net was now rapidly closing. Reynolds and Mallet-Prevost were sifting the final evidence in preparation for the trial. The chief justice of the Court of Private Land Claims had fixed the opening date of the trial at Santa Fe for May 30, 1895.

Poor Reavis had learned little of what had been going on during the past few months. He was pursued by ill luck such as he had never experienced before. Before embarking on the protracted trial of the Peralta case, the Santa Fe court had in quick succession dealt with a series of minor claims, and one after another was dismissed. In several judgments the court pronounced that "claims based on fraudulent evidence would inevitably result in criminal prosecution of the perpetrators."

The warning was understood by Reavis backers, as well as by his attorneys. One by one deserted him. Even Harvey S. Brown, who had represented him for more than sixteen years, ever since he first met him at Huntington's and Crocker's offices, and who had become his close personal friend, notified the court that he was withdrawing from the case without as much as bothering to tell Reavis about it beforehand.

Reavis had given up his sumptuous offices at the Dunhoe Building in San Francisco; he could not afford the rent or the salaries for his clerks. From a modest apartment house, where he now lived with his wife and the twins, he indefatigably wrote letter after letter to his influential friends in New York, Washington, St. Louis, and Los Angeles. Most of these letters remained unanswered. The men who had once eagerly and greedily backed his fantastic schemes had seen the red light and chose to forget their dealings with the Baron of Arizona. They preferred to write off the money they had advanced rather than become involved in criminal proceedings, as it now seemed to be almost certain.

Newspaper reporters had ferreted out information from Reynolds and Mallet-Prevost and predicted a sticky end for the baron. Reavis tried in vain to enlist once again the help of Huntington, Crocker, and the other California tycoons. Their doors remained firmly shut for him.

Such mail as arrived brought only news of woe. Unable to pay mortgage instalments and interests for loans he had raised on his houses in Chihuahua and St. Louis and being in arrears with land taxes and other duties, he saw his properties put up for auction by his creditors and municipal authorities. He had long since disposed of his mansion in Spain and had sold his wife's jewels. By the spring of 1895 he was almost penniless.

On top of all this, Reavis learned—probably with a wry smile—that a committee had been formed of 106 persons residing in many parts of the United States, all named Peralta, all insisting on being direct descendants of the legendary baron, and all claiming a share in the Barony of Arizona. It was not exactly to the credit of the legal profession when a distinguished lawyer, Judge J. T. Kinney, of San Diego, accepted the brief to represent the Peralta claim at the Santa Fe trial, although in fairness it must be added that he withdrew on the opening day, as soon as he had glanced through the evidence submitted by Attorney Reynolds.

When the opening date of the trial arrived, Reavis found himself without a legal adviser, even without an attorney to go with him to Santa Fe.

12

The Trial

It was a cruel twist of fate that the trial which destroyed the Baron of Arizona was held at the city founded nearly 300 years before by a real Peralta. For more than 200 years La Villa Real de la Santa Fe de San Francisco de Assisi was the capital of the vast Spanish provinces ruled by sixty governors, protecting the Spanish empire in America from the Indians and the encroaching French, English, and American invaders from the north.

The flags of royal Spain, of Emperor Augustín of Mexico, of the Mexican Republic, the American Confederacy, and the United States of America have flown over the *palacio* which Don Pedro de Peralta, third governor of Nuevo Mejico, had built in 1609 at a spot which the Pueblo Indians called "the place of the shell beads near the water." His palace still stands on the north side of the plaza, symbol of the ancient history of Santa Fe, the oldest capital within the boundaries of the United States.

The Court of Private Land Claims assembled at ten o'clock in the morning on Monday, June 3, 1895, at the Federal Building in Lincoln Avenue, only two blocks from the Peralta palace. With the last chime of the hour still booming from the nearby Cathedral of San Francisco, the five judges filed into the courtroom. Chief Justice Joseph R. Reed, a dignified bearded figure, led his associate judges Thomas C. Fuller, William W. Murray, Henry C. Sluss, and Wilbur F. Stone.

The usher called the case: "James Addison Peraltareavis, Doña Sofía Loreta Micaela Reavis, and Clinton F. Farrell* against the United States of America." There was a hush in the crowded court, where the throng of newspaper reporters had overflowed from the press benches into the public gallery, as everybody looked toward the door for the entry of the Baron of Arizona and his wife. But although the names of the plaintiffs were thrice called, there was no response. The clerk then announced that the Honorable Matthew Given Reynolds, assisted by Mr. Summers Burkhart and special counsel Severo Mallet-Prevost appeared for the defendant, the Government of the United States.

The presiding judge inquired whether the claimants were represented by counsel, but the clerk said that none had appeared on their behalf. Chief Justice Reed then ordered the adjournment of the court until two o'clock in the afternoon.

When the court resumed, there was still no sight of Reavis or anyone to plead on the claimants' behalf. The presiding judge then invited the government attorney to present his case.

Matthew Reynolds made a brief opening statement, reserving his right to make a fuller submission at a later stage. He said that the claim covered an area of 12,100,000 acres in Arizona and parts of two counties in southwestern New Mexico, Fertile valleys like those of the Salt and Gila Rivers, the White Mountains, the San Carlos, Pima, and Maricopa Indian reservations, and such cities and towns as Phoenix, Florence, Maricopa, Globe, Solomonsville, and Clifton, and numerous settlements

---

* Farrell was the trustee of one of the syndicates which had financed the claim. Although he did not appear in the case, his name remained on the docket.

in western New Mexico were included within its boundaries. Its value was about $95,000,000.

"This claim is a fraud and I am prepared to prove it," he said quietly. "The chief claimants are James Addison Reavis, formerly of St. Louis, and his wife, who is alleged to be the great-granddaughter and only living heir of Baron Miguel de Peralta who had received a grant to these lands from the king of Spain.

"The Government's submission to this court is," Reynolds continued, "that no such Spaniard as Miguel de Peralta ever existed; that such a grant was never decreed by the king of Spain or located in Arizona by the viceroy of New Spain; that Mrs. Sofía Loreta Micaela Peraltareavis, the wife of James Addison Peraltareavis, the alleged sole heir of the imaginary Baron Miguel de Peralta, is really the daughter of one John A. Treadway and a Digger Indian squaw known as Kate, and that she was born in Sherwood Valley, Mendocino County, California, and is in no wise related to any Spanish family; that every document and record submitted or filed by the plaintiffs is manufactured or was forged and surreptitiously inserted in the various archives of Spain and Mexico; that James Addison Peraltareavis was in 1886 in Spain discovered in the act of attempting to leave among the archive files forged evidence of title, that proceedings against him were taken in Spain, and that having made his escape, the said James Addison Peraltareavis is a fugitive from justice."

While most of the Government attorney's submissions were already known, his disclosure of Reavis' alleged misdemeanor in Spain caused a stir in the courtroom. Reynolds' statement that Reavis was "a fugitive from justice," even though only from Spanish justice, was immediately interpreted to mean that the Baron of Arizona might be facing arrest and criminal proceedings. Indeed, this was one of the main reasons why Harvey S. Brown, the last of his lawyers, had withdrawn from the case on the instruction of the Big Four as soon as they had seen the Brief for the Defendant, circulated by Reynolds in February.

Next to rise was Judge J. T. Kinney, of San Diego, repersenting 106 ex parte claimants, all of them relatives of the real Miguel Peralta, the prospector is Wickenburg who in 1864 or later had made the deal, true or imaginary, with Willing. Kenney addressed the court:

"I feel as though it was due to this honorable court and due to my clients and due to myself that I make a statement of the position I occupy. The case I had the honor of commencing on behalf of the Peralta relatives and the one filed by Mr. Reavis have been consolidated and must be tried together. So far we have relied entirely upon Mr. Reavis to collect the testimony to establish the grant which he claims. I represent what are known as the Peralta heirs, lineal descendants of Miguel Peralta. Before assuming the position of these persons, who live five hundred miles from where I reside, I had them all gathered together and personally spent a number of days in ascertaining that they were without doubt such lineal descendants of Mr. Miguel Peralta of Wickenburg.

"That was about three years ago, and they were induced to take this step from the fact that Mr. Reavis had published to the world through the newspapers that he had indubitable evidence that there was a grant made by the viceroy of New Spain to a Don Miguel de Peralta. Proceeding upon this basis, my clients instituted this suit, and not being financially able themselves to accumulate the evidence to establish this grant, they depended entirely upon Mr. Reavis' evidence.

"Now, if twenty years of labor and something like a quarter of a million dollars, which is said to have been expended, have failed to establish the existence of such a grant, then we necessarily fall with it, for we based and predicted our hopes and expectations upon the grant being established by Mr. Reavis. Now, if Your Honors please, the government attorney yesterday afternoon placed in my hands the printed evidence upon which he largely depends, and to my mind it did seem, even from a cursory examination, as though the grant, or supposed grant, was a fabrication, and if such it turns out to be before this honorable court. I want it distinctly understood that we have nothing to do with it.

"We wash our hands of all of it," Kinney said, raising his voice. To make it quite clear that he now wanted no truck with the Baron of Arizona, he added, "I only saw Mr. Reavis once in my life, and that was at Tucson for three or four minutes, and in that conversation I called upon him to get his book of evidence, which he refused to give me. He also insulted my clients by saying that their petition was nothing but a blackmailing affair."

In his concluding statement Kinney was somewhat confused, saying that he and his clients disclaimed any connection with Reavis and the frauds that he might have committed and that the case was a source of embarrassment to him. This was very obvious from his demeanor, but Kinney added, "If the grant was to be established by this honorable court, then the Peralta clients as heirs of Miguel Peralta would investigate their rights in the lower courts."

The respected Judge Kinney of San Diego had, of course, been greatly perturbed about the possible damage to his reputation which his appearance in the Peralta case could have caused. By washing his hands of the case, he prejudged it without waiting for the court's decision, but it seemed that he still wanted to keep the door ajar. Nevertheless, with a deep bow he withdrew and was never seen again in the courtroom, taking the next train to San Diego. Nor was anything ever again heard of the 106 Peralta heirs.

The court could now turn to more serious business. On Tuesday morning, still without Reavis or counsel for the claimants present, the sitting was occupied with the presentation of documents by the defense and the submission of translations made by government experts. These translations were compared with those submitted with the claimants' written evidence. Reynolds called Severo Mallet-Prevost.

The Government's Spanish expert told the court: "One of the important features of this case is the difference between the translations of ancient documents which have been presented by the petitioners and the correct translations of these documents as submitted on behalf of the government. The plaintiffs' translations contain Spanish words and phrases which were absolutely unknown at the time and are absolutely unknown today. The plaintiffs' translators made what is called free translations; they evidently desired that the English should read as smoothly as possible and that the documents should be made to appear [to bring] certain results. A careful comparison of these translations with the original documents shows that they entirely fail to bring out many inaccuracies and grammatical and other errors which are contained in the so-called originals."

Mallet-Prevost implied that the original documents were forged in whole or in part and could not have been written by Spanish scribes at the courts of Madrid or Mexico. He gave many examples of errors and grammatical mistakes. He pointed out that in a number of documents, purported to come from the viceroyal chancery, the indicative was used whereas the subjunctive should have been used in Spanish. Some of the words had no meaning at all, he insisted; others were wrongly used, and some were misspelled.

So far the proceedings had been rather tedious, and interest on the press benches and on the public gallery had begun to flag. But when Reynolds called to the stand William N. Tipton, the audience became electrified. Tipton was the graphology expert, and his opening statement caused a sensation. Holding up the "original documents," which Reavis had filed in 1883 with Surveyor General Johnson at Tucson, and which represented the cedulas of the grant and the report of Father Pauer of 1758, the witness said, "Your Honors, my opinion is that everything appearing upon the title leaf is genuine and that the words appearing thereon were written at the period which they purport to have been."

There was a gasp in court. For a moment, everybody believed that the witness called by the Government had decided to exonerate Reavis. But it was only a dramatic start, perhaps made by Tipton on Reynolds' advice.

"However, this title leaf must have been purloined by the claimant from a Spanish or Mexican archive, and in fact, it has no bearing on the Peralta Grant at all," Tipton continued. "This leaf has been partially covered by a thin piece of yellowish tissue, which has been pasted on. The portion to which I refer is in the words *Relato de la concesión al Señor Don Miguel de Peralta, Caballero de los Colorados.* It is these words which alone on this leaf refer to the Peralta Grant."

The graphologist paused for a moment, cleared his throat, and said, "It is my opinion that these words are written in a modern writing fluid and with a steel pen, and written necessarily at a period much later than the words composing the title page were written.

"The printed cedula following the title page, I have to say, is printed in a modern type—that is, it is not printed in type which was in use in the year 1748, and to the eye of one who is accustomed to the examination of printed Spanish cedulas of that period, there is no resemblance to the genuine cedulas of that time.

"The remainder of the document, which consists of five written pages, is, in my opinion, of the same character as the signature and writing of the first page. . . . It is so poor a simulation of the style of writing then in the vogue in Spanish countries as to make it ridiculous to anyone accustomed to the examination of writings of that kind to set up a claim of its genuineness."

Tipton then told of the seal attached to the second leaf of the document, the royal seal confirming the grant. Again, he described it as perfectly genuine, but added that it had not been impressed on the paper, but had obviously been attached to it at some later date by the use of some adhesive substance. One by one, Reavis' handiworks were thus destroyed by this expert.

For several hours he went on to tell of his investigations at the Ayuntamiento archives at Guadalajara. He told of the folder "discovered" by Reavis, containing papers of the notary Diego de la Sierra y Dueñes dating from the years 1697 and 1698, in which documents relating to the Peralta Grant were found. He said these documents must have been inserted on some recent date into this old folder, and he described them as "patent forgeries."

On the following day Severo Mallet-Prevost took the stand and gave evidence of his visit in Spain and his investigations at the archives at Seville and Madrid. They concerned documents filed by Reavis in 1887. In great detail the witness described these papers and, like Tipton, testified that they presented a mixture of genuine papers and cleverly forged ones. Those which the witness accepted as genuine had, in their original state, nothing to do with the Peralta Grant, but referred to other land grants. Wherever the words "Miguel de Peralta" or references to the Peralta Grant appeared, these words and paragraphs had been written in over erasures. Genuine documents had been purloined and faked to produce evidence of the Peralta Grant.

Some of the sheets were of different paper, but they had been carefully inserted between document leaves which were genuine and bore genuine signatures and seals and had then been sewed together into a book, which was represented as the original of the Peralta Grant. Document after document was now piled on the table in front of the judges. Tipton was recalled and gave a lengthy opinion on several of the documents, spreading before the court papers bearing royal and viceroyal signatures, with attached lead and wax seals. Some were emblazoned with the seal bearing the Peralta coat of arms, and Tipton again insisted that these and much of the writing were forgeries.

It seemed that little more was needed in order to brand Reavis as a crook and his claim as a fraud, but Matthew Reynolds was determined to lead the case to its bitter end for the claimants. He told the court that twenty witnesses would be put on the stand and that Mallet-Prevost would introduce the testimony requisitioned from the archivists at Seville, showing how Reavis had inserted documents and had been caught in the act.

Suddenly there was a commotion at the back of the court. A messenger appeared and handed a telegram to the clerk. Chief Justice Reed put on his spectacles and read the missive. It was a scene like one of those in a Perry Mason courtroom drama.

The judge called Matthew Reynolds, and they had a brief whispered conversation. The Government attorney then addressed the court: "If Your Honors please, in view of the telegram from Mr. Reavis to the chief justice requesting that the trial of this case be continued until Monday the tenth, to enable him to get here, the government is perfectly willing to stop the case and wait until Mr. Reavis can get here. The government is not disposed to push this case unreasonably, and if he comes, we are willing to begin the case over again. If he does not come, we can go right ahead where we have left off."

Chief Justice Reed announced that the court would allow the plaintiff's request and adjourned the session until the next Monday, June 10, at ten o'clock. Previously, sometime before the beginning of the trial, the court had received a letter from Reavis, pleading for a continuance of the case until November.

The letter, which showed the pathetic situation in which Reavis found himself after all his legal advisers had deserted him, read:

You are hereby informed that it is impossible for Plaintiffs to appear at the examination . . . since the Hon. Harvey S. Brown and Hon. Phil. B. Thompson Jr. have withdrawn from the said case as counsel owing to inability to attend the said examination, and since Hon. James O. Broadhead, Minister to Berne, Switzerland, is prohibited by virtue of his office from appearing. . . . Hon. John H. Knabel withdrew peremptorily. . . . It is impossible for the Plaintiffs to appear personally on account of illness and incompetency to proceed without counsel, therefore we pray to adjourn the examination . . . until such time, reasonable, as will enable your Petitioners to secure the service of counsel. They are surprised at the resignation and withdrawal of their attorneys and counsel, which has been sudden and without warning.

But the court was then not prepared to adjourn the case for several months, and the trial began like a performance of *Hamlet* without the prince. On June 6, the day following the adjournment, the Santa Fe *New Mexican* reported:

James Addison Reavis arrived this morning from California, but is not ready to take up the fight. He appeared informally today at the court and asked for a still further continuance of his case. The application is based upon the lack of counsel. His former attorneys all have abandoned him. The judges have not announced a decision, but the Bar believe the matter will go on trial next Monday, as set.

And so it did. On Monday, a week after the trial had begun, the Baron of Arizona made his entry into the courtroom. Every neck was craned, and the presiding judge had to use his gavel repeatedly to restore order and silence.

Dressed in a black frock coat, his silver beard parted into two carefully trimmed long side whiskers, a bulky leather case in his hand, the Baron of Arizona walked erectly the length of the aisle between the seats of the counsel, gravely bowed to the court, and, mounting the step in front of the bench, shook hands first with the chief justice and then with each of the four other judges. He looked dignified and completely composed, and when he stepped back and addressed the court in a loud and solemn voice, he gave the impression, not of a man accused of fraud and forgery, but of a distinguished lawyer addressing his equals.

In a brief fluent speech he repeated his application for an adjournment of the hearing on the grounds that he was without counsel and needed more time for preparing the case. He said he had a complete answer to all the statements made by the Government attorney and the witnesses so far heard for the defense—statements, he said, which he had only read in the press and which were such that he refused to believe they were correct reports of what had been said.

After a brief consultation with the judges, Chief Justice Reed announced that the petition was denied, and he reminded Reavis that his case had been on the docket since February 1, 1893, and had been set for trial since February, 1895. This was regarded as ample time for preparation.

Whether it was a calculated move or Reavis, annoyed by the refusal to postpone the trial, did it on the spur of the moment, he now made a statement that caused a sensation in the court-room and even took the judges aback.

He jumped up and said, "I beg to move that Your Honors dismiss this case."

After years of his fight for recognition and after his having prepared for the trial at extravagant expense for more than four years, this sudden motion looked like utter capitulation. Was he earnest about acting as the gravedigger of the great Peralta claim? Or had he decided that dismissal of the case and an end to further litigation were the only way to escape criminal indictment. He gave no further explanation and, in fact, never disclosed the motives which had prompted him.

His motion was instantly rejected. Chief Justice Reed sternly told him that "important matters of this nature, voluntarily brought before the Court of Private Land Claims, and where titles to large tracts of land were involved, could not be dismissed at the pleasure of claimants, but must be adjudicated." The judge added, "Therefore I order the hearing of the case to continue at ten o'clock tomorrow morning."

The baron took this decision with good grace. He bowed to the judges, gathered his files, and, smiling at the newspaper reporters, left the courtroom in the same dignified manner as that in which he had entered it.

THE BARON OF ARIZONA IS KNOCKED OUT and REAVIS IS IN THE DOCK proclaimed newspaper headlines the following morning. He certainly did not have a good press. When the court reassembled the next day and Matthew Reynolds put him on the stand and for two and a half days subjected him to a merciless examination, everything Reavis said was reported with bitter contempt and gruff sarcasm. Even simple statements about his life and career were twisted into paragraphs damaging the hapless baron who was fighting his desperate battle without a friend and counsel.

But if headlines such as REAVIS SKINNED BY GOVERNMENT ATTORNEY, THE KING OF FRAUDS ENTANGLED IN HIS OWN NET, and THE END OF THE WOULD-BE MONTE CRISTO implied that he was cowed, cringing, and groggy and helplessly taking blow after blow, such an impression was unrelated to what was really happening in court. For many days Reavis dominated the proceedings, making long and involved speeches in a stentorian voice, which, one reporter noted, "could be heard through open windows two blocks away from the courthouse." He dashed back and forth between the witness stand and his table, which was covered with the paper debris of the Peralta Grant, interrupted judges, shouted down Reynolds, and cajoled and abused witnesses; but he also surprised his audience by shrewd observations and amused it by the sparkle of his wit. He fought his last-ditch battle right out to the end, never conceding defeat.

Although he must have known from the start that his case was now irretrievably lost and although all that time he must have been in fear of arrest—since his arrival at Santa Fe he was constantly watched and followed by U.S. Marshal Page B. Otero's detectives—Reavis never flagged. The judges and even Reynolds were impressed by his pluck and his intelligent grasp of legal procedure, and when on several occasions witnesses accused him of fraud and he asked for protection from "such malicious and baseless attacks," the court granted him protection.

When he took the stand he made a long statement about his early career, saying he had been brought up in a happy home and had received a good education and mentioning his meritorious military service during the Civil War. With great skill and fluency he skipped over events in his life which would cast a shadow on his activities, described his prosperous business in St. Louis, and told of his first meeting and subsequent partnership with Dr. George M. Willing, from whom he first learned of the existence of the Peralta Grant.

He proudly recounted his work for the San Francisco *Examiner,* his editorship of the Sacramento weekly paper, and his acquaintance and business deals with Collis P. Huntington, with Senator Stanford, and later with Senator Hearst. "The Southern Pacific Company," he said, "made a contract with me for one-half of the Peralta Grant and had paid me fifty thousand dollars advance money. But afterwards the company broke the contract, and Mr. Huntington and Mr. Crocker told me that the money paid would be for the right of way of their railroad through my estates."

The disclosure that the Big Four had actually been his

partners in the exploitation of the claim, a fact mercifully unmentioned by the Government attorney, made at least for a moment the impression on the court which Reavis obviously intended. Although many newspapers, fearing Huntington's wrath, suppressed this statement, William Randolph Hearst made the most of it in his San Francisco *Examiner*. Hearst was by then engaged in a feud with Huntington, and Reavis' disclosures were splashed across the front pages of the Hearst papers.

Reavis obviously enjoyed telling the visibly embarrassed judges that the late Senator Conkling had been his legal adviser, as had been James Broadhead, and that Robert Green Ingersoll was still the president of several of the Casa Grande companies. Reavis was not in the mood to spare his faithless friends who had deserted him in the hour of his misfortune: "I was in partnership with Mr. Charles Crocker, Mr. Ingersoll, Mr. Henry Porter of the American Bank Note Company, with John W. Mackay, with Ed Stokes, John S. Benson—"

He rattled off names which were household words on Wall Street and at the American Bar. "They, like the late Senator Conkling and many Congressmen, had examined my claim and had found it good and well founded."

He revealed that he and his companies had, at one time, held payments and notes to the value of $5,300,000, given by Arizona settlers and companies, such as the Silver King Mining Company, in recognition of this title to the land they used. Carried away by the stories of his glorious past and enumerating his success and exploits, Reavis made the mistake of thus admitting that for almost fifteen years he had been involved in machinations which the Government attorneys were now only too eager to prove were confidence tricks and criminal frauds.

A reporter for the *Phoenix Gazette,* sending his special dispatches to Phoenix, described the court scene "as intensely dramatic" and wrote: "At times Reavis seems to be hardly in his sober senses, his statements and answers are marked by the most intense excitement."

Reynolds let him rant. He was biding his time to confront Reavis with witnesses and then proceed to administer the *coup de grâce*. The opportunity was soon to come. The attorney began to question him about the Willing papers and his visit to Guadalajara. Reavis gave an account with apparent frankness. He admitted he did not attach too great an importance to the Willing documents.

"But, however spurious these papers might be, they could not have originated in themselves. When I showed the documents I had found in Dr. Willing's gunnysack to Justino Rubio [the custodian of the archives in Mexico City], he said that the signature of the king was a forgery, simply because he had not an original in his archives. I had in Guadalajara a discussion with Don Manuel Cordero [an archivist], and he maintained the king's signature was a stamp. I had no means to contradict him, and I yielded a great deal to his judgment. While we were talking Señor Baltrand, his chief, came into the office, and he identified the document. He said he knew all about it, it had been executed there, and he gave me his card and told me if I needed evidence on that subject and if the Peralta family desired any evidence, he would testify. He mentioned W. W. Gitt, a former resident of St. Louis, Missouri, as being instrumental in proving this evidence. I knew Gitt; he was the man who had rendered the title to me."

"Why did you doubt the genuineness [of the Willing documents]?" Reynolds asked.

"I was in doubt because of what some of the archivists had told me. But then I yielded to Baltrand rather than to Rubio. Baltrand said he knew the documents had been gotten up in that office and that Gitt had the supervision of it. That was very many years ago, soon after the American invasion of Mexico, there were many Americans in that office, and many discrepancies and irregularities occurred."

"You knew Gitt?"

"Yes, Dr. Willing introduced him to me. Gitt was known in St. Louis as the Spanish Land Grant Gitt. Through him I had purchased several Spanish land grants in St. Louis [which had nothing to do with the Peralta Grant], and I made a great deal of money out of these. For that reason I had great confidence in him."

"Do you know what Gitt's reputation was, with reference to grants?"

"Doubtful," Reavis admitted.

"Very doubtful, wasn't it?"

"I know that Gitt had spent several years as a refugee, on account of some transactions. He stated to me that he had served as a surgeon in the Mexican army* and that he knew this family of Peralta, because his service was in Sonora and Jalisco. He vouched for the documents in every way. He was regarded as a very learned man in these matters. Had Señor Baltrand at Guadalajara told me that the title was spurious and that Gitt had gotten it up, I should have had nothing more to do with the Peralta case, but Baltrand said that the originals were there [in the archives]."†

---

* Gitt was a medical man before embarking on his legal career.

† Donald M. Powell, who made a very close study of the Peralta Grant, said that "if anywhere, Reavis here came close to revealing the true origin of the Peralta claim. It probably all began in 1847, when Gitt was involved in a New Madrid land claim. It was discovered that the signer of the deed to Gitt had been dead some time before the deed was made. A warrant was issued for Gitt's arrest, but he escaped, leaving his wife and family behind, eventually got to Mexico and turned up at Guadalajara, where he spent a great deal of time examining records. In Guadalajara, Gitt married again and raised a second family. When he finally left the city, it was found that he had removed some twenty pages from a volume of land records and had substituted an equal number. It is likely that at that time Gitt assembled some of the 'original' Peralta papers, and on his return to St. Louis disposed of them to Dr. Willing. Willing, to complete the chain of possession, had sought out a man by the name of Miguel Peralta in Arizona and obtained from him a deed which made the connection between Gitt's papers and himself."

Thus, the original forgeries would have originated from Gitt who used the drunken former medico as a cat's-paw. He sent him to Reavis with the story of the purchase of the documents from the "old Mexican" across the campfire at the Black Canyon, and Gitt appeared at Reavis' office only after the latter agreed

On the fourth day of the trial Reynolds turned for the first time to the creation of the real heiress and began questioning Reavis about the entries of the birth of the twins and the death of Doña Sofía Peralta de Maso in the San Salvador church register.

Reavis' first answer created a sensation. He firmly denied that he had ever entered the mission house or the Church of San Salvador or had ever met any of the priests.

"But you admitted to have visited the place?" Reynolds asked, for a moment taken aback by this statement.

"Yes, but when I went to San Bernardino, I asked a Mexican barber to go to the church and ask the priest for a certificate of certain entries in the register. I gave the barber five dollars for this."

"How did you know that there were entries of interest to you?"

"I knew, of course, that my wife was born there."

"Why did you not go and get the certificates yourself?"

"Because I didn't wish anybody to know I was looking for them. I have been informed that Father Stockman was a villain of the first water, sir, and I did not wish him to know I had anything to do with this case at all."

Later, when Father Stockman and Father O'Reilly were put on the stand, there was a fantastic scene, Reavis abusing the priests and calling them villains and liars.

Father P. J. Stockman, rector of the Church of San Salvador, an elderly dignified priest, repeated in substance what he had told Secret Service Agent Levi Hughes, when he had called to examine the church books.

---

with Willing to exploit the Peralta Grant. This is the most plausible explanation, although it will never be known whether Reavis actually knew that the "original" documents had been fabricated by Gitt. Probably he did not; otherwise he would not have waited for years to retrieve the papers from Willing's gunnysack at Prescott. The later forgeries, of course, Reavis made himself, and they were greatly superior to Gitt's.

He said that in 1891 or 1892, when he had been absent from
the mission, two men had borrowed the church registers from
his curate, Father Joseph O'Reilly. The priest had brought the
books to court, and he showed them to the judges. He said that
one was of baptisms and the other of burials and that both had
been doctored by the removal of certain leaves and the substitution of others. The handwriting of the entries recording the
births of the Maso twins and the burials of Doña Sofía Peralta
de Maso and her infant son, José Ramón Carveen, had been
well imitated. Father Stockman confirmed that there were no
corresponding entries in the separate index, which Father
O'Reilly had not given his visitors. Instead, the index contained
names of two different babies born on the date under which the
forged entries for the Maso twins had been made. He testified
that there was no trace of any graves in the San Salvador graveyard which could be ascribed to a Doña Sofía Peralta de Maso
or her newborn child.

Father O'Reilly followed his rector to the stand. He took the
oath on the Catholic Bible and made the sign of the cross before
answering Reynolds' first question.

"Do you recognize the gentleman sitting at the end of that
table?"

"Yes, sir," was the priest's reply. "I believe I met him at San
Bernardino."

"Did he call upon you while you had charge of the parish
during Father Stockman's absence?"

"He did, with another man."

"And he asked to see these record books?"

"Yes, sir."

Reavis jumped up and, greatly agitated, began to shout abuse
at the priest. The usher intervened, and Reynolds continued,
"Did he give you his name?"

"Yes, sir. I don't know whether he gave his first name, but he
gave me the name Peraltareavis."

"Did you let him have these books?"

"Yes, sir. Having at that time been only a short time in the West, I was unacquainted with its wickedness," the priest replied with disarming naïvité, which caused an outburst of laughter in court.

"How long did they have them?"

"I could not positively say, but I think it might have been for two or three weeks, probably a month. They were then brought back by another man."

"The index book they did not have?"

"No, sir."

Reavis now rose to cross-examine the priest. "I have never seen you before in my life," he began. "I have never been to your church and never received any books from you. Why are you lying?"

The priest was not easily intimidated. "I well remember you and also your name," he said. "I understood it was Reeves, and I thought it was an Irish name. I wondered within myself why an Irishman should marry a Mexican, as I thought you needed the certificate for marriage bans. Then you told me that your name was Reavis, not Reeves—"

"All lies," shouted Reavis. But in spite of many more questions and denials, he was unable to shake the priest's identification of him.

Reavis grew extremely agitated, and when Reynolds rose to call William Tipton to testify about his findings on the handwriting in the church books, he jumped up and addressed the judges: "Please, Your Honors, I do not think it necessary for me to be here and listen to these lies. If Your Honors will excuse me, I should like to be absent. I shall offer my objections later and have the opportunity to cross-examine this witness before the close of the trial." He stormed out of the courtroom.

Tipton and Severo Mallet-Prevost continued the evidence related to the forgeries of the first baron's testament and the elaborate genealogical tree of the Peraltas which Reavis had discovered at Seville.

Tipton showed the testament to the justices and explained how he had found that a genuine document, a probate application by two brothers named Escobadoz, of Guadalajara, had been partially used for producing the testament. The first leaf had been cleverly faked by minute erasures and insertions so that the genuine petitioners mentioned on it, the said Escobadoz, now appeared to be witnesses to the notary's endorsement. The signature of the notary Ballesteros had been cleverly forged, but this was not particularly difficult to do, Tipton explained, because there were many papers in the Guadalajara archives with this signature—the notary must have been a busy man at his time—and it could be copied by a skilled forger.

A document, dated 1742, was the decree appointing Don Miguel de Peralta as *visitador del rey* in Mexico. This was the appointment which put that gentleman of Cádiz on the road to his fortune in America. Tipton showed the document to the judges, saying that it was a completely genuine ancient document apparently purloined from Spanish or Mexican archives. However, it was the appointment of someone else, not of Señor de Peralta. The original name and rank had been erased and replaced by those of Don Miguel. It was an excellent forgery, but the ink of the substitution was slightly darker. Tipton told the court that after prolonged examination he believed he had deciphered the original writing. Where the word *visitador* (inspector) was now written, there had been the word *virrey* (viceroy), and under the name of the Baron de Arizonac, there had been that of the Conde de Fuenclara. In fact, this was a decree of the appointment of the count to his office as viceroy of New Mexico. Tipton described the document as one of great historical interest, cruelly defaced and spoiled by the forger.

The titles and high orders of Don Miguel de Peralta, mentioned in many of the documents, were then discussed at length. Reynolds and his assistants had gone to the trouble of producing ancient registers and lists from the royal chancery in Madrid, containing the names of all grandees, bearers of such titles, knights of the Order of the Golden Fleece, of the Order of Montesa, of the Order of Our Lady of Guadalupe, and so on. None of these lists contained the name of Miguel de Peralta or any other Peralta who lived at the period in question.

A lengthy discussion ensued about the first baron's astoundingly long life. According to the documents produced by the claimants, the great-grandfather of the real heiress was born in 1708 and died in 1824, reaching the age of one hundred and sixteen years. Mallet-Prevost submitted that the reason for making the first baron into a Methuselah was to avoid the difficult task of having to forge yet more documents by introducing a baron of a generation between the first and the second. Reavis realized the weakness of the lineage which he devised, but never at a loss for an explanation, he tried to brush off the accusations by saying that birthdates on late-eighteenth and early-nineteenth-century documents were notoriously unreliable. It could have been that the first baron had been born much later. But he had no answer when told that all searches for records of the baron's death and burial or for his grave at the Belén cemetery had remained completely fruitless.

Suddenly Reavis jumped up and challenged Mallet-Prevost's contention that Don Miguel de Peralta's name could not be found among the knights of the Order of the Golden Fleece. He demanded to see the list, and after thumping the pages, he stretched out his arms in a dramatic gesture. "Of course, here it is. If it pleases Your Honors, here is the very entry!"

The list was passed around and inspected by the judges and Mallet-Prevost. The name to which Reavis had pointed was that of a Duke of Santistebán.

"But that's Santistebán and not Peralta," said Mallet-Prevost.

"Exactly," Reavis declared triumphantly. "That was, of course, the Baron de Peralta's second title." Then, turning to the attorney, he said with deadly sarcasm, "I assume you don't speak Spanish?"

"That may be so," replied the famous Spanish scholar.

"Well, seeing is knowing, is it not? Who was that Spanish grandee?"

"Indeed, I do not know," Mallet-Prevost modestly admitted.

"I thought you wouldn't. That is just what is the matter with you. You wouldn't know it if you could see it."

Chief Justice Reed intervened: "Please stop this kind of proceeding, Mr. Reavis." No one fell for the baron's histrionics anymore.

But Reavis persisted. "You could not say, Mr. Mallet-Prevost, that the Duke of Santistebán was none other than Don Miguel Nemecio Silva de Peralta y de la—"

"No, but I am certain of one thing, Mr. Reavis. If he had been a duke, you would have got 'duke' into all your documents." The audience was greatly amused.

Reavis asked, "Would you believe that there was such a man as Don Miguel Nemecio Silva de Peralta and Duke of Santistebán, if you saw his name on a tombstone with the date of his birth and death? Would you, Mr. Mallet-Prevost?"

The hilarity in court persisted for a minute or two when the Government expert crisply replied, "Not if you had been at that tombstone first, Mr. Reavis."

In regard to stones, almost half a day was spent in discussing the famous Initial Monument, the rock engraved with the *diseño* of the Peralta Grant, from which the first baron, in the company of Father Pauer and the two hidalgos who produced the delineation of his estates, had surveyed the Gila Valley on May 13, 1758, and which had been so conveniently discovered by Reavis after his return from Spain in the autumn of 1887. Photographs of the rock, with the real heiress posing in front of it, were shown to the judges, and although Reynolds tried his best to cast doubts on its genuineness and insinuated that Reavis or someone in his employ had executed the carving, the stone memorial to the Peralta glory remained immovable and irrefutable evidence in Reavis' favor.

Reavis was closely questioned about the events at Seville in 1886. Reynolds produced lengthy testimony from the custodian José Quintano and the clerk Antonio Juárez of the *Archives de Indias,* as well as the charge sheet of the Seville police accusing Reavis of having tried to insert forged documents into a *legajo* and of having stolen other documents from the archives.

These accusations were brushed off by Reavis. He told the court that Quintano had denounced him because he, Reavis, reported the custodian to the directors of the archives after Quintano had tried to blackmail him.

"Quintano, having found out that I was looking for documents which would enable me to complete the evidence for a claim of great value, attempted to blackmail me into large payments of money, in return for the procurement of such documents. When I refused, he wrongly accused me to the police. With the help of my friend, the United States minister in Madrid, I had been able to have the blackmailer suspended. The charges were withdrawn."

When Reynolds insisted that a warrant for his arrest had been issued and that the Spanish authorities regarded him as a fugitive, Reavis repeated again and again, "This is false, quite false."

Several witnesses filed through the stand. One of them was the surveyor general of Arizona, Royal A. Johnson. He gave a detailed account of his protracted ordeal of probing the Peralta claim, ever since Reavis first registered it in 1883. Scores of letters exchanged between him and Reavis and Johnson's correspondence with the General Land Office, the Secretary of the

Interior, and other authorities in Washington were produced. Reavis rose to cross-examine the witness.

He approached him with well-acted courtesy. "Mr. Johnson, sir, you have maintained the reputation of Arizona exceedingly well. I did not want to trouble you with my questions at all, but I shall ask you just one or two small questions. The first is about that hallucination that naturally surrounds the good folk of Arizona—"

"I am at your service, Mr. Reavis," Johnson said.

"I am greatly obliged. Now, as you have reported so adversely on my claim, do you remember that you sent to Mexico and got a seal?"

"Yes, sir."

"Such seals could be furnished very easily and without any inconvenience at the archives?"

"I am not speaking of a metal seal, I am speaking of the seal on paper," the surveyor general replied.

"Now, then, Mr. Johnson," Reavis said with biting irony, "I didn't know you knew the difference."

Reavis tried hard to make the surveyor general appear a fool and a man ignorant of the legal complexities of the case. But he did not succeed.

"How long have you lived in Arizona, Mr. Johnson?" he asked with a sweet smile.

"About thirteen years."

"Well, you won't have to live much longer to sustain the reputation of Arizona."

"I would not have lived there any longer, if I had accepted your proposition," Johnson answered. Whether this was a hint that Reavis had tried to bribe him was left unsaid.

"You said, Mr. Johnson, I have stolen the Willing papers from Judge Fleury in Prescott. How did you come to make that strange assumption?"

"I took your word for it that you had stolen them, Baron," was the reply.

Reavis wanted to know why Johnson had stated that he had pressed him for a favorable report, after he had filed his first claim.

"Well, you used to come to my office frequently and demanded I make a report and confirm what you and Mr. Hopkins had found in Mexico. You sure did that."

"Does not your memory fail you, Mr. Johnson. Was it not an attorney named Cox you're thinking of?"

"No," Johnson replied. "I was thinking of you, Baron. You pestered me for years."

"Oh, well, poor Cox is dead," Reavis remarked, implying that he could prove Johnson a liar if Cox were alive.

At that moment an elderly burly man rose in the back of the court. "Your Honors," he said, "Mr. Cox is alive and well, or at least he was when I left Phoenix last week."

Reavis wheeled around and recognized the interrupter as James D. Monihon, the former mayor of Phoenix, who had been summoned as a witness by Reynolds.

When Rufus Hopkins, the chief clerk at the surveyor general's office at Tucson in the 1880's was put on the stand, Severo Mallet-Prevost took over the examination. Hopkins, who had traveled with Reavis to Mexico in 1883 and, having enjoyed the baron's hospitality, had made a favorable report about the documents found at Guadalajara, was now an old man, over eighty. His hearing was impaired, and his reactions were slow. He admitted that the translations of the documents which he had made officially for the surveyor general and also privately for Reavis were not literal; he had tried to convey the sense of the wording, rather than to give a strict rendering. He presented a pathetic figure, and the Government attorney spared the old man further embarrassment.

James D. Monihon's examination was accentuated by mo-

ments of hilarity. The old pioneer, who had known Doc Willing in the roaring days of the Southwest, brought a breath of
the sharp Arizona air into the stuffy courtroom.

"You did not like my claim to the Peralta estates, Mr.
Monihon?" asked Reavis. "Your concern was that it would
impair the interest of the citizens of Phoenix?"

"By heck, I didn't like the whole crooked business," replied
Monihon with a broad grin.

"And you tried to discourage me? You even threatened me
with lynching and hanging? Did you not?"

"No, but I gave you a well-meant warning that you would
meet with just fate if you attempted this foolish business."

To questions by Reynolds, the former mayor told how Doc
Willing had come to him, sometime in the 1860's, and proposed
that they go in together into that floating grant business and try
bleeding the mining companies and settlers.

"I told the Doc it was a pretty bad business trying to get the
people's homes away from them, and I refused to have anything
to do with this business. I had long forgotten all about it when
some twelve years or so later this gentleman here came along.
He said he was the correspondent of the San Francisco *Examiner,* never mentioned that he had a claim, but wanted to see
the valley. I took him in hand and showed him around, as one
would do for a friendly stranger. Only then he mentioned this
claim, and I advised him to keep off it. Some years afterwards I
met him on a train. He was the baron now and dressed so finely
in broadcloth and high hat that he looked like one. He told me
that he would change boundaries of the grant to avoid hostility
in Phoenix and a row with the Phoenix Canal Company,
which, he said, was too strong for him."

Realizing that Monihon was getting the better of him, Reavis
gave up the cross-examination.

The trial was now in its second week, but the climax, im-
patiently awaited by the spectators and newspaper reporters,

was still to come. On Friday, June 14, the Santa Fe newspapers reported that Mrs. Reavis, the Baroness de Peralta, had arrived with their children from Denver, where she now resided, and that she would testify early next week. Long lines formed on Monday morning in front of the building; everybody wanted to have a glance at the legendary heiress.

Two marshals had to clear the way when she arrived in court, leading her two little boys by the hands. She was dressed in black, her attractive face was pale, and her large dark eyes had an expression of bewilderment and hardly concealed anxiety. But she retained her poise, which had so enchanted the worldly gentlemen and courtiers of Madrid and London. She was ushered to a seat near the witness stand. The twins at first stood next to her, but a little later began to explore the courtroom, playing hide-and-seek around the chairs and the balusters of the railing in front of the judges' bench.

Reavis came over to greet his wife, and they exchanged a few words while he bent down to pat the heads of his two little boys. It later transpired that the baron and baroness had been separated for several months; he had been living in San Francisco, while she had moved with the children to Denver, Colorado, where a friend had offered her hospitality.

Matthew Reynolds called the baroness to the stand. He asked her about her name, her childhood memories, and her life in Sherwood Valley. At first she gave brief and hesitant replies, in a pleasant but almost inaudible voice. Her English was fluent, with no trace of foreign accent. Reynolds invited her to tell about her childhood in her own way.

The baroness remained silent for a long while. Then when Chief Justice Reed addressed her with a few words of encouragement, she said, "I remember little about my early childhood. I remember my grandmother, Doña Carmelita Maso, who cared for me. Later I lived with Mr. Sherwood, and for some reasons I do not know, I was called Carmelita Treadwell—"

"You mean Treadway, do you not, Mrs. Reavis?" Reynolds asked.

"No, sir. Treadwell," the baroness said quietly, but firmly.

She paused, again and to a question about her education she replied, "I had not much education as a child. Perhaps only three months' schooling."

"You lived at Mr. Alfred Sherwood's house in Mendocino County. You did not attend school then?"

"No, sir. I had some schooling later, after I met my husband. At a convent."

"You used the name Treadway, after you left Sherwood Valley and worked as a milliner or dressmaker?" Reynolds persisted.

"No, sir, I called myself Treadwell. It was just a name I went by, although I knew my real name was Maso, but I had no papers in that name."

Reynolds suddenly switched to her visit with her husband to Sherwood Valley in 1887, after their return from Spain.

"You went to Mr. Sherwood, and you asked him for the return of a picture. A photograph of John A. Treadway, did you not?"

"Mr. Sherwood brought it out, with my father's picture."

"Your father's picture? John Treadway's picture! But you said you never heard of him. What was the necessity of asking for Mr. Treadway's picture if you did not know him?" Reynolds shot the questions into Carmelita's face.

She began to sob. "No, I made a mistake," she whispered. "You asked me too quickly. That was the first time I ever heard of Treadway, as I said before. That was after my husband had told me of Treadway . . . he said . . . and that was for the first time . . . I really heard John Treadway's name . . . I had it mixed up with Treadwell—"

She had been fighting her tears but could no longer control

herself. She bent her head and tried to wipe the tears flowing down her cheeks, her body trembling.

Reavis jumped up. "If Your Honors please, I must demand that the witness be protected." There was a great commotion in court. Here was the drama for which the public had waited so long. The reporters scribbled their notes. Judge Sluss said the witness should be protected and asked the Government attorney not to distress her. Reynolds bowed to the court and did not persist in pressing the subject.

An usher brought a glass of water, and after taking a few sips, the baroness composed herself. The twins had taken advantage of the commotion, when all attention centered on their mother. They had crawled up the steps of the bench and were playing around the judges' legs. Judge Sluss, a kindly grandfatherly man, made them sit on the bench next to him, and there they remained, quiet and well behaved, for the next two hours during their mother's ordeal.

The baroness had regained her self-control, and she now answered questions in a straightforward manner and a firm voice. This later caused Attorney Reynolds to pay her the compliment that "in spite of your frequent and material deviations from the truth, you are a remarkable woman, and you fully sustain the wisdom of Mr. Reavis in selecting you to pose as his baroness."

To questions of how she had met her husband, she gave vague replies, saying it had been an accidental meeting, but she insisted she had known before she had met him that she was the heiress to the Peralta estates in Arizona.

Her statement that she had gone alone to Spain, in 1875 or 1876—she could not remember the exact year—caused a sensation. Reynolds remarked that it was surprising that a young girl should have traveled alone to Europe, but she replied that she went to visit her relatives there, the Peraltas, Masos, and Ibarras.

Reynolds asked her whether she could speak Spanish.

"Yes, I always could. I learned Spanish from my grandmother, Doña Carmelita Maso. I always spoke Spanish with her, as a child."

"Did you ever speak that language when you lived with Mrs. John Snowball, who spoke Spanish as she came to California from New Mexico?" Reynolds asked.

"I tried not to, because she forbade me to speak Spanish and nearly broke my head when I did. She would not have it. She was determined to brand me as an Indian. She told me I was an Indian, and an Indian she would have me."

Reavis never took his eyes off his wife. He stared at her with a steely blue glare, as if he wanted to exercise some hypnotic powers. But Carmelita was telling her story to his full satisfaction:

"I was later living with Mrs. Bradshaw, who kept a dressmaking store, and I had mentioned to her, and also to Mr. and Mrs. Snowball, that I had a large amount of property; but they would never let me talk about it. I had always known that my grandfather, Don Miguel de Peralta, was an honest man, who had been wealthy, and that he had gone with my father to Spain and died there. That was after my mother died, soon after I was born."

"But is not the truth that the very first time you ever heard of your property or inheritance was when you met your present husband?" Reynolds asked.

"No, it is not true," she replied firmly. "I did not hear it for the first time from Mr. Reavis. I knew it as long as I can remember, and I must have been told about it by my grandmother."

"Did you not hear about it from Mr. Reavis, who showed you some documents and told you that you were the heiress?" Reynolds asked again.

"I was young when they were shown to me, I assume by my

grandmother. But when my husband did show me some documents before we were married, I recognized a paper, with a seal thereon, which I had seen as a child. My husband said that this was the title paper, upon which I later claimed the grant, which was filed at the office of the surveyor general of Arizona."

Being pressed by Reynolds to read and examine some of the documents which he brought to the witness stand, Carmelita said, "The plain fact is that I am not an educated woman. I do not understand these things." And suddenly growing angry, she said in a loud voice, "If I do not get through today, I will never come back here again."

When Reynolds repeated his questions, Carmelita broke down again and burst out crying. By then the sympathy of the audience had definitely turned in her favor. There were hisses in the public gallery when Reynolds tried to continue the examination.

After another pause, Carmelita recovered. There was no repetition of a scene until the end of her examination.

Reynolds addressed her more kindly: "Please do not distress yourself. Just answer my questions. Is it not true that you are impersonating the granddaughter of that Miguel de Peralta, a person who never existed, and that you do so, at your danger, on the incitement of your husband?"

"No, it is not true. I am all I represent myself to be," she replied calmly and with dignity, every inch the real heiress.

Reynolds then turned to Carmelita's sojourn in Spain in 1887 and asked whether she had been with her husband at Seville, where an unpleasant event had taken place.

Her answers sounded plausible and not only bore out Reavis' statements, but greatly strengthened his case. She said that when her husband was conducting his studies of ancient documents relating to her inheritance, they had met a young man, named José Quintano, one of the archives' clerks.

"Quintano came to our house and demanded at first five

thousand dollars and later even more money, I believe seven thousand dollars before he would allow my husband to examine the records. Quintano told us that if we paid that amount, he would help us in every way and make for us all the copies we wanted without trouble. But Mr. Reavis refused to be black-mailed, and Quintano then told a pack of lies to the police. That was how the trouble in Seville started."

Reavis cross-examined his wife only briefly. He tried to bring out some of the salient points she had made about her knowl-edge of her inheritance long before she had met him, indeed when she was still a child. Several more witnesses followed the baroness onto the stand. They included the Archbishop of Santa Fe and the former Bishop of Tucson John B. Salpointe, who testified about the search Reavis had made in the records of the Mission of San Xavier del Bac. He denied that there were any documents relating to the Peralta family among these records.

Reynolds then presented the sworn statements of Alfred Sherwood, John Snowball, and other California witnesses ex-amined at the various testimony takings about Carmelita's childhood. He described the testimony of Miguel Noe, Andrés Sandoval, and José Ramón Valencia, who had insisted on hav-ing known the second baron and José Maso, as obvious perjuries and announced that after the trial, criminal proceedings would be instituted against these witnesses.

This grave announcement did not, however, discourage Reavis from mounting the stand once again. He told the court that he desired to clear up a number of misunderstandings which had crept into the proceedings. He once more recapitu-lated the story of his first meeting with his wife, trying to impress on the court that Carmelita had known all about her inheritance before they met.

"You kept up your acquaintance with your wife from the time you claim to have first discovered her on the train in 1877 or 1878?" Reynolds asked.

"Yes, sir."

"You suspected by reason of her appearance that she was of Spanish origin? That was not a particular reason for speaking to her on the train?"

"Certainly. That was the only inducement for speaking to her."

"Maybe because you were then looking to find a long-lost heiress to the Peralta property?"

"No, the idea had not occurred to me when I first spoke to her. It was simply that she was a Spanish beauty and I a young man . . . It was quite natural to pay a compliment to a beautiful girl on a long train journey," Reavis declared with a smile.

"How did you connect her after that with the Peraltas?"

"Because she interested me when she told me that her father's name was Massol or Maso."

"Is it not true, Mr. Reavis, that you met your wife very much later, perhaps only in 1882, when you were roaming the country in search of a suitable young woman whom you could present as the heiress?" the Government attorney asked.

"No, sir. I met her in 1878, we remained in touch, and I married her in 1882."

Reynolds leaned across the barrier, looking straight into Reavis' eyes.

"Did you or did you not take out a marriage license to marry another lady in southern California in 1882?"

"Another lady?" Reavis pretended to be greatly surprised. "What was her name?"

"Miss Laura Bridger."

"Oh, yes, I did," Reavis suddenly remembered.

"Where did she reside?"

"In Pomona or in Los Angeles. You asked me whether this was in 1882, did you?"

"Yes, Mr. Reavis. It was after the signing of your marriage contract with your present wife. Was it not strange taking out a marriage license to marry another lady after you had married the present Mrs. Reavis, or did you not marry her in 1882 at all?" Reynolds insisted.

The long-winded explanation Reavis now gave only confused the issue even more. "Oh, well, it was only a bluff. Miss Bridger and I had been engaged for a long time. My wife understood the situation thoroughly, when I went down to accomplish the purpose. That was the reason why we started on a secret marriage. After making the marriage contract with my wife, I went down to see Miss Bridger. We had quite a little disturbance, and I thought it was time to put an end to it."

It was never established at the trial when Reavis had really met Carmelita, when he had married her, and whether she was Sofía Treadway. Nor was it ever established when and where she was born. Even Reynolds' contention that she was the natural daughter of John Treadway and his Indian squaw was never proved. If, as it was said, Carmelita was born in 1862 or 1863, she could not have been Treadway's child, because he died on November 21, 1861, and yet Alfred Sherwood had testified on oath that it was Treadway who had brought the few-weeks-old girl to his house.

On the last day of the trial Reavis still tried to bamboozle the judges. He asked for permission to clarify another misunderstanding.

"It was said that the name of Peralta did not occur in the lists of Spanish nobility and holders of titles and orders," he said. "This misunderstanding can easily be explained. Often this family went by the name of Peralta, as a nom de plume, as titled people often do. In fact the titles of Santistebán and Peralta are synonymous and belong to the family of the Córdobas. Sometimes we find it as Santistebán—I should say the Duke of Santistebán—sometimes as the barons of Peralta and Córdoba."

But it was too late in the day to introduce yet more ducal

grandees of Spain from whom Carmelita could trace her ancestry. The judges dismissed this attempt with amused smiles.

Reavis was not yet prepared to throw in the towel. He asked to be excused for a moment, dashed out of the courtroom, and reappeared at the head of a small procession. Two attendants brought in a large black trunk studded with copper nails and secured with leather belts. It took him a few minutes to unlock and open it, and he was watched with great curiosity by everyone present. Even the judges leaned forward to see what new and surprising evidence would emerge out of the trunk.

The baron was unpacking a collection of oil paintings, pictures, and photographs. He marched to the judges' table and spread the exhibits in front of them.

"I will now take up the chief action and present Your Honors with most important evidence," he solemnly announced. "Here is a portrait that we have of Don Miguel Nemecio Silva de Peralta y de la Córdoba, the young Duke de Santistebán, at the age of three years and five months."

He marched to the seats where his wife and the twins were sitting and, grasping little Miguel by the hand, led the child to the front of the judges' bench.

"If Your Honors please, I would like to call the attention of the court to the remarkable resemblance between that childhood portrait of Don Miguel Nemecio and my boy, Miguel, one of the twins. My boy is stouter, though he is only a little over two years old, but Your Honors admit that this portrait is a perfect image of him. Nature seems to have aided us very much in our fight!"

The judges could hardly suppress their amusement. Reporters and people in the public enclosure were on their feet to catch a glance of the Peralta portrait gallery. There were paintings and miniatures, drawings and sketches, and photographs, portraits of the first and second barons de Peralta, of the Baroness de Córdoba, of Doña Juana Laura Ibarra, and a few of the family of the dukes of Santistebán. While the pictures were being shown around, Reavis tried to catch little Miguel, who, having become frightened by all the commotion, began to run up and down in front of the judges' bench, crying, "Mama, Mama!" Judge Fuller lifted the child onto his lap, and the little boy began to play with the judge's frock coat tail and watch chain and quieted down.

After all the acrimonious scenes and bitter exchanges during the past days, the atmosphere in the courtroom became easy and almost friendly, like that at a family gathering.

Reavis lifted up a large, heavily framed painting, which, he said, represented Doña Francisca María de García de la Córdoba y Muniz de Pérez, mother of the first Baron de Peralta. The melodious names and titles rolled easily from his tongue.

"This is a genuine oil painting by the famous Spanish artist Bartolemé Murillo, who lived in Seville in the seventeenth century," he proudly announced, holding the picture high above his head and turning it round, as if he were putting it up for auction.

"Eh, a real Murillo?" asked Severo Mallet-Prevost. "It must be worth a fortune. Have you got it insured, Mr. Reavis?"

"I would not have brought it where you were, if I had not," Reavis parried the attorney's irony.

At last the inspection of the portraits was concluded, and Chief Justice Reed announced that the court would reassemble on the next morning, Wednesday, June 19, to hear the final submissions. On that last day of the trial, which, including the recess, had lasted for two weeks, Attorney Reynolds told the court that he had decided to waive his right to submit a final argument. The evidence against the claim was so overwhelming, he said, that he did not wish to trouble the court with any further statements.

Reavis, however, introduced fifty-two objections against testimony given by witnesses called by the Government and made a long speech recapitulating many of his contentions in favor of the claim. It seemed that he just could not tear himself away from the courtroom, enjoying every moment of his appearance as his own counsel. Chief Justice Reed announced that the judgment would be pronounced within a week.

Reavis remained at Santa Fe and was present on Friday, June 28, at the rendering of the judgment. It is probable that he had been warned by the marshal that he would be arrested if he tried to leave town. He listened quietly when Chief Justice Joseph R. Reed announced that the petition of the claimants had been dismissed and the cross-petition filed by the Government allowed. Reavis briskly jotted down notes as the judge began to read the lengthy text of the formal decision, and he displayed no emotion.

"This is the decree of the court," Chief Justice Reed began, "that in the cause of James Addison Peraltareavis and Doña Sofía Loreta Micaela de Peraltareavis, née Maso y Silva de Peralta y de la Córdoba, Mr. Clinton F. Farrell having withdrawn, coming on to be heard upon the amended petition filed on the sixth day of November, 1893, and the answer and cross-petition duly filed by the Government of the United States on the third day of June, 1895, and after hearing and considering all of the evidence presented by the plaintiffs in opposition thereto, and after considering the objections presented by the plaintiffs to the testimony offered by the Government, the court overrules the same.

"The court finds from the evidence that said grant or claim is not entitled to confirmation in the name of the alleged grantee, Don Miguel Nemecio Silva de Peralta y de la Córdoba, nor in the name of anyone else claiming an interest therein.

"That the claim is wholly fictitious and fraudulent, and that the various documents upon which the same is based, as well as those tending to establish the plaintiff Doña Sofía Loreta Micaela Silva de Peralta as the great-granddaughter of said Don

Miguel Nemecio Silva de Peralta and the granddaughter of Don Miguel Silva Jesús de Peralta are each and all of them forged, manufactured, and have been surreptitiously introduced into the records and archives at Madrid and Seville in the kingdom of Spain and into the records and archives in the city of Guadalajara in the state of Jalisco in the republic of Mexico.

"And the court further finds that the baptismal and burial records of the parish of San Bernardino and San Salvador in the county of San Bernardino in the state of California, copies of which were introduced in evidence of plaintiffs in support of their claim, for the purpose of establishing the identity of one of the petitioners herein, namely Doña Sofía Loreta Micaela Silva de Peralta as the daughter of Doña Sofía Laura Micaela de Peralta y de Maso and Don José Ramón Carmen Maso, are forgeries and have been surreptitiously inserted in the records of said parish mission.

"And the court further finds that no such person as Don Miguel Nemecio Silva de Peralta y de la Córdoba, bearing the various titles of nobility and official relations with the kings of Spain, as set forth in said amended petition, and to whom said grant is alleged to have been made, ever existed, or that he had a son, Don Miguel Silva Jesús de Peralta, to whom he willed said property so alleged to have been granted.

"And the court further finds that the plaintiff, Doña Sofía Loreta Micaela Silva de Peralta de la Córdoba and her husband, James Addison Reavis, now styling himself James Addison Peraltareavis, are not in any wise related to, or connected with said alleged original grantee, the alleged Don Miguel Nemecio Silva de Peralta y de la Córdoba, either by privity of blood or estate, but that they and each of them are fraudulent and fictitious claimants for said property described in the amended petition.

"It is therefore ordered, adjudged, and decreed that the claim to the property which is commonly known and called the

Peralta Grant, situated in the territories of Arizona and New Mexico, is hereby rejected."

There was complete silence in the courtroom when the chief justice finished reading. He then added:

"The evidence adduced conclusively proved that the so-called Peralta Grant was purely fictitious, being clearly founded on fraud, forgery, and perjury. It was, however, necessary to go into the question as to the ancestry of Mrs. Peraltareavis. So far as she was concerned, the court was persuaded from her appearance and for other reasons that she was of Spanish origin, but whether or not she was a descendant of one Miguel Peralta was a question that could not be passed upon by this court, nor did it concern the court as to its present judgment."

This final remark of the chief justice was as surprising as it was significant. The court had rejected the submission of the Government attorney that Carmelita was the daughter of John Treadway and an Indian squaw, and it left the mystery of her ancestry unsolved.

During the week he had been waiting at Santa Fe for the judgment, Reavis stayed at the La Fonda Hotel on San Francisco Street, the famous inn which, since Spanish Trail days, had been the rendezvous of New Mexican traders, rancheros, and politicians. There he held court to reporters who had come for his trial from many cities of the United States. He was still talking about his great plans for developing Arizona:

"So far as the Peralta Grant is concerned, I don't care a snap of my fingers for it. If it is confirmed, it would be an incumbrance to my plans. The capitalists who are interested with me in the great irrigation schemes would be glad to have the grant beaten and the land disposed of. They feel that way because there is a great deal more for us in the development of the water system and in the sale of water rights than could possibly have been made if we had obtained title to the land."

He was still confident that even after the claim was rejected, as everybody expected it would be after the damning evidence submitted by the Government attorneys, he could go on with his great schemes. When the judgment was pronounced, Reavis immediately arose in court and asked leave to file a bill of exceptions, which meant that he intended to carry the case to an appeal before the Supreme Court. He said this would be based on the fifty-two objections to the testimony of witnesses. The chief justice informed him that if the bill were properly prepared and presented, he would accept it.

It was Reavis' final grandiloquent gesture. The great cardhouse he had elaborately built of forged documents had collapsed.

After he had bowed to the court and the judges filed out, Reavis, talking to the newspapermen, left the building and crossed to the shady side of the sunbaked plaza.

There he was approached by the United States Marshal Page B. Otero. The officer showed him a warrant for his arrest on a charge of attempted fraud. He told him his orders were to bring him before the United States Court Commissioner W. H. Pope. Accompanied by the marshal, he returned to the Federal Building he had left only a few minutes before. There he was taken into custody.

He asked to be allowed to send a messenger to the famous Santa Fe lawyer James Catron, whom he wanted to brief for his defense at the preliminary hearing fixed for 2 P.M. But Catron was not available, and a young attorney, Charles A. Spiess, accepted the brief. Matthew Reynolds and Assistant District Attorney George P. Money appeared for the prosecution.

Reavis pleaded not guilty to the charge that on the 18th day of February, 1893, in the city of Santa Fe, Territory of New Mexico, he filed in the United States Court of Private Land Claims a claim against the United States, said claim being filed for the purpose of falsely, fictitiously and fraudulently obtaining from the Government of the United States, through a judgment of said court, a large sum of money, to wit exceeding $100,000.

The accused asked for release from custody on bail, and Commissioner Pope fixed a bond of $10,000, to await trial. But Reavis told him that all he could deposit was "about $2,000 at the moment." He was allowed to send several cables to friends in San Francisco and New York, asking them to stand bond security for him. He cabled Ingersoll, Crocker, Harvey Brown, and several of his former backers and partners. But no replies were received. He was taken to the city jail and there he remained until the criminal trial took place more than twelve months later.

The trial was on June 27, 1896, before Judge Loughlin and a jury, composed mainly of Spanish-speaking citizens. On the whole, the evidence submitted by the district attorney was a recapitulation of that which Matthew Reynolds and Severo Mallet-Prevost had produced a year earlier.

But this time there appeared for the prosecution two important witnesses: Andrés Sandoval, the boardinghouse keeper of San Francisco in the 1860's, and his waiter, José Ramón Valencia, who had five years before testified that they had known the second Baron de Peralta and José Maso, the alleged father of Carmelita. They had since made full confessions that their testimony was fictitious and that they had committed perjury.

Both had been promised pardons by the prosecution, and Valencia, in particular, said on the witness stand that all the stories he had dished up at the testimony takings were inventions. He had been coached by Miguel Noe and Reavis. He produced a contract letter by which he had been promised in 1891 to be paid by Reavis $20,000 for his false testimony if the case went in favor of Reavis, but he had been paid only $1,000 "on account of this payment."

The district attorney told Judge Loughlin that a warrant for the arrest of Miguel Noe on the charge of conspiracy and fraud was in force but that Noe had escaped to Mexico and that all efforts to have him extradited by the Mexican authorities had been fruitless. The district attorney demanded imprisonment of between six and ten years and a substantial fine.

Reavis put up a spirited defense, and the sympathy of the jurors of Santa Fe, where more than half the population was of Spanish descent, seemed to be on his side. Nevertheless, he was found "guilty as charged in the indictment to defraud the United States Government out of parts of its public lands in connection with the effort to establish the fictitious and fraudulent Peralta Grant."

The jury added a recommendation for leniency. Judge Loughlin announced that sentence would be pronounced on July 17. When on that day James Addison Peraltareavis was brought before the court, he heard a sentence which must have surprised him.

The sentence was unexpectedly mild: two years in the federal penitentiary and a fine of $5,000.

After hearing the sentence, Reavis turned to his attorney, Charles A. Spiess, and said, "I shall ask you to prepare an appeal to the Supreme Court. I am sure this decision will be reversed."

On second thought, he did not make an appeal, and he served his term at the Santa Fe Penitentiary, being granted a remission for exemplary conduct during his imprisonment. He was released on April 19, 1898.

The day after his release he traveled to Denver to see his wife and his children. To a reporter of the *New Mexican* who saw him off at the railroad station, he said that he was "returning to the world of business. I am still on deck, and I am prepared to assert my rights. The Casa Grande Development and Land Improvement Company still exists, and it has controlled, since 1884, all the water storage reservoir sites on the Salt and Gila

Rivers north of Phoenix and Florence. I shall proceed, after a short rest with my family, to New York and confer with my associates. Then I shall go to Arizona and make arrangements to carry forward the irrigation enterprises my company had planned."

The former Baron of Arizona had fully regained the self-assurance which had marked his fantastic life of fraud. He was a preposterous crook, but he also had a clear vision of Arizona's future as a land of plenty.

Epilogue

Occasionally, there emerges a criminal of genius. His exploits though antisocial, have the golden touch of high adventure born of superb imagination. The hero-villain of this story was a man of this type, strangely neglected by the biographer and film producer, perhaps because the contemporaries this fraudsman had duped were influential enough to see to it that he should soon be forgotten.

Reavis never succeeded in repeating his success, however hard he tried. Not in New York, in Washington, or later in San Francisco, where he spent many months knocking at many doors, did he ever again find men willing to finance his great development schemes in Arizona. His many Casa Grande companies were wound up by official receivers in bankruptcy.

He returned penniless to Denver, where he lived for a time with his wife and the twins in a dingy apartment in Latimer Street, among some of the brittle yellowing documents of the Peralta Grant and with the paintings and pictures of the Spanish grandees, which he had bought at the Madrid flea market at the Rastro and had presented as those of his wife's ancestors. Mrs. Reavis, her Cinderella-life now a broken dream, supported the family, eking out a pathetic livelihood as a milliner.

The old volcano in his mind was not entirely extinguished.

In 1900, still only fifty-seven, but gaunt and badly nourished, in threadbare clothes which had seen better days, he traveled to San Francisco. There he found a man, Dr. A. T. Sherwood, a relative of the Alfred Sherwood of Mendocino County, Carmelita's foster father, who took pity on the former Baron of Arizona. He supported him for a while, and Reavis made some money by selling his memoirs to the San Francisco *Call*. Several installments of "The Confessions of the Baron of Arizona" were published. He began his story thus:

I am of Scotch-Welsh and Spanish antecedents, with a traditional Spanish extraction in the remote generations. Three of my great grandparents fought in the Revolution. I was reared in Henry County, Missouri. In May 1861, at the age of 18, I enlisted in the Confederate Army, and during my life as a soldier committed my first crime. I forged an order and, being successful in this, I forged many more. After the war . . . I opened a real estate office in St. Louis. I was successful in forging a deed to sustain a tax title to some valuable land I had bought and carried out other frauds . . . but these are incidents in which there is little interest. However, success in these early years sowed the seed that later sprang forth into the most gigantic fraud of the century.

The plan to secure the Peralta Grant and defraud the Government out of land valued at $100,000,000 was not conceived in a day. It was the result of a series of crimes extending over nearly a score of years. At first the stake was small, but it grew and grew in magnitude until even I sometimes was appalled at the thought of the possibilities.

I was playing a game which to win meant greater wealth than that of a Vanderbilt. My hand constantly gained strength, noted men pleaded my cause, and unlimited capital was at my command. My opponent was the Government, and I baffled its agents at every turn. Gradually I became absolutely sure of success.

As I neared the verge of triumph I was exultant and sure. Until the very moment of my downfall I gave no thought to failure. But my sins found me out and as in the twinkle of an eye I saw the millions which had seemed already in my grasp fade away and I heard the courts doom me to a prison cell.

Now I am growing old and the thing hangs upon me like a nightmare until I am driven to make a clean breast of it all, that I may end my days in peace.

But he never made a clean breast of it. The cunning "Prince of Confidence-Men," as the San Francisco *Call* described him in announcing the publication of his memoirs, succeeded in duping even the editor of that newspaper and his readers. All that he revealed was old stuff, well known to those who had followed the trial reports. He repeated *ad nauseam* the evidence submitted by Matthew Reynolds and Severo Mallet-Prevost, accepting most of it, rejecting some; but he never disclosed his real secrets, never told how he found the real heiress and how he forged the documents—all 200 of them—and never revealed Carmelita's real identity, if he knew it at all.

He probably wanted to keep these scoops for another publication, which he started with the money he had received from the *Call* editor for his apocryphal memoirs.

On July 5, 1900, he issued the first number of a magazine, *Peraltareavis Real Life Illustrated.* The first issue was adorned by his and his wife's portraits, one showing him as he looked in the heydays of his barony, in a frock coat, wing collar, black silk cravat, and luxuriant side whiskers; the other, of Carmelita, in a silk gown, her head covered with a Spanish lace mantilla, as she appeared at the court of Madrid.

On the title page was an announcement that *"The romance of the Peralta Grant will begin with a later issue,"* but no other issue of his *Real Life Illustrated* ever appeared.

In the only issue ever published, Reavis devoted all the space to fulminant descriptions of the development and irrigation schemes in Arizona, which he was still pursuing.

"Twenty years ago," he wrote, "I found this arid region a bower of wild luxurious flowers of every hue and delicacy of tint—there were two springtimes then, at every swing of mother

earth around the sun, beginning with each soltice. But the old
adage that 'seasons change' has been written indelibly upon the
face of country and man during those too brief years I spent in
Arizona. . . ."

So it went on, in a style alternating from poetic clichés to
bombastic claims that he, and only he, held the secret of
bringing great prosperity to Arizona, until the publication
became nothing but a business prospectus, obviously intended
to hook people credulous enough to entrust their money to the
former baron. He explained at length that "the ever present
oxidized iron in Arizona's soil gives a porous condition easily
soluble in water, hence admirably adapted to irrigation processes in this torrid climate, without baking irretrievably nor
[sic] drying into hardpan with great fissures zigzagging the
whole country. . . ."

Nothing came of all his efforts to find finance for his schemes.
After a year or two he was down to his last dime, although he
had earned some money as a free-lance journalist. Whenever he
had a few dollars to spare, he traveled to Arizona. The once
hated baron, threatened by the enraged citizens with lynching,
was received with pity and friendliness in Phoenix. Indeed, the
Arizonans seemed to be proud of their baron, who had put their
country on the map, and although it was a questionable sort of
fame he had achieved for Arizona, fame it still was.

Reavis had quickly aged beyond his years. A tired emaciated
old man, he ambled through the streets of Phoenix, which had
grown into a large and modern city beyond all recognition of
the days when the baron's agents had extorted his tribute. He
spent his days at the public library, rummaging among old
books and documents and still talking of his great development
schemes. Good-hearted people gave him a few dollars and stood
him a drink in the saloons. He had deserted his wife and the
twins, who had remained in Denver, and in June, 1902, Mrs.

Reavis obtained a divorce on the grounds of desertion and nonsupport.

The last few years of his life the Baron of Arizona spent as an inmate of public institutions, living on public charity. In 1913 he was in the Los Angeles County Poor House. He must have known that his days were numbered, and he wanted to see Carmelita and his sons, perhaps, for the last time. He was given some money from public funds and traveled to Denver.

There, on November 20, 1914, suffering from bronchitis, at the age of seventy-one, he died and was buried in a pauper's grave.

His wife survived him by twenty years. The twins had grown up into manhood and both served honorably their country in the First World War in France. Carmelita died on April 4, 1934, in Denver. The following brief notice was published in the Denver *Rocky Mountain News:*

> Mrs. Lola Micaela Reavis, aged 71, a resident of Denver for thirty-eight years, died last night in the Presbyterian Hospital, following a stroke of paralysis which she suffered ten days ago. Mrs. Reavis was born in San Francisco, California, where she spent her childhood. Her husband J. A. Reavis died in Denver twenty years ago. She leaves two sons.*

There may be some old documents and faded pictures of Spanish nobles in a dusty attic somewhere in Denver, and if there are, they are all that is left of the Barony of Arizona.

* April 5, 1934.

Documentation and Selected Bibliography

Records, documents, and manuscripts at the General Land Office, the Department of the Interior and the Department of Justice (in the U. S. National Archives, Washington, D.C.) ; at the U. S. Land Office, Phoenix, Arizona (microfilm copies in the Department of Library and Archives, Phoenix, and in the University of Arizona Library, Tucson) ; at the Arizona Pioneers' Historical Society, Tucson, and the City of Phoenix Public Library; at the State Records Center and Archives of New Mexico, Santa Fe, the Zimmerman Library of the University of New Mexico, Albuquerque, and the U. S. Land Office, Santa Fe; at the University of California Library and Stanford University, Palo Alto, California.

U. S. Congressional Record, Library of Congress, Washington, D.C.

Muniments of the Barony of Arizona (microfilms in the Zimmerman Library of the University of New Mexico, Albuquerque).

Brief and Argument of the Petitioner in the Peralta Grant Case. San Francisco, Bancroft, 1884.

Petition of Claimants, J. A. Peralta Reavis and others, In the Court of Claims of the United States. Washington, Gibson Bros., 1890.

Petition of Claimants, J. A. Peraltareavis and Sofía Loreta Micaela Peraltareavis vs. The United States of America (stylographed), San Francisco, 1892.

Brief for the Defendants, in the Court of Private Land Claims, J. A. Peraltareavis and Sofía Loreta Micaela Peraltareavis vs. The United States of America (stylographed), Santa Fe, 1895.

Transcripts of proceedings at the trials before the U. S. Court of Private Land Claims (June 3 to 25, 1895) and the U. S. District Court, Santa Fe (July 18, 1896).

Altamira, R., *Historia de España*. Madrid, 1900–1902.

Bancroft, H. H., *History of Arizona and New Mexico*. San Francisco, Bancroft, 1889.

Bechdolt, F. R., *When the West Was Young*. New York, Century, 1922.

Blasco, E., *Historia de Corte de Madrid*. Madrid, 1904

Bruce, J., *Gaudy Century*. New York, Random House, 1948.

Cleland, R. G., *California in Our Time*. New York, Knopf, 1947.

———, *From Wilderness to Empire*, New York, Knopf, 1949.

Corle, E., *The Gila River*. New York, Rinehart, 1951.

Crane, H., "He Fooled a Nation." *Sunday Referee* (October 21, 1937).

Dagett, S., *Chapters in the History of the Southern Pacific*. New York, 1922.

Dodge, I. F., *Our Arizona*. New York, Scribner's, 1929.

Farish, G. H., *History of Arizona*. San Francisco, Filmer, 1915.

Farish, T. E., *The Gold Hunters of California*. Chicago, 1904.

Federal Writers' Project, *Arizona*. New York, Hastings House, 1950, 1952, and other editions.

Foreman, G. (edit.), *A Pathfinder in the Southwest, The Itinerary of Lt. A. W. Whipple*. Norman, University of Oklahoma Press, 1940.

Forrest, E. R., *Arizona's Dark and Bloody Ground*. Caldwell, Ida., Caxton, 1936.

Fugate, F. L., *The Spanish Heritage of the Southwest*. El Paso, Tex., Western Press, 1952.

Hepburn, A., *Complete Guide to the Southwest*. New York, Doubleday, 1963.

Hinton, R. J., *Hand-Book of Arizona*. San Francisco, Upham, 1878.

Hoffman, O., *Reports on Land Cases*. San Francisco, Numa Hubert, about 1892.

Hollon, W. E., *The Southwest Old and New*. New York, Knopf, 1961.

Hopkins, R. C., *Muniments of Title of the Barony of Arizona and Translation into English*. San Francisco, Bancroft, 1893.

Hunt, R. D., *California and the Californians*. San Francisco, 1926.

Johnson, R. A., *Report of the Surveyor General upon the Alleged Peralta Grant*. Phoenix, Arizona Gazette Book and Job Office, 1890.

Jones, W. C., *Report on the Subject of Land Titles, etc.* Washington, D.C., Gideon, 1860.

Kelland, C. B., "The Red Baron of Arizona." *Saturday Evening Post* (October 11, 1947).

Kelly, G. H., *Legislative History of Arizona 1864–1912*. Phoenix, 1926.

Kerby, R. L., *The Confederate Invasion of New Mexico and Arizona*. Los Angeles, Westernlore, 1958.

Lee, J. M., *A History of American Journalism*. Boston, 1917.

Leighton, P., "The Baron of Arizona." *Everybody's Magazine* (May, 1951).

Lewis, O., *The Big Four*. New York, Knopf, 1958.

Lockwood, F. C., *Arizona Characters*. Los Angeles, Times-Mirror, 1928.

———, *Pioneer Days in Arizona*. New York, Macmillan, 1932.

Lyman, G. D., *The Saga of the Comstock Lode*. New York, Scribner's, 1934.

McClintock, J. H., *Arizona*. Chicago, Clarke Co., 1916.

Mitchell, J. D., *Lost Mines of the Southwest*. Phoenix, Journal Co., 1933.
Powell, D. M., *The Peralta Grant*. Norman, University of Oklahoma Press, 1960.
Reynolds, M. G., *Spanish and Mexican Land Laws*. St. Louis, Buxton, 1895.
Rickard, T. A., *A History of American Mining*. New York, McGraw, 1932.
Rockefellow, J. A., *Log of an Arizona Blazer*. Tucson, Acme Co., 1932.
Sloan, R. E., *Memories of an Arizona Judge*. Palo Alto, Stanford University Press, 1932.
Strover, W., "Story of the Red Baron." *Arizona Magazine,* Vol. X (September, 1919).
Swanberg, W. A., *Citizen Hearst*. London, Longmans, 1962.
Tipton, W. M., "The Prince of Impostors." *Land of Sunshine,* Vol. 8 (February and March, 1891).
Vassili, Count A., *La Société de Madrid*. Paris, 1888.
White, S. E., *Arizona Nights*. New York, McClure, 1907.
Wright, H. B., *When a Man's Was a Man*. New York, Burt, 1918.

Newspapers and Periodicals

Denver *Rocky Mountain News*
Florence *Arizona Weekly Enterprise*
Globe *Arizona Silver Belt*
London (England) *Times*
——— *Pall Mall Gazette*
——— *Morning Post*
Los Angeles *Herald*
Madrid *La Época*
——— *La Correspondencia*
——— *Illustracion*
Menlo Park (California) *Sunset*
The New York Times
Phoenix *Arizona Gazette*
——— *Herald*
——— *Arizona Republic*
Prescott *Arizona Miner*
Sacramento *Advertiser*
St. Louis *Post-Dispatch*
Safford *Graham County News*
San Francisco *Call*
——— *Examiner*
Santa Fe *New Mexican*
Tucson *Citizen* (full name: *Arizona Daily Citizen*)
——— *Star* (full name: *Arizona Daily Star*)

Index